83

89 93 97

0

The Critical
Evaluation of
African Literature

The Critical Evaluation of African Literature

Essays by
Edgar Wright
W. J. Howard
Dan Izevbaye
Eldred Jones
John Povey
Clive Wake
Peter Young

Edited by
Edgar Wright

INSCAPE/Publishers/Washington, D. C.

Library of Congress Catalog Card Number 76-6048
International Standard Book Number ISBN 0-87953-404-4

CIP

Library of Congress Cataloging in Publication Data

Wright, Edgar, 1920—
The critical evaluation of African literature.

Includes bibliographical references and index.
I. African literature (English)—History and criticism—
Addresses, essays, lectures. 2. Criticism.

I. Title.
PR9340.5.W7 1976   820'.9   76-6048
ISBN 0-87953-404-4

1. African literature (English)—History and criticism—Addresses, essays, lectures. 2. Criticism.

1. African literature (English)—History and criticism—Addresses, essays, lectures. 2. Criticism.

Contents

▼▼▼▼▼▼▼▼▼▼▼▼▼▼▼▼▼▼▼▼▼▼▼▼▼▼▼▼▼▼▼▼▼▼▼

Acknowledgements

▼▼▼▼▼▼▼▼▼▼▼▼▼▼▼▼▼▼▼▼▼▼▼▼▼▼▼▼▼▼▼▼▼▼▼▼

For permission to reproduce material in this book we are grateful to the following:

Editions Gallimard, Paris, for 'Vivre' and 'Echanges' by J. Supervielle (*Gravitations*, Collection Poesie, 1966); and 'Que je meure Ramatoa' by J. Paulhan (*Les Hains-Tenys*, 1939). Oxford University Press, London, for excerpts from *The Swamp Dwellers* by Wole Soyinka (*Three Short Plays*, 1969). Weidenfeld & Nicolson, London and Macmillan Publishing Co., Inc., New York for excerpts from *The Rise and Fall of the Man of Letters* by John Gross (1969). It has not been possible to trace the copyright in all cases. The publishers apologise for any omissions and would be glad to hear from any such unacknowledged copyright holders.

Introduction

▼▼▼▼▼▼▼▼▼▼▼▼▼▼▼▼▼▼▼▼▼▼▼▼▼▼▼▼▼▼▼▼▼▼▼

THE relationship between a literature and the critical comment that develops about it is never static. Any new literature or literary movement of value is not only subject to existing critical approaches but may itself act as a powerful agent in modifying those approaches; there is a continuous dialogue between literature and criticism. The purpose of the essays in this volume is to discuss some of the more important elements of this dialogue as it relates to modern African writing, and to provide examples of ways in which contemporary critical approaches can be employed and modified, critically examining particular authors or aspects of literature.

Written African literature can be said to be in general terms a post-war phenomenon. It is true that a historical survey will include writing by Africans from earlier periods. It is also true that one important element – the work of Senghor, Césaire and others of the early *négritude* period – developed in the 'thirties, although anglophone writing has no comparable development. This volume concentrates on literature in English, with the exception of the final essay, which I will comment on later. The real beginnings of African literature in English occur in the 'fifties, and it was not until the middle 'sixties that a sizeable body of work was available for critical comparison. Jahn's bibliography published in 1965[1] presented the first comprehensive view of what was available, and was able to do it quite comfortably in one volume while including a large amount of related material. At this point a necessary qualification is that oral literature has not so far been mentioned.

Critical comment followed hard on publication, but on the whole is a development of the 'sixties. For some time it was a comment limited in tone and range, confining itself mainly to description and explanation, while avoiding much serious excursion into evaluation. There were some good reasons for this. Among them were the desire to foster and encourage African writing, a wish to support the political, cultural and emotional attitudes for which the literature was often a vehicle, the reluctance of white critics to

[1] Jahn, Janheinz, *A Bibliography of Neo-African Literature: from Africa, America and the Caribbean* (Deutsch, London, 1965).

appear hostile or condescending, the lack of Africans with much training or experience in literary discussion, and, of necessity, the absence of a critical tradition, other than the European one, to handle the new elements appearing in African writing. A basis of critical comment slowly developed, the periodicals *Présence Africaine* and *Black Orpheus* playing a major part in the initial stages, while African critics began to emerge from the universities and from the equally important formative discussions in clubs and bars and cafés. The literature itself grew at a rapid if uneven rate as publishing houses encouraged new writers and helped to establish publishing bases on the African continent. A world-wide interest in all things African created a 'band-wagon' which carried African literature with it as a subject of study and discussion into the western world, and at the same time, with the growth of educational institutions, into the African educational pattern.

The critical methodology and theory available to begin with was on the whole what had developed from and around the literary tradition of the western world. Its traditional concerns with themes and content, style, plot and character-analysis served well enough initially for descriptive and broadly interpretative comment. But these were soon felt to be inadequate. The intentions and techniques of the writers were rapidly becoming more complex, absorbing contemporary ideas while bringing in concepts and methods from a living tradition of oral literature. Modern criticism had developed new theories and methodologies, which provided an increasing stock of critical tools for more refined forms of analysis, and in turn the use of more refined and specialized critical techniques could often discover values and subtleties in earlier writers that had been ignored by descriptive methods. So re-evaluation and more stringent critical analysis developed, to build on earlier comment. As criticism developed around African literature it found itself having to allow for elements that it had not so far been able to deal with in any methodical fashion, although the consciousness of them had been present from the beginning. Two aspects can be emphasized. The first concerned the differences between African and western literature, differences deriving from cultural and linguistic backgrounds which were capable of producing modes of thought and effects of technique strange to western criticism. The second aspect is really part of this, but is important enough to warrant separate mention; it concerned the growing realization of the importance of an oral literary tradition. Yet at the same time critics were beginning to trace more clearly and closely the influences of western writers and literary methods on African literature.

Such a brief survey, unsatisfactory as it must be, provides some idea of the context out of which these essays developed. Each contributor has gone his own way, but each has consciously attempted to bring to bear on his chosen topic a knowledge and experience of critical methods and standards gained from English literature in general, while being also experienced in the problems and values deriving from the African tradition and background. The first two essays discuss some of the critical problems directly. Each of the remaining essays focuses on a particular writer, possibly on a selected aspect of that writer's work, applying a selected critical method and making comparisons or passing judgements according to the standards that would apply to any work of literature. To put it another way, these essays attempt to show how general critical techniques can be applied to African literature given a knowledge of the problems that may occur for criticism because of the interaction of two literary, linguistic and cultural traditions.

The final essay by Clive Wake breaks away from the anglophone emphasis to deal with a francophone poet. It is easy to forget that parallel developments were producing an equally important corpus of new literature from French-speaking Africa, and not only from the Paris-centred group that I mentioned earlier. It is useful to be reminded that a literary renaissance developed from within Africa in French as well as in English (and for that matter in Portuguese). The growth of literature in the African languages is yet another story.

It should be noted that Ngugi has dropped James Ngugi, the name under which he published his first books, and now uses his birthname of Ngugi wa Thiong'o.

Every effort has been made by individual contributors to acknowledge all sources of reference. I would like to thank Jean Hardwick for her invaluable secretarial help. Finally I would like to thank the Canada Council, whose assistance in providing a travel and study grant enabled me to do some of the necessary work and research in preparation for this volume.

EDGAR WRIGHT

1 Critical Procedures and the Evaluation of African Literature

▼▼▼▼▼▼▼▼▼▼▼▼▼▼▼▼▼▼▼▼▼▼▼▼▼▼▼▼▼▼▼

EDGAR WRIGHT

S ERIOUS critics of English language literature, as well as those whose interests extend to comparative literature, are beginning to show by reference and comment an increasing realization that modern African literature is a part of contemporary literature in English. But there is also a need to be aware that African literature poses many special problems for the critic, especially since theories, methodologies and standards of criticism as we normally use them have developed largely within a western context. It is possible to distinguish a number of the main problems, such as those related to language use and to cultural distinctiveness, and to discuss the extent to which a responsible criticism should modify itself on their account. In doing this it becomes necessary to ask how far these are, in fact, new problems, and if so, to what degree. It is possible that they can be regarded as variants of problems that criticism and editorial practice have already learned to handle. An examination of the way in which critical and editorial practice have handled past problems, together with a look at the methods of some modern African writers, can provide us with some idea of how far we may or may not need to adjust normal critical techniques.

Edgar Wright has taught and published work on Victorian literature and on language, as well as on African literature. He was on the staff of University College, Nairobi, Kenya, for many years. He is now Professor of English at Laurentian University, Canada.

The problem I want to examine has begun to be noted by critics of English literature over the last few years. John Gross has stated a number of its features as he surveys the present state of 'letters'. Having argued that the modern world has no room any more for the profession of 'man of letters' he goes on to point out that any parochial or insular view of English literature is also impossible.

Science, sociology, the cinema – the kind of forces which have been mentioned so far are at work throughout the entire more-or-less civilized world.
But there is one further development which affects English critics specifically. Since the war it has inevitably been brought home to them far more
forcibly than ever before that there are many other authors writing in
English besides Englishmen. In practice that means, overwhelmingly,
Americans. But in addition writers from Commonwealth or ex-Common-
wealth countries – figures as different as A. D. Hope and Chinua Achebe –
are at least beginning to count for English readers in their own right, not as
curiosities or poor relations, and this is going to be more and more the case
as time goes on. The English literary scene itself, too, would be noticeably
poorer if it were not for some of the Commonwealth writers who have
settled here in recent years. At first sight it may not seem as though all this
has any particular bearing on the role of the critic. Nor does it, perhaps, in
immediate practical terms. But I think it is true to say that in the past
month English critics have been fortified by the idea, whether explicitly
formulated or not, that by right of birth they are the guardians and interpreters of one of the world's great literary traditions. Put that bluntly, it
may make them sound as though they were the custodians of the Crown
Jewels, and no doubt a good deal of inferior criticism has often been a form
of patriotic advertising. But the question goes much deeper than that. One
need only consider the part played by the idea of English tradition in the
thought of Leavis, or, more recently, Raymond Williams. Or take F. W.
Bateson, a critic who certainly qualifies, both in literature and politics, as a
progressive. In *English Poetry: A Critical Introduction* (which in general
seems to me an admirable book) he observes that 'in modern times a society,
in the sense of a linguistic unit, rarely overflows the boundaries of the
nation-state'.[1]

Gross does not unfortunately attempt to deal with the issue of criticism; he is
content to raise it and then to comment on the impact of American writing.
This shift is really a ducking of the problem, for American culture has common roots with English culture.[2]

[1] *The Rise and Fall of the Man of Letters* (Macmillan, London, 1969), pp.
288–9.

[2] American literature has been, until very recently, the literature of white
America. The tendency of contemporary criticism is to treat white and black
American literature as two culturally distinct areas; partly at least because
many Negro writers themselves insist on their Afro–American heritage. The
whole question of the context in which recent American writing should be
judged raises its own particular problems, but these reflect in many ways the
issues under discussion here, notably the desire for a recognized cultural
separateness on the part of a race that is consciously rejecting its previous

In spite of the standard jokes about England and America being divided by a common language, the degree to which both language and the social experiences communicated by language are shared creates a major tie. The appearance of the term 'mid-Atlantic' to describe a type of English dialect indicates a good deal of this growing approximation.

The question of the nature and use of English as a language in various parts of the world has also been noted, more however by linguists than by literary critics, though the state of affairs has been put, with some over-emphasis, by George Steiner:

> 'The great energies of the language now enter into play outside England ... African English, Australian English, the rich speech of West Indian and Anglo–Indian writers, represent a complicated polycentric field of linguistic force, in which the language taught and written on this island is no longer the inevitable authority or focus.'[3]

But Steiner also misses an important point: by running together the various versions of 'English' as a group he blurs the fact that at least three quite distinct types of English are under discussion: (*a*) English as a mother tongue, e.g. Australian English, South African English, American English. (*b*) English as a second language, e.g. English in Africa where the first language is a vernacular, and the actual English spoken (e.g. Ghanaian, Nigerian) will be influenced by regional languages and contacts. (*c*) English that has been, or is in the process of becoming, 'creolized', e.g. West Indian English. In such cases a new language is being created, which may be close or not so close to English.

Even these distinctions need a good deal more discussion, and I shall return to the language problem later. The immediate point to note is that where English is being used as a second language, a problem by no means easy to handle is created for the literary critic who wishes to analyse or discuss the style of a writer. It is very possible that Steiner deliberately chose to blur the differences in order to focus on the fact of variety, which of course is important. But for African literature, which is wholly 'second-language' in its use of English, the distinctions are necessary.

[3] Article in *The Listener*, 21 October 1965.

---

domination by another race. In practice I doubt whether any important writing by white or black in America today can be uninfluenced by the 'other culture'. The deliberate turning towards black Africa by American Negroes is also having an effect in many areas; one can instance fashions in clothes and hair, the growth in the teaching of Swahili, the recent formation of the African Heritage Studies Association as a counter to the African Studies Association. But these issues, though important, lie outside my present argument.

Both Gross and Steiner do, however, show that the road of the traditional critic becomes full of mines and booby-traps when it leads him into the territory of African literature. The question of critical authority is raised, and raised too justly to be ignored.

One obvious response is to reject the whole apparatus of western criticism and western standards. Joseph Okpaku moves to this extreme.

> The present practice of judging African literature by Western standards is not only invalid, it is also potentially dangerous to a development of African arts. It presupposes that there is one absolute artistic standard and that, of course, is the Western standard. Consequently, good African literature is taken to be that which most approximates to Western literature.[4]

So far, so good; the point is well and energetically made. But the conclusion he arrives at a couple of pages later is that western culture is totally irrelevant.

> The primary criticism of African arts must come from Africans using African standards. We cannot accept either of the existing two approaches to criticism of African literature. It is as undesirable to plead for leniency in criticizing African works as it is absurd for Lewis Nkosi to ask that Western critical standards be used. Western critical standards are developed in the Western tradition and are applied by Western critics to interpret and criticise Western Literature to the Western audience. Thus, when a critic says of the Western writer that he smacks of Conrad, he immediately invokes a whole concept of Conradism with which the Western reader is acquainted as part of his cultural education. So, when the Western critic looks at an African work he immediately tries to find out which Western works it best resembles so he can use this to establish communication with the Western reader. His comparisons are made against the background of Western Literature and, therefore, Western Culture. By the same token, an African critic trying to relate African Literature or any literature to Africa must do so against the background of African Culture. He must draw upon the patterns of the African aesthetic. In other words, he must use African critical standards.[5]

Okpaku does quote, a few sentences earlier, Soyinka's statement, which carries the argument not in terms of critical traditions but of art: 'Soyinka says we do not want to be African writers but writers.' Now such an attitude as Okpaku's, however justified by exasperation at the insularity of some western critics or by

---

[4] 'Tradition, Culture and Criticism', *Présence Africaine*, no. 70, 1969, p. 139.
[5] Ibid. p. 141.

national or racial pride, seems to me to throw away the baby with the bath water. The references to Lewis Nkosi and Soyinka show also that African writers are by no means agreed on this approach.

The problem remains. Both in matter and manner, content and style, culture and language, interests and expression (to use some of the common critical terms of opposition), modern African literature in English has roots and contexts that lie outside the traditional cultural and linguistic soil which has nourished the literature of the west. The western world, not simply the English-speaking elements but the whole European tradition, has been influenced by Greek thought; the study of Greek and Latin literature, thought, even grammar, was the basis of all education from the renaissance until the end of the nineteenth century. Aristotle and others are (quite rightly and legitimately) alive and well in the literary theories of the west, though now jostled and sometimes ignored by a swarm of later arrivals. Today the west is just beginning to find out that the cultural and, more narrowly, the literary heritages of Africans are also extensive and rooted in living traditions. The view that oral literature consists of collections of naïve or simple folktales, though stubbornly entrenched, is rapidly becoming untenable; some real beginnings have been made in examining the complexity of the artistic reality.[6]

Yet it is impossible to avoid recognizing that writers using English produce work that moves into the current of 'world literature' in English. There was an early critical honeymoon when virtually any work by an African author was treated kindly, either because of its novelty or because encouragement is necessary to a developing literature. The situation is now greatly changed. African literature is reviewed as a matter of course, albeit scantily, in general periodicals and papers along with other English-language literature; at the same time critical discussion has a home in a large and growing number of specialist journals dealing with African affairs. But there are no common or agreed standards for evaluation, nor are the problems involved in achieving such standards widely understood. I shall not presume to suggest the standards. I can attempt to show the problems in some detail and perhaps clarify a little the issue of whether, or how far, modern African literature in English should be judged by the criteria and standards that have developed over centuries to handle English literature.

To begin with it is necessary to have some working definition of 'African literature'. This itself is not easy. A geographical definition would appear to be simple, but problems of race and culture appear, even so. (Europeans are native to South Africa, Arabs to North Africa, for example.) Some critics

---

[6] The most comprehensive treatment so far is Ruth Finnegan's contribution to the Oxford Library of African Literature, *Oral Literature in Africa* (Oxford University Press, 1970).

favour an extremely loose definition, which would include West Indians and North American Negroes on grounds of influences and affinities. For the purpose of this discussion I shall stay within the limits that I have proposed elsewhere and confine the term to writers from the non-Arabic countries of the African continent, excluding those who are of European descent.[7] For those using English this implies the former colonies of Britain, plus Ethiopia. (Botswana, Ethiopia, Ghana, Kenya, Lesotho, Malawi, Nigeria, Rhodesia, Sierra Leone, Somalia, South Africa, Tanzania, Uganda.) Such a working definition has the advantage that it presents a group of countries in all of which there are vernaculars that are vigorous and alive, carrying oral traditions independent of western ideas or cultures, yet in which the use of English as a second language is also strongly developed.

Even when so defined – and any broader definition seems to me to make the use of the word 'African' hopelessly vague – the term is still misleading. Most of the writers themselves, and most critics who have discussed the literature, would agree that we are dealing with a number of national literatures that have certain elements in common, distinguishing them from the literatures of countries that are in direct lineal descent from English-speaking culture. These elements can be fairly easily listed, though for any one country there will inevitably be exceptions or variations. The degree of commonness is more important than any exception related to a particular aspect.

(i)   There is at most only a brief history of written literature, but a strong tradition of oral literature that is still alive.

(ii) The vernaculars (there may be many within one country) are still actively used at all levels of normal social and family life.

(iii) English is the second language common throughout the country, used as a medium of education (at higher if not at lower levels) and as the medium of communication with other countries in Africa and beyond.

[7] E. Wright, 'African Literature I: Problems of Criticism', *The Journal of Commonwealth Literature*, vol. 2, 1966. The counter-argument can be vigorous, as in this quotation from a paper by the South African Mazisi Kunene, 'Revolutionary Challenges & Cultural Perspectives', given at the 1969 Algiers Festival, reported in the *Journal of the New African Literature and the Arts*, nos. 7/8, 1970, p. 96.

In order to divide Africa, which is obviously in their interest, they [imperialists] have propagated a myth based on racial division. Much attention has been paid to what is called Africa north of the Sahara and Africa south of the Sahara (one wonders what would happen if the Sahara became cultivable once again). This differentiation is true to the Fascist colonial mentality based on race, racism being an institution or a superstition arising out of a colonial situation.

(iv) The past history is that of a colonial territory subject to cultural, political and missionary as well as linguistic influence from Britain.

(v) The present history is one of achieved independence, with a growing awareness of both national identity and modern problems.

(vi) There is an acute racial awareness based on colour.

(vii) Traditional culture (possibly a number of individual cultures) is a major influence on the development of the contemporary national culture and its accompanying attitudes and beliefs.

Some of the exceptions are important enough to be noted in general terms. Ethiopia in particular has a long history of independence and national identity; its brief period as a colony was under Italian rule; it has long been Christianized and it had a written literature. Swahili in East Africa is a supra-national language, and one with a written tradition. The political situation in South Africa ranks as still colonial for its non-white population. And so on: no one country is a copy of the past or present pattern of another; the dis-similarities form part of the individuality that goes to the creation of a national literature, or possibly, in the African situation, of a regional literature within the national literature, when a regional vernacular and culture flourishes side by side with the national consciousness and the general use of English. Ibo authors in Nigeria and perhaps Luo authors in Kenya provide examples of such individuality; in some ways such regions may be considered as equi-valents of Scotland at the end of the eighteenth century, when Scottish literature flourished.[8]

These common elements can themselves be roughly grouped, though with considerable overlap, as cultural, political and linguistic. If we accept tem-porarily and for convenience the critical habit of creating a dichotomy between matter and manner, then we have on the one side the cultural and political life of the community as providing the content (the 'matter'), while the relationships between English as the language of writing and the verna-cular as the language of daily life provide the linguistic area or 'manner'. Such a division is inadequate, but provides a basis for further analysis. If we carry on with our rough-and-ready division, then we shall need to include 'form' under 'manner', and straight away we run into a problem that hardly exists for written literature but is crucial for an oral tradition. Oral literature is so intimately related to a socio-cultural context for performance that the linguis-tic element is only one of many elements that make up the 'manner' of narra-tion. Oral literature is discussed elsewhere; the literary critic faced with the printed page should be aware of how and when forms and techniques have

[8] For general comment on this situation see for example W. L. Renwick, *English Literature 1789–1815*, Oxford History of English Literature, vol. 9 (Oxford University Press, 1963), ch. 7.

been taken over from the oral tradition, deliberately or unconsciously, as well as of the effect they will leave on the African reader who links directly with the tradition.

Two further questions face the western critic of modern African literature. The first is whether any general critical theory, e.g. a mythopoeic or a Freudian approach, can work when applied to a culture that is totally distinct in its origins from the one that supplied the source material for the theory. How universal are such theories? The second relates to the reading public and the author's intention. Who, ultimately, is the writer writing for, and who can best appreciate or evaluate his purpose and methods?

The question of the transmissibility of culture has troubled critics for a long time. It developed originally with the question of translation, particularly concerning the Greek classics. Robert Browning posed it in *Aristophanes' Apology* (1875), when Balaustion asks what may happen if, after Greek civilization is finished, its art arrives:

> In novel lands as strange, where, all the same,
> Their men and women yet behold, as we.
> Blue heaven, black earth, and love, hate, hope and fear ...

and imagines the people of the Kassiterides (Britain) complaining that the subject-matter of a painting is peculiar, the behaviour shown indecent:

> Each hair too indistinct – for, see our own!
> Hands, not skin-coloured as these hands we have ...
> Shows wrestlers, wrestling at the public games,
> Atrociously exposed from head to foot.

The fear is that however fine the art:

> Such strangers may judge feebly, stranger like.[9]

In practice the problem has been recognized as wider than one of translated classics. Home-bred classics also need their culture explained for the modern reader; the annotation of Shakespeare or Milton, for example, is necessary. The background of reference and cultural content has altered in important

[9] *The Poetical Works of Robert Browning* (Smith, Elder & Co., 1900), vol. 1, p. 704.

ways, and though the reader can understand much of the language there is still a good deal that requires interpretation. Yet we are still within a tradition, though one that has changed and is changing possibly even faster today; even with the Greek classics we are still within a tradition of western culture. A reversal of it has been created by the spread of the English language; the fear voiced by Balaustion also applies to English literature itself, carried overseas. But the real twist has been created by the growth of English as a second language. The words and the syntax are, by and large, the same, but the culture of reference is different. The English tradition is there, carried by the language and by the forces that brought the language; so are other traditions that share no part of western culture.

The novelist Anthony Burgess recalls his own experience of this as a translator:

> My first big effort was a Malay version of *The Waste Land* – difficult to do, since, in the tropics, April is no more or less cruel than any other month, and summer cannot surprise one if it is summer all the year round. Translation, as anthropological linguists keep telling us, is not just a matter of words.
>
> Given a language like French, however ... it is mostly words, and the turning of a French novel into English is essentially a matter of Part One of the big Harrap, a little book called *Beyond the Dictionary in French* and the marshalling of what elegance one can find in oneself.[10]

There are other facets to the problem, but we can perhaps pause here to note that editorial techniques have been developed to deal with certain difficulties. The footnote, the glossary, the explanatory preface can cope with most of the barriers to understanding at what we may call the informational level. These techniques have been gradually accepted for normal editions of contemporary writing, so that it is now common for a new book by an African author to carry a minimum amount of 'apparatus' to eliminate most of the obstructions caused by the use of strange words or references, whether the apparatus is supplied editorially or by the author.

The use of notes in this way developed steadily in the nineteenth century, and for reasons that apply to the present discussion. Literature in general, with the novel rapidly becoming the dominant form, was the medium of vision through which the reading public was made aware of the world around it. I suppose that Sir Walter Scott must always remain the great example in this development because of the way in which, first in poetry and then with his novels, he revealed Scotland as a place and a culture; describing it, exploring

[10] 'Bless Thee, Bottom,' *The Times Literary Supplement*, 18 September 1970, p. 1024.

and analysing its history and its relationship with England, treating its inhabitants as worthy of being heroes and heroines in fiction, presenting its dialect as a natural form of language that could and should be used for serious as well as comic effect. Scott himself had no qualms about giving explanatory notes occasionally, while for a long time standard editions have glossed dialect terms and explained references to people, customs, tradition. (The accuracy of Scott's presentation, the selection of items and events that he put forward to represent Scotland, is not the issue here.)

One obvious point has to be emphasized: Scott was a supreme narrative artist. Editorial techniques are no substitute for literary skill or creative imagination, and the writer who relies on them has probably mistaken his *métier*: as has the writer who churns out naïve social anthropology under the guise of fiction, a literary mode all too wearily common in the modern African novel. But the questions relating the writer's art to presentation of content will be discussed in more detail later. Throughout the nineteenth century and up to the present day, literature has continued to convey not simply information, but the imaginative experience of other worlds and other cultures. To support it there has been the booming popularity of travel books. And 'ex Africa semper aliquid novi' – there was always something new out of Africa, as Pliny is reported to have remarked. To follow the explanations and descriptions of the earlier travellers there came, in the twentieth century, journalism, radio, film and television; the pictured scene and the (more or less) expert commentator.

My point is that strangeness is no stranger to literature. The common reader, if such a statistical vagary still exists, has down the generations acquired the habit of moving into strange worlds, and has had an ever-increasing intensity of formal and informal education to support his reading. The question for us is where, if anywhere, we can be expected to place the limits of imaginative or rational comprehension; or, to put it more pointedly, how far can a white man ever really understand or experience the world of the African (or vice versa)? Standard editorial techniques and the impact of educational systems and communications media combine to remove a lot of the difficulty at the factual or informational level. Can or should the reader expect more from the writer, from the editor, or from his own knowledge or experience – before he can claim to understand or be in a position to criticize a piece of African writing? The aspects of language and literary art may be distinguished for the moment as separate in order that we may concentrate on this concept of culture.

The response varies with individual writers and critics. If there are areas of sensibility and experience in each culture that are inevitably and permanently inaccessible to those outside the culture, they lie, as Burgess noted in the extract quoted earlier, in something that 'is not just a matter of words'. We move into the areas of morality, of aesthetics, of social relationships; into worlds of connotations and awarenesses that flesh out the words used to express them. For example:

> It is possible for someone fully to understand, and to be able to use correctly, the idioms of conventional morality, while rejecting this whole terminology as superstitious or in some other way inadequate . . . He is then in a position similar to (but not the same as) that of the anthropologist, or the student of comparative religion, who learns to use or to understand a language, or part of a language, while denying that many of the distinctions or classifications involved in the language correspond to any reality.[11]

One can apply this argument both to the critic looking at a second-language literature and to the writer using the second language. The critic applies a complex of acquired concepts within which any one of the terms he uses will be understood and will work. This may be illustrated at a technical level with the term 'form'. 'Form' is a generalization, induced from existing forms (we speak of 'the form of the novel') and from the possibility of future forms that may be relatable to existing ones. Produce something whose relationships are dubious, or are related to other complexes, and doubts arise, as they have done with Tutuola's *The Palm-wine Drinkard*. Here the relationships lie with a narrative tradition (oral, not written) and a culture (non-western, non-Christian) that make judgements of the form of the work difficult if we wish to relate it to or compare it with other novels in English. Or, in a novel whose form or language presents no problem, so that we can follow a total pattern of behaviour – for example Achebe's *Arrow of God* – we could reject the pattern itself as psychologically nonsensical, meaning that we could not accept such a pattern within our range of meaning of psychology. Since Achebe uses, and uses very well, the techniques of western fiction for the presentation and development of Ezeulu's character (context of social background and relationships, dialogue, interior monologue, analysis of motivation, authorial presence, etc.) the reader will probably accept, although he may not sympathize with, the pattern of behaviour. A more subtle danger is that we may *assume* we understand the pattern since we are at home with the method of presentation, while in fact we miss the real significance because we have imposed one of our own on it. With a writer such as Achebe the danger is minimized because of his control over the skills and art of the form he is using, and because of his own ease of movement in both Ibo and western cultures. It is also important that Achebe's preferred theme is that of transition, of the impact of one culture on another, so that his viewpoint has been to some extent that of the

[11] Stuart Hampshire, 'The Interpretation of Language: Words and Concepts', *British Philosophy in the Mid-Century* (Allen & Unwin, London, 1966), p. 271.

middle ground. Tutuola's presentation and subject-matter is, language apart, from within the Ibo culture; the reader is left to observe and emphasize as best he can or wishes to. The result is that for most western readers the formal category for Tutuola is the quaint or folksy fantasy.

Against the view that would stress the gulf rather than the bridges, we can place a writer such as Soyinka, who is not prepared to accept that because a writer is initially bound by the culture of his roots, he must also be chained and padlocked by it.

> I borrow seasons from an alien land
> In brotherhood of ill, pride of race around me
> Strewn in sunlit shards. I borrow alien lands
> To stay the season of a mind.[12]

Soyinka points up the interchangeability of cultural experience, the use of one culture to cope with experiences or events in another. The views expressed here should be matched against Burgess's comments on the handling of seasons.

The discussion at this point tends to spill over into a matter of ideologies. *Négritude* developed from a felt need to emphasize distinctness, to pull away and stand apart from the white man's culture. It did distinguish, it is true, between fundamental and more superficial aspects of culture, although less sophisticated supporters of *négritude* stressed the aspects of traditionalism. *Négritude* itself was concerned, especially at its beginning, with literature as a medium for asserting the cultural affinities of the African spirit to a particular regional culture, and at the same time to other Africans in general. But the arguments for separateness quickly and naturally merged with political and racial attitudes and antagonisms. Much of the theory that developed in the mid-'sixties led back finally to emotional attitudes and political facts to do with independence, racism, and neo-colonialism. It tended to reject any interpretation, let alone any attempt at critical evaluation, from what was seen as an antagonistic or patronizing culture. Opponents of *négritude* rejected the need for and the viability of an all-embracing theory; preferring to acknowledge political and racial situations that had common elements across the African content, and in situations of racial conflict, while stopping short of a generalized mystique of African culture. It would probably be accepted fairly generally today that *négritude* is no longer a powerful force, but the critical attitudes and ideas it fostered, though often attacked, are still influential.[13]

---

[12] Wole Soyinka, 'Massacre, October '66', *Idanre* (Methuen, London, 1967), p. 52.

[13] See, for example, the theory of Neo-African Literature developed by Janheinz Jahn.

There are, then, various motives for emphasizing or making little of the question of crossing over cultures. The difficulties certainly exist; in practice they can be important but not, I think, insuperable. If we wish to work from extremes then it is incontestably true that no one individual can ever understand or share fully the experiences of another. (In the same way, as I shall point out later, no individual speaks precisely the same language as any other.) Yet we accept for all practical purposes the existence of a good deal of common experience and understanding shared by members of a community, who in turn have common ground with other communities and families of communities. And so on. Time, familiarity and the spread of knowledge continually spread this range of commonness. Literature is still a prime medium for acting on the minds and imaginations of readers in such a way as to make them understand through vicarious experience customs, behaviour, emotions that were formerly strange or unknown to them. It may be that certain types of experience, certain emotions or attitudes in one culture are too far at the limits of imagination for members of another culture to grasp, but before accepting such a notion it will be at least wise to ask whether the failure to 'come across' is not a failure in the art of presentation rather than some fixed and eternal cultural gulf.

One should also take into account the myths that have been fastened on to Africa and still befuddle western attitudes. Africa has come to the foreground too rapidly for easy and informed comprehension. It is only a generation ago that the Africa of popular imagination and wide belief was the Africa created by Rider Haggard and Edgar Wallace and Edgar Rice Burroughs. It was a fantasy world for Europeans before science fiction came along, inhabited by witch-doctors and mysterious beings, or dominated by a literally swinging Tarzan. Where realism was attempted, the picture was often of a child-like race controlled by a superior one. Pseudo-scientific myths (the lesser brain power, the sexual prowess) were and still are current. It is easy to claim that the intelligent critic – you or I, that is – is too mature, too well informed to be affected by such habits of popular thinking; it may be well occasionally to check within oneself.

> ... communication requires the use of *language* (that is, of the area of overlap between two or more people's usage) rather than the use of personal language. Now in order to have an overlap you have to decide whom you are going to overlap with.[14]

Personal language is earlier referred to, in Le Page's article, as the verbal behaviour of the individual. The writer, in deliberately setting out to publish

[14] R. B. Le Page, 'Dialect in West Indian Literature', *Journal of Commonwealth literature*, no. 7, July 1969, p. 3.

his work, or even in acquiescing to a request for publication, will normally be making certain assumptions, not only about the accessibility of his language to others – the use of *language*, the area of overlap – but about the nature of those others, his reading public. And to some extent the writer, if he has a skilful enough control of style, can set his own priorities in choosing that reading public. He can decide to overlap primarily with language-users of his own community or country, or with language-users in countries where English is the native language. Many modern African novelists lack sufficient linguistic range and control to make such a choice; they are then necessarily confined to using the form of English of the region in which they live. To modify a term being used as the basis for a description of modern British English, 'standard educated English', educated Nigerian English, or educated Kenyan English, and so on, will be the language used.

Such writing may still become popular beyond the linguistic boundaries from which it developed, and this for many possible reasons, ranging from innate values to a fashionable interest in a particular area or a desire by readers for novelty. But critical comment will probably vary from one linguistic area to another, since the local critic can recognize a clumsy or false style immediately, while the non-local critic sometimes has no means of differentiating between clumsiness and creativeness. The writings of Tutuola and Okara are of interest here, and I shall look at them briefly before turning to see how such critical problems arise in an examination of Okot p'Bitek's *Song of Lawino* and its sequel, *Song of Ocol*.

The case of Tutuola has already been mentioned. *The Palm-wine Drinkard* was extravagantly praised by western critics when it first appeared in 1952, and was then vehemently attacked as an articulate core of Nigerian criticism developed.[15] To many western critics Tutuola's language was delightfully fresh, a naïve 'non-English' that was an admirable vehicle for a non-western, and by implication African world of imaginative fantasy. It is a language that does not rely on dialect markers of pronunciation or vocabulary; its non-Englishness relies on a quaint usage and syntactical order rather than on incorrectness. But for Nigerian critics also Tutuola's language was strange. It is not the English of Nigeria; it is neither the pidgin nor any level of educated English used for communication within Nigeria or between Nigeria and other countries. Nigerian writers were suspicious of what they suspected to be patronizing overtones in the praise that had been meted out. Local opposition

[15] For a useful assessment of past arguments, and a basis for revaluation, see O. Leslie, '"The Palm-wine Drinkard": A Reassessment of Amos Tutuola', and B. Lindfors, 'Amos Tutuola and D. O. Fagunwa', *Journal of Commonwealth Literature*, No. 9, 1970. Taban lo Liyong's comments in 'Tutuola, son of Zinjanthropus', *The Last Word* (East African Publishing House, Nairobi, 1969), p. 158, present an interesting East African viewpoint.

to Tutuola had good reason to exist; his emergence as the first successful Nigerian writer created anticipations about the development of African literature that had then to be denied. Nigerian writers were about to face some difficult choices about the presentation of reality, whether they wished to examine their past or their present, and some equally difficult choices about readership and the audience they wanted to 'overlap' with. Tutuola's style was tied to the world of imaginative fantasy that was one aspect of Yoruba oral literature; the writers who immediately followed him had not only to create viable styles of their own grounded in more normal usage, but had also to face comparisons with Tutuola's use of the language. Now that there has been time to come to terms with it against a varied and solid achievement of creative writing across the African continent, it can be seen more clearly as a 'loner' in the field, and such work is always especially difficult to evaluate.

The real problem is that Tutuola's language represents nothing but Tutuola. It is a literary artefact inasmuch as it is peculiar to Tutuola.[16] It lies in a linguistic limbo, appropriate to its subject-matter; it does not communicate a contemporary reality.

There is yet another point that criticism should perhaps consider at some stage; the extent of editorial intervention where second-language writing is concerned. Geoffrey Parrinder, in his introduction to a later novel by Tutuola, stated: 'The book has been edited to remove the grosser mistakes, clear up some ambiguities, and curtail some repetition. But the original flavour of the style has been left to produce its own effect.'[17] Since the style of *My Life in the Bush of Ghosts* is similar to that of the earlier novel, we can assume that a similar process was at work there. If so, Tutuola's verbal behaviour, his style, is not even fully his own; a non-Nigerian polish has been given to it. It is common knowledge that well-known English writers have had their style helped along by publishers' readers, but the impact can be crucial when judgements are made of the stylistic efforts of second-language English. The work will stand or fall, rightly, by the effect that it produces in its published form, but critical comment on the development of language styles may go wildly astray if editorialized texts are used as the examples.

But to return briefly to the language question, we may generalize Tutuola's solutions to the stylistic problems discussed by saying that he gets his registers right. The register he adopts is in harmony with the level of limited complexity

---

[16] It is, of course, perfectly possible to analyse the linguistic constituents of Tutuola's style. The articles referred to in the previous note examine a number of these. My comments are confined to the impact made by the style and to the early response of literary critics.

[17] Amos Tutuola, *My Life in the Bush of Ghosts* (Faber & Faber, London, 1964), p. 15. (The novel was first published in 1954.)

at which the story content, episodic structure and the characters operate. It may not be 'natural' to any real language world, but it is natural within the created world. The case with Gabriel Okara in *The Voice*[18] is, I suspect, one of an experimental writer who has failed to create any unified style. He also opts out of the linguistic framework of a standard English; deliberately aiming at and claiming to recreate the rhythms of Ijaw. He also 'translates' idioms and usages. It becomes necessary to illustrate:

'Listen. Asking the bottom of things in this town will take you no place. Hook this with your little finger. Put it in your inside's box and lock it up.'
'Your teaching words do not enter my inside.' (p. 29)

'Say nothing more on this matter. This wanted-to-happen thing, on my head it should have fallen. The rain and storm they came and passed away because I the god begged. And this nearly ourselves lost in water. It is my bad head. Talk no more of my son's wife, talk no more, of this matter, talk no more.' (p. 73)

These are real people, but they talk an artificial language. It is not Ijaw. The rhythms may be – I cannot judge; but the base language remains indubitably English. The elected readership for the novel is English-speaking, whether African or non-African, and therefore it is largely unable to pass judgement on Okara's claim. Instead it will pass judgement on the only thing available, the style itself. And here we are constantly being jolted, with little apparent contextual reason, from ordinary colloquial to 'other-idiomatic' to various degrees of formality. The syntactical order is strained, but not with any regularity, e.g. in the second extract the order is subject, object, verb transitive – 'I the god begged.' The SOV sequence occurs three times. But in the first extract we get SVO (or V (imp) O) in all sentences. Similarly the novel throughout mixes formal and informal; the prosaic and the poetic. Okara has failed, in my view, to handle the registers and their implications of mood and social context that are inextricably involved in the use of language, nor has he, like Tutuola, been able to skip the difficulty by creating a consistent style, easily comprehensible but clear of language-tied social or emotional overtones, that creates its own level of register. To be fair to Okara it must be stated that some sensitive and well-informed critics have praised *The Voice* and claimed it as a successful experiment in language. My purpose in dealing with it here is to draw attention to the particular difficulties that face the experimental writer when he is deliberately drawing on the capacities of not one but two languages

[18] Gabriel Okara, *The Voice* (Deutsch, London, 1964 and Heinemann, London, African Writers Series 1970).

and attempting to conflate them realistically. The difficulties are even more acute for the critic who has to interpret the result from the basis of only one language.

Okot p'Bitek's first English publication, the long narrative poem *Song of Lawino*,[19] was a popular and critical success with English-speaking readers, although not in the spectacular manner of Tutuola's first novel. The mere novelty factor of something interesting out of Africa had worn off by the time of its appearance in 1966. There was instead a sufficient body of literature to allow some judgements to be made. A few writers, mainly novelists, were acknowledged to be good, although there was still a tendency to avoid labelling others as bad. Certain genres had become hackneyed, especially the auto-biographical anthropological narrative with its stock scenes of village child-hood, school life and the tensions involved in growing up under the influence of an alien colonial culture. Enough good writing was available also to show up work whose use of language was faulty or naïve. It is worth considering the poem, and its successor, *Song of Ocol*, which appeared in 1970, to ask why it was so well received, and what types of problem it poses.

The type of problem that arises with the poetry of Okot p'Bitek is of quite a different order from what we have been discussing. There is virtually no language difficulty. We are given the occasional linguistic reminder of Afri-canness by the use of an Acoli word, printed in italics, whose precise meaning is either contextualized or is unimportant:

> He says I am silly
> Like the *ojuu* insects that sit on the beer pot
>
> *(Song of Lawino* p. 16)

Occasionally an explanatory note is offered. The question of register is settled by giving Lawino and Ocol, as the basic style for their long monologues, a slightly formal, correct type of speech. This establishes, by the nature of English-language usage, a context of respect or inherent dignity, which can be modulated by colloquialism or emotion. This solution is, in fact, similar to the one used by earlier English writers when they wished readers to forget class implications about characters and to accept them in their roles as heroes or heroines; Oliver Twist and Jane Eyre use standard English and received pronunciation instead of slang or dialect. Okot p'Bitek uses this linguistic literary convention to equalize the relationship between Lawino and Ocol, since Ocol accuses his wife of being an ignorant rustic. Their real speech

[19] East African Publishing House, Nairobi, 1966.

environment is Acoli, but they come to us through the medium of English and
are presented as speech equals without any markers of class or educational
distinction, which English can handle through dialect forms and syntax. As
far as the English-language use is concerned, Lawino is Ocol's equal, within
the Acoli cultural context. Since p'Bitek is his own translator and has the
sophisticated competence in English that results from years of residence and
higher education in England, he presumably realizes this.

Within that style we can recognize discriminations as we would in other
English-language poems, even while description and comment enable us to see
European manners through non-European eyes. When, for example, Lawino
comments on the westernized Clementine who is her husband's mistress

> Her breasts are completely shrivelled up,
> They are all folded dry skins,
> They have made nests of cotton wool
> And she folds the bits of cow-hide
> In the nests
> And calls them breasts! ...
> The modern type sleep with their nests
> Tied firmly on their chests
>
> (*Song of Lawino* p. 25)

the effect is not just satirical; it reveals Lawino's pride in her own body and,
more abstractly, in a way of life that rejects the type of falseness symbolized by
a padded brassière. It also indirectly comments on the stupidity of her
husband Ocol, who allows himself to be caught by such a contraption. Yet
superficially the description is naïve; a reflection of Lawino's lack of sophistication. In another section of the poem she comments on her inability to tell
the time:

> Ocol has brought home
> A large clock
> It goes tock-tock-tock-tock
> And it rings a bell ...
> I wonder what causes
> The noise inside it!
> And what makes it go!
>
> (*Song of Lawino* p. 86)

Here the vocabulary and syntax reflect her own simplicity, and the ignorance
that angers Ocol. But when she comments on death she can turn to her own

experience; the same simplicity can then take on a note of authority and imaginative perception.

> When Death comes
> To fetch you
> She comes unannounced,
> She comes suddenly
> Like the vomit of dogs,
> And when she comes
> The wind keeps blowing
> The birds go on singing
> And the flowers
> Do not hang their heads.
>
> (*Song of Lawino* p. 172–3)

The *Song of Lawino* is subtitled 'A Lament'. The occasion for it is Lawino's rejection by her husband. Ocol has been to high school and university, he has become a 'black European' sedulously imitating western ways, moving into the politics of independence, acquiring a westernized mistress. But the long monologue is much more than a lament. It develops into a vigorous defence of traditional life and values, contrasting Ocol's attitudes with her own. Eventually it creates a similitude between Ocol's choice and the cultural attitudes developing in the Uhuru (independence) movement. All this has been embodied in a traditional Acoli form, the 'lament'. The non-Acoli reader has no way of judging how successfully the form has been adopted or re-created, he has no way of judging the realities of the situation presented except by reference to other African writing dealing with aspects of the theme of transition and its impact.

The critic need be little concerned with the form in relation to its original, unless he wishes to move deliberately into the field of comparative criticism. We ask the question 'Does the form work for the poem?' and, according to our judgement, we give the answer. We have a long poem in thirteen sections, each section after the first developing a particular aspect of Ocol's resentment against Lawino and bringing in behind the personal reaction the developing picture of traditional Acoli culture. So we move from domestic and sexual relationships through such aspects as education and religion to the notion of Ocol and Lawino as representing two contrasting sets of values, a choice for the Acoli, although the wider contrast is never allowed to cut loose from the frame of personal reference. Within this form the two characters develop (three if one includes the satiric references to Clementine). It is a form that, to my mind, is successfully flexible for the discursive treatment of the content and emotions that it presents; the poem has a unity and inner pattern that does not require any knowledge of the original form. What may be missed is any meaning carried by the form itself as denoting a particular genre and the feelings conventionally associated with that genre.

Something similar may be said of the content, the 'lament' itself. Given Lawino's point of view, the poem has an emotional unity and integrity. Her pleas, her anger and pride, her love for Ocol and her love for her way of life, all are presented with a self-sufficiency and emotional relevance very far from the naïvely didactic type of sociological explanation that has been too commonly passed off as good coin of fiction or poetry in African literature. Unless the critic is at home in the particular cultural situation, however, he cannot bring to bear on the poem any judgement of the 'truth' of the values and attitudes in contention.

These are the grounds of the objections raised by Taban Lo Liyong, an Acoli writer and critic whose own educational background in the western world equals that of p'Bitek. For Lo Liyong takes sides with Ocol and Clementine against what he sees as a belated *négritudinist* poem defending a worn-out tradition of backwardness that should have been discarded long ago.

> To ask if we had culture is to ask an elementary question. After it has been answered with a 'yes' – does that conclude the discussion? Should it? What needs answering is: what sort of culture had we? . . . Did this general spirit allow for the utmost individual search for himself and his expression of his individual spirit – unhampered by social, cultural, moral, governmental restrictions? Did it have within it mechanisms for survival . . .?[20]

and at the end he comments that until we have equal statements from Ocol and Clementine, 'the triptych picture of modern Africa will remain incomplete'.[21]

He also raises other questions. He claims that Acoli proverbs have been weakened in translation; that figures of speech have lost their liveliness, that Acoli word-play vanishes, that for him it becomes prolix in some of its detail. He admires the section on politics (section 11) because it has to do with politics, then claims it is an interpolation added to the original poem after Uganda became independent. While allowing the poem considerable merit in certain aspects, he attacks it on grounds that are simply not available to the western critic; in details relating to language the grounds are not available to a non-Acoli African. But the western critic can raise in turn the interesting

[20] *The Last Word* (East African Publishing House, Nairobi, 1969), p. 153. Lo Liyong notes (p. 142) that the name 'Ocol' means 'son of Black', i.e. African – a note that certainly adds to our awareness of how the poem could or should be read.
[21] *The Last Word*, p. 156.

question of whether many of these comments are relevant to the English-language poem that we read. The most serious problem, however, comes from Lo Liyong's reading of the content and his total lack of sympathy for Lawino. We can gather from the article that he is opposed to p'Bitek's views, so we may be reasonably assured in assuming a reading of the poem that sees Lawino sympathetically. But there is a problem of cultural values involved that will depend on the reader's cultural background and sympathies for evaluation.

Whether or no urged on by comments such as those of Lo Liyong, p'Bitek did write a companion piece, the *Song of Ocol* (1970), which is Ocol's side of the argument. It would hardly satisfy Lo Liyong, since the speaker, as in a Browning monologue, betrays his own weaknesses as he speaks, while occasional images seem to be used with ironic symbolism, as when Ocol praises the new farming techniques:

> Look at that prize bull,
> Black, hornless and without a hump.
>
> (*Song of Ocol* p. 61)

In my view the poem is less successful, a rather forced treatment of an argument for the sake of producing a sequel. But the reasons for this judgement are based on the criteria I have used in discussing the earlier poem; the same possible limitations to such an evaluation would apply.

The examples I have chosen for discussion are necessarily limited and arbitrary: not only do they leave questions unanswered, they leave many more questions unasked. Yet this is itself an indication of the range and variety that modern African literature now presents; it has emerged to a state where it deserves and demands the careful consideration that is given to any other writing in English, and is best served by having applied to it standards and procedures as carefully considered as those we apply to literatures whose norms and traditions have already been thoroughly understood. It is a literature that shares many of these norms and traditions, while incorporating others that will be better understood as the literature becomes more widely known and develops further. It is moving through a phase that in some ways presents criticism with problems it has formerly encountered, and still does encounter, with the development of, say, American or Australian or Canadian literature. Yet a closer comparison might be achieved in saying that it presents a particular problem within the broad field of literature in English; one that is in many ways related to problems associated with comparative literature, even while it interacts with and itself begins to influence the written literary tradition of the English language. Warren and Wellek, concluding a detailed discussion of the problems of comparative and national literatures related to the fundamental problems of the study of literature itself, observe that 'Only when we have reached decisions on these problems shall we be able to write histories of national literature which are not simply geographical or linguistic categories.'[22] We should by now be aware of the problems, and by taking heed of them contribute to the growth of informed critical standards for modern African literature.

[22] René Wellek and Austin Warren, *Theory of Literature* (Harvest Books, 1960), p. 41.

2 Tradition, Language and the Reintegration of Identity in West African Literature in English

▼▼▼▼▼▼▼▼▼▼▼▼▼▼▼▼▼▼▼▼▼▼▼▼▼▼▼▼▼

PETER YOUNG

THE question of choice of language leads to a consideration of the stimuli that produced writing in French and English by the eighteenth- and nineteenth-century African writers. In the twentieth century there has developed a growing consciousness of cultural or linguistic identity, along with or as part of the feeling for social and political independence that has moved through the continent. As a corollary authors are turning to explore their own, mainly oral traditions, as well as writing to inform the world outside Africa about their cultures and attitudes. An examination of the West African scene shows that authors there have a number of problems to solve – personal, literary, linguistic – when they begin to make choices about the way in which they write and the things that they write about. Some of these problems are considered in detail and related to individual authors. Underlying the whole argument is the transition from an oral literature and tradition to a written literature in communication with other traditions.

Peter Young spent five years lecturing in English at Fourah Bay College in Sierra Leone and at Ibadan in Nigeria. He is now the head of the English department at one of Norway's new regional university colleges.

In the criticism of African literature the influence of the oral tradition and the specifically 'African' experience of language have been points of major concern. They are there for all to see, to be sure, and yet comment has largely confined itself to the obvious manifestations of a highly complex problem of criticism. This is not intended as an accusation of critical evasion in the past. Much of the critic's hesitation has been due to the fact that an enormous amount of preliminary research remains to be done before he can be fully at ease in the assessment of the literature that has appeared at a bewildering rate since the early 1950s. The African critic, while he can sometimes take much more for granted than his European counterpart, when considering literature produced outside his own region has come up equally sharply against the diversity of African cultures and languages. Much criticism by European and African critics alike has necessarily remained at the level of noble drudgery or inspired crossword-solving. The situation cannot change overnight. I feel nevertheless that we have now a sufficient body of West African creative writing to be able to look for patterns in the handling of language and the oral tradition and to make critical comparisons within the literature.

Until quite recently – say 1966, the year after Soyinka's *The Interpreters*, and the year of Achebe's *A Man of the People* – the comparison of techniques has generally had to go outside the immediate bounds of African literature. Now African writers can be set one against the other, rather than against European literary reminiscence. The paradox of this shortening of the critical paradigms for African literature is that far from rendering criticism parochial it allows for the first time a fair degree of criticism on the literature's manifest terms and a consequently greater freedom from inhibition about 'universal' critical value-judgments, which might in any case be expected to establish their own relativity.

An adequate criticism of African literature, like that of any other literature, presupposes the establishment and acceptance of a set of precritical criteria between writer and reader.[1] The acceptance of these criteria in most literary circumstances is to be taken for granted by both writer and reader, and the creative element that singles out a good writer from a bad one, though in itself ultimately unanalysable, can none the less rely confidently for its effect on a fund of cultural and linguistic experience shared by reader and writer. This holds good for as long as a literature remains national and monolingual; the matter becomes more difficult, more demanding of effort in a large part of the readership, when a literature becomes in any true sense international and multilingual.

We cannot here discuss the rightness or wrongness of the African writer's choice of an international rather than a national literature, but must accept that this is the choice he has most often made. The debate over the choice of a language has been long and bitter and continues still, a little muted, fighting over ground covered by writers such as Achebe, Ekwensi and, on the other side, Obi Wali.[2] Wali's passionate, and outspoken, conviction and no small

---

[1] There is an illuminating study of the relationships of European criticism to African literature in Dan Izevbaye, 'The Relevance of Modern Literary Theory in English to Poetry and Fiction in English-speaking West Africa', unpublished Ph.D. thesis, University of Ibadan, 1968.

[2] For example, C. Achebe, 'Handicaps of Writing in a Second Language', *Spear*, August 1964, pp. 43–5; 'English and the African Writer', *Transition*, 18, 1965, pp. 27–30. Cyprian Ekwensi, 'The Dilemma of the African Writer', *West African Review*, 27, 346, July 1956, pp. 701–4. For the other side,

courage brought him to write his novel *Ngozi dili Chukwu* (1963) in Igbo, a deliberate withdrawal into a linguistic and cultural privacy, which he felt to be the only situation in which creative integrity is truly possible. At the same time *Ngozi dili Chukwu* must gleam a jewel unseen by most readers, not a few of them Ibo, and Wali in the eyes of a great many remains an honest and spirited anachronism.[3] Wali would no doubt say that a gem remains a gem, seen or no, but this invites only a critical stalemate. African dignity might well be importantly reasserted from within in Wali's way, or more outwardly directed as in the case of other writers. Again, a writer will choose a language that suits his several duties and creative ambitions best according to his own idea of them. I shall leave the matter there for the present.[4]

Any division between the influences of a language and the culture of which it is at the same time the vehicle and a part is never wholly satisfactory. When, to take a simpler type of example, an Ibo writer chooses to transfer into his use of English certain words for which there are no suitable translation equivalents in the language (such as names of foods, clothing and other culturally bound objects), he is not so much being influenced by his mother tongue as being compelled by simple denotational necessity. When, however, he transfers such a word as *dibia*, for which none of the possible English translation equivalents will do (for example 'priest', 'doctor', or even the collocation 'native doctor', which in its West African use is nearer than either of the other two), he is up against a more difficult problem. None of the possible British, or West African, English equivalents may carry the proper degree of solemnity or imply a sufficient sense of the respect in which the *dibia* is held. And yet he is unable by simple transference of the word into English to achieve the effect that prompted the decision with any but another Ibo reader. Attempts to surmount problems of this kind have had a profound effect on the stylistic freedom, and thus the 'quality', of African writing in English, and I shall

[3] Wali's novel, published by Osu Freeman's Press at Nsukka in 1963, was reviewed by Dr A. J. Shelton, 'The New African Novel', *Transition*, 12, January–February 1964, p. 8.

[4] I have made some attempt to consider the linguistic and critical problems raised by this debate in 'An Approach to Style in the West African Novel in English', 9th West African Languages Congress, Freetown, 1970. There is a challenging article from a sociological point of view on the adverse effects of using a European language as a second language by Pierre Van den Berghe, 'European Languages and Black Mandarins', *Transition*, 34, December–January 1968, pp. 19–23. Presumably these effects would arise from the use of any other language by the élite which is not shared by the whole population.

Obiajunwa Wali, 'The Dead End of African Literature?', *Transition*, 10, September 1963, pp. 13–15; 'A Reply to the Critics from Obi Wali', *Transition*, 12, January–February 1964, p. 7. See also *Transition*, 11, November 1963, for some idea of the storm Wali's views provoked at the time.

return to some discussion of it later. The point to be made at the moment is on a rather more general level and concerns the tendency general among critics to imply a separateness for the oral tradition as an influence in the African writer's work. Just as it is unsatisfactory to divorce a language from so intimate a part of it as the oral tradition, it is equally unsatisfactory to imply a division between the oral tradition and the total complex of culture that makes the writer the man he is, expecting or hoping to achieve certain effects upon his readers. A quickness to make such divisions is, I think, largely behind the readiness to dismiss cultural content as 'local colour', whereas it is probably more often than not due to a breakdown in response and communication between the impatient European, who is frequently inclined to think of the *dibia* as a 'witch-doctor' in any case, and, for instance, Achebe or Flora Nwapa, who are trying to convey what the *dibia* is to an Ibo. Once again, the problem must be dealt with by an appeal to the reader to make a larger pre-critical effort than he normally expects to make in his armchair. The caution is doubly important in that for many writers cultural content does remain at the level of 'local colour'. It is this that is an important difference between the 'poorer' and the 'better' writers, those who write out of a form of card-index experience and those who write out of the total cultural self. This division in the handling of cultural experience, which can be verified easily enough, reflects, perhaps even rests on, the historical background of modern African writing in English.

The earliest African writing in the European languages is largely a product of cultural dispossession, or, put another way, assimilation to European cultures. Writers such as Afonso Alvares or Juan Latino are, were it not for largely external reference to their African origins, indistinguishable from their contemporaries in Portugal or Spain.[5] Allowing for an increasing interest in foreign parts and Africa in particular on the part of the reading public, very much the same is true for the African writers of the eighteenth century. There are, of course, frequent hints of an awakening racial awareness in their writing, though modern critics have tended to see these more in the light of recent experience than in eighteenth-century terms.[6] But it is less important to

---

[5] For further discussion of such writers see Janheinz Jahn, *A History of Neo-African Literature* [1966] (Faber, London, 1968), pp. 15, 30–4.

[6] E.g. Paul Edwards, ed., *Equiano's Travels* (Heinemann, African Writers Series, London, 1967), pp. ix, xiv–xv. Jahn, op. cit. p. 41, attempts to justify the irregularities in Jupiter Hammon's poem 'An Evening Thought' in a similar way:

> . . . sung polyrhythmically as a sort of spiritual, it would not sound at all laboured. Jupiter Hammon could do without metre; there is a rhythm swinging through his verse, no doubt a strongly African rhythm.

Without challenging the questionable distinction of prosody, I find it even more difficult to speculate about the language of Hammon, who was born at

ignore the voice of Pope in Phillis Wheatley's poetry, or her close similarity in this and other respects to other Colonial American poets, or to deny Sterne in Ignatius Sancho's *Letters*, than it is to recognize the assertion of an independence of mind through the most accessible means. It is altogether natural towards the end of the century and the peak of the abolition debate, when the African began to move more clearly as the personification of the fate of his race, that writers such as Cuguano and Equniao should be the first to include, however sketchily, autobiographical details of their African childhoods. As yet the terms of expression are firmly established, like the economic and Christian arguments of the abolition debate as a whole, on European opinion and taste.

The nineteenth century was above all the age of the establishment of the African man of letters as external to Europe. The resettlements at Sierra Leone and the transference of the evangelistic effort to Africa itself were potent forces in shaping the pattern of the future in this respect. Most of all, perhaps, the linguistic rediscovery of African languages, first for their practical necessity in spreading the Gospel and inevitably later for their own sake, revealed for all thinking people the undeniable richness of African cultures.

The rediscovery by those Africans caught up in the western intrusion of a literary inheritance of dignity and worth did much to add fire to the emerging nationalist consciousness in the West Africa of the last three decades of the nineteenth century. For Blyden, Horton and Bishop James 'Holy' Johnson, as well as many others less well known, the past had become clearer and the vision of the future more intense. For the most part they wrote still as propagandists, but it is on the foundation of independence they laid that modern African literature in the European languages rests. The transition from them to the modern world is made by Casely Hayford's *Ethiopia Unbound* (1911), a linking work, half propaganda and half the progenitor of the culture-conflict novel.

In francophone writing, in spite of apparently incompatible differences, the pattern has been essentially similar. For in *négritude* the process of rediscovery and the creative expression of African awareness are worked out side by side. The insistence of such men as Senghor and Birago Diop on the establishment of African patterns of rhythm and language in French and the overall concept of *négritude* echo more clearly than is usually noticed, though in far more intimately literary terms, the voices of Blyden, 'Holy' Johnson, Hayford, and the men of their age. Aimé Césaire's much cited debt to the Surrealists, for example, goes far beyond the accident of their being to hand in

---

Long Island, New York, than I do about Equiano's or Phillis Wheatley's. However, for a general impression of the Afro–American speech situation in the eighteenth century see, e.g. A. W. Read, 'The Speech of Negroes in Colonial America', *Journal of Negro History*, XXIV, 3, 1939, pp. 247–58.

the Paris of the 1920s and 1930s, just as Edward Wilmot Blyden's debts to the rhetoric of Exeter Hall and such eighteenth-century abolitionists as Benezet and Clarkson goes beyond the imitative. It is a clear part of the historical logic of the liberation of African literary consciousness that if Surrealism had not offered fashionable approval for the assertion of subjective response over an increasingly cold and detached reason in the African's argument for his dignity, Césaire would have made his point no less clear. Without taking the point too far, there are certainly ways in which the poets of *négritude* belong to the same phase of African literature as the anglophone writers of the late nineteenth century. As with them, the business of the *négritudinists* has been the examination and assertion of felt cultural difference rather than a firm sureness in the intuitive expression of African consciousness. Facts such as that when Senghor's famous *Anthologie de la nouvelle poésie nègre et malgache* appeared in 1948 it contained very little work by writers actually born on the continent of Africa, and the relative silence of both Césaire and Senghor over the last two decades, suggest not only a parallel with Anglophone writing in terms of historical development and the geographical origins of writers of the first phase but also the writers' own awareness of their historical role in the emergence of a literary consciousness by now more secure in itself. It is probably revealing that when Césaire finally broke his long creative silence he should have chosen to do so through the more direct and general exposition made possible by the drama rather than through a poetry from which, though it owes him much, he has become estranged. The irony which he has confronted is perhaps that of *négritude* as a movement in general, for arising out of cultural estrangement in a search towards intimacy it must finally be denied that intimacy in the very estrangement that gave it birth.

In South Africa there was a similar pattern of development discernible at the same time, for though the African writer there had not gone through the same process of cultural repatriation from Europe, direct confrontation with white supremacy had been more bloody and traumatic.[7] Writers in the indigenous languages looked back to a heroic past. S. T. Plaatje's *Mhudi*, published in 1930 but certainly written much earlier, is a story of heroic action and love. Like Casely Hayford before him, Plaatje brought together in his 'epic of South African native life a hundred years ago', imaginative narrative, propaganda, and cultural documentation. Thomas Mofolo's historical novel *Chaka* (1925), first written in Sotho and later translated by Mofolo into English, is even more interesting. Using the techniques and mythology of the oral literary tradition, Mofolo goes beyond narrative to a fascinating revelation of

[7] A useful anthology, which gives an idea of the patterns of development in African literature in the European languages as a whole, is, O. R. Dathorne and Willfried Feuser (eds.), *Africa in Prose* (Penguin African Library, Harmondsworth, 1969).

the psychology of Chaka's complex personality; alienated child, heroic warrior and nation-builder, shrewd and bloody tyrant. As a revelation of the profound possibilities of the oral tradition, *Chaka* must be said to remain in its own way one of the most important works in modern African literature.

In West Africa the collection of oral tradition and the study of African societies increased dramatically in the 1920s, and it is quite fitting in terms of the time that thorough documentation should have given rise to the first anthropological novel from West Africa. Some idea of the effects of the discovery of Africa's cultural wealth is conveyed by the fact that the author was not himself an African. It is generally forgotten that R. S. Rattray, best known for his works on the Ashanti, wrote a novel, *The Leopard Priestess* (1934), based on his knowledge of Ashanti social and oral tradition.

The Leopard Priestess is fascinating for the student of African literature, though it must be admitted that it is not particularly fascinating as a novel. The task Rattray set himself was openly didactic; to reveal Ashanti culture not only to Europeans but also to westernized Africans who had withdrawn from the old ways into mockery or simply indifference. It is a paternalistic gesture that rather takes one's breath away today. Yet Rattray was no sun-helmeted stereotype, for he came as close as most men could, certainly closer than any of his contemporaries, to entering into the culture he studied. *The Leopard Priestess* is an impressive testimony to his sincerity.

What Rattray was trying to do is not essentially different from what Achebe has said he has tried to do in his novels towards revealing the Ibo past to his own people.[8] This change of direction in the informational content of African literature from one that was exclusively outwardly directed in the early days of protest took a very long time to occur after 'Holy' Johnson had so forcefully indicated the need for it in an article in *The Negro* as early as 1873.

Of course, Rattray could never have hoped to go further than he did. Even if he could ever have achieved total assimilation into Ashanti culture he had still set out to instruct and to do so in English. *The Leopard Priestess* inevitably moves at the informational level, and Rattray's technical problems of language and characterization are still faced by many African writers today. His need to carefully elucidate transferred or culturally bound words and expressions or to inform his reader about relevant cultural background almost, but not quite, turns a beautifully conceived story of defiant love into a handbook.

Paradoxically, Rattray, an Englishman, marks the break-away of British and West African English literary traditions. Whereas Joyce Cary, from *Aissa Saved* (1931) to *Mister Johnson* (1939), makes the European writer's first real attempt to interpret African characters as truly living beings, Rattray

[8] Achebe states his views on the subject clearly in 'The Novelist as Teacher', in G. D. Killam (ed.) *African Writers on African Writing* (Heinemann, London, 1973), pp. 201–5 (also in *New Statesman*, 69, 29 January 1965, pp. 161 ff.).

indicated the African's own choice. Both Cary and Rattray failed, and both for much the same reason: a paternalism that was probably unconscious. There was a difference. Cary's *Mister Johnson* is a failure as the culturally circumscribed interpretation of an African character, though it remains legitimate on the strength of its point of view. Rattray failed because, a sincere man like others before and since, he mistook the possessive love of paternalism for cultural assimilation.

By the time of Rattray and Cary the pattern of African literature is aleady set. Absence, reminiscence, rediscovery and propaganda remain characteristic of African literature today, and when the first true West African novel, the Ghanaian R. E. Obeng's *Eighteenpence*, appeared in 1943 it maintained a deliberately propagandist tone. But didacticism and propaganda have become decreasingly outwardly directed, and Achebe's projection of his image of the Ibo past towards Ibos and such internally preoccupying political concepts as Pan-Africanism in such novels as William Conton's *The African* (1960) and Cyprian Ekwensi's *Beautiful Feathers* (1963) have begun to replace the inevitably outward-directed propaganda of anti-colonialism. The essential thing is not that the tract continues on occasion to usurp the novel, but that in the turning inwards of African literary consciousness at every level, from the paradoxes of *négritude* onwards, the major phase of African literature has begun. Emphasis had necessarily been since the earliest days on African externalization from Europe, but it has at last turned from the protestation to the examination of difference, and from the culturally general to the personally particular. The record of this literary integration of the informational and the interpretative is in the way in which recent African writers in English have handled language and the oral tradition.[9]

Amos Tutuola's novels – to call them fantasies, while accurate enough, shows greater certainty about the nature of the African novel than the present state of flux really permits – are the most extended as well as the most consistent use of the oral tradition in West African writing in English. Even to say this much is misleading, for Tutuola does not so much use the oral tradition as

---

[9] This departure is emphasized by the resolution of the most extreme examples of informationalism into what can be called 'narrative anthropology', where the preservation and publication of material is mainly directed by anthropological motives. The first example is, interestingly, of the same year as Cary's *Mister Johnson*, the Tiv *Akiga's Story*, translated and annotated by Rupert East (Oxford University Press for the International African Institute 1939, reprinted 1965). The most recent, and slightly less directly informational, is Mary Smith's *Baba of Karo; A Woman of the Moslem Hausa* (Faber, London, 1954). The tradition has had its offshoot in *Return to Laughter*, a little known and greatly underrated novel by Dr Laura Bohannan, whose studies of the Tiv, with the work of her husband Paul Bohannan, have done much to revive interest in Akiga.

continue it in writing. It does not matter that his rendering of the Yoruba tradition is less faithful than that of the late Chief D. O. Fagunwa, or that it is handled with less critical intellectualism in facing the problems of setting it down in English than Soyinka has shown in his translation of one of Fagunwa's novels, *The Forest of a Thousand Daemons* (1968).

Tutuola's own idea of his function is essentially that of the traditional story-teller, with the additional duty of passing on the tradition he has inherited to as wide an audience as possible before it is too late. Specific uses of the tradition are obvious enough: the common quest of a mortal to the land of the gods to secure the return of a dead person as in *The Palm-wine Drinkard* (1952), or the strange creatures and demi-gods of the hunters' sagas in *Simbi and the Satyr of the Dark Jungle* (1955) or *The Brave African Huntress* (1958).

The heated debate over Tutuola's use of English is also less important if it is seen in the same light. The argument about his language has ranged from the first review of *The Palm-wine Drinkard* by Dylan Thomas in *The Observer* to a reception at home which, according to J. P. Clark in his remarks on Tutuola in *Black Orpheus* in 1968, caused some Nigerian mothers to ban the novels to their children. It is certainly true, especially among Yoruba-speakers, that Nigerians are less enchanted on the whole by Tutuola than are Europeans. First of all, they have the oral tradition at first hand and as a living force, and it is inevitable that they should judge him at least partly in the light of this. Moreover, is there not about the language Tutuola uses a quaintness which, for all its happy accidents, draws much of its charm from specifically European preconceptions? In Yngvar Ustvedt's recent collection of essays on African and Latin–American literature, *Stemmer fra den tredje verden* (Gyldendal, Oslo, 1970), Helge Rønning attempts a translation of parts of *The Drinkard* not into *riksmål*, the urban, Danish-based language, but into New Norwegian. Whether or not New Norwegian was chosen because of some sense of corresponding linguistic vigour in Tutuola's English, or because the translator noted similarities to his own reaction to the language of rural Norway, does not much matter. But it is clear that little of lasting value is to be gained from carrying into the criticism of African literature still more of our unease about our own cultures. Hope must rest on a receptivity to change and a recognition that however much enjoyment we may have in Tutuola – and he *is* still to be enjoyed – it has perhaps little to do with the real business of modern African written literature. Another example of this kind of unease from one of the best European critics of African literature is Gerald Moore's reference in his article on Tutuola in Beier's *Introduction to African Literature* to Tutuola's use of the word 'lady' in a particular situation in *Simbi and the Satyr of the Dark Jungle*, where he feels it 'heightens the comedy'. However, 'lady' in everyday Nigerian English is closely equivalent to 'woman' as it is used in British English. One readily agrees with Mr Moore that such semantic overlaps can be amusing, but the relevance of the amusement is immediate rather than general, European rather than African.

The European enthusiasm for what I once heard very revealingly, if unoriginally, described as Tutuola's 'native woodnotes wild' probably does reveal, as Soyinka once suggested, Anglo–Saxon boredom with English. But that just remark and the more violent denunciations of his syntax have obscured the essential fact that it is the immediately oral effect of Tutuola's linguistic individualism that is so compelling. I greatly admire Soyinka's technical and artistic achievement in *The Forest of a Thousand Daemons*, and the possibilities he has revealed in the English language gives that book prophetic importance, but I must reluctantly admit that there are times when I would gladly trade some of Akara Ogun's Old Testament rhetoric for some of the happier linguistic offences of the Drinkard. Soyinka probably found as near an accurate equivalent as was likely to be ready to hand, but since there are no strict equivalents in English, Tutuola, accidentally or not, provided a limited alternative.

Since Dylan Thomas's rapturous review of the Drinkard's 'grisly and bewitching tale' on its appearance in 1952, Tutuola has been hailed as a visionary and comic genius,[10] and he certainly has a visual imagination, a faculty of humour and narrative gift that justify his place as the most widely known of Yoruba story-tellers. The qualities for which he is praised are no less valued in the Yoruba story-teller than they are by European critics, but there may well be many equally skilled who have not told their tales in English. Chief Fagunwa's work would certainly indicate as much. On the other hand, the fact that Tutuola has written in English reveals for all to see the international possibilities of the oral tradition. Tutuola is also enormously entertaining and imaginatively challenging. It is a pity that it cannot be left at that, but some of the objections to Tutuola reveal much that is important about the wider West African literary effort and the role that the indigenous language and the oral traditions have to play in it.

Apart from the rather schoolmasterly attacks on Tutuola's English – after all for a good part of the anglophone world prescriptive schoolmasterliness is closely associated with the English language – the most concerted critical attacks on him have come from African critics. He is often condemned as unrepresentative of the oral tradition, for enthusiasm for anything other than faithful reproduction, an extraordinarily difficult demand to meet, has been taken as a rather tactless invasion of privacy on the part of the English language. Indeed, there was something equivocally indulgent about much of the early enthusiasm for Tutuola. However, the most critically satisfactory objection is

[10] Dylan Thomas, *The Observer*, 6 July 1952, p. 7. Also, G. Moore, 'Amos Tutuola. A Nigerian Visionary', in U. Beier (ed.), *Introduction to African Literature* (Longmans, London, 1967), pp. 173–84.

the one that has been almost passed over: that Tutuola presents something of a dead end for the writer already convinced of the value of the oral tradition as part of his total cultural self and trying to establish the creative reintegration of the modern African. Objections would probably have been fairer if Tutuola's choice had been seen from the beginning to be in quite a different direction from the rest of West African literature in English. As it is they were probably unnecessary, for in his most recent novel, *Ajaiyi and His Inherited Poverty* (1967), oral immediacy has given way to a form of the language still highly individual but irrevocably closer to the written standard of English. Though his imaginative power has not slackened, as Tutuola has changed his art has become static.

While Tutuola's work may offer a direct promise, it is not one that he sets out to fulfil; nor is it one that can fully satisfy the African writer's creative needs, as these are historically and currently presented. It may prove that the artistic integrity of the literature will depend on some form of linguistic and cultural withdrawal from westernization, but it cannot, as the very idea of withdrawal for such a reason insists, be an isolation of the writer from the creative and profoundly personal implications of establishing his relationship to his modern world. Protest will remain necessary for as long as the world outside Africa continues to make it necessary, and yet the partial realization of the objects of protest in the last decade and a half no longer requires protest as the necessary companion to art. As the African writer has turned inward to self-examination and self-questioning, so has he logically turned from protest and externally direct propaganda to exposition and satire of Africa, its institutions and internal political ideals, for Africans. The failure of Wali's courageous committal to his novel *Chukwu*, it seems to me, is not at all that he wrote it in Igbo but that the artistic privacy he sought was already assured. If, in the necessity of protest, the African writer has in the past been unable to direct his whole creative resourcefulness inwards to the point of consistent art, he can now as never before turn to the reconciliation of self. Not the least part of the incalculable price of colonialism is surely that unlike any other writer in history the African has been compelled to found his art not on the established cultural and linguistic premises of his people but on the distractions of protest and the heuristics of identity in the most basic sense. The felt fact of culture conflict, no less painful or relevant for its familiarity, itself assures a sharpened introspective awareness of the divisions in the writer's mind and art. The business of the modern African writer is the reintegration of identity, and this is clearly reflected in the cultural, formal and linguistic reintegration of his art. The process has been no less critically democratic than literary movements usually are, and the signs are to be found in the worst as well as in the best contemporary writing from West Africa.

Onuora Nzekwu's *Wand of Noble Wood* (1961) is among the most frankly informational of recent West African novels, and it is at the same time one – N. U. Akpan's *The Wooden Gong* (1965) is another – in which the division of theme, content and language is at its most evident. Some idea of Nzekwu's concentration on the informational level can be obtained by a comparison of the thoroughness of cultural documentation in *Wand of Noble Wood* with one of his own anthropological articles.[11] However, the significance of this first novel lies more in the attempt at the creative integration of the theme, basically the urban rural exposition of culture conflict, and the informational motive, than in the artistically superficial attempt to reach a more general and more popular readership than that for anthropology. The dominance of the informational motive in the novel precludes the possibility of artistic unity, and this is clearly seen in Nzekwu's use of language, which is as documentary as one might expect. This is no doubt reinforced by the coincidental dominance in his experience of forms of the language appropriate to the exposition of a social science; partly too by the fact that he is only accidentally a novelist. Whether or not these points are true, the failure was already determined by the extensiveness of the dominant motivation. The following exchange, for example, takes place between friends over a drink as an aside to a long disquisition on the cultural gap between generations by Peter Obiesie, the hero of *Wand of Noble Wood*.

'What does [the *ofo* staff] look like?' 'It is a short piece of stick', Reg explained, 'cut from the *ofo* plant (*Detarium Senegalense*), which, when consecrated, is a symbol of authority and a guarantee of truth. Freshly obtained, it is consecrated and becomes dynamized. There are different kinds of *ofo* – the family *ofo*, which is the one we are now discussing; the personal *ofo*; the *ofo* used by medicine men; the cult *ofo*; and so on. The family *ofo* are of two types. . . .'[12]

The artistic restrictions of this passage, which is representative of the novel, are self-evident. They become far more serious when they affect not only such casual moments in the action, but also destroy what is potentially the most moving of the novel's situations. Peter Obiesie's love for Nneka, a girl in his home town, is made impossible by the curse of the *iyi ocha* which she bears. Peter goes to the shrine of the powerful *iyi ocha* 'deity' to ask for the curse to be lifted. He obeys the oracle's instructions for lifting the curse so that he can marry Nneka, but Ikem Ono, who once was to have married her himself, removes the sacred stone (without which the oracle is powerless) from the

---

[11] For example, 'Initiation into the Agbalanze Society', *Nigeria Magazine*, 82, September 1964, pp. 173–84.

[12] *Wand of Noble Wood* [1961] (Signet Edition, New York, 1963), p. 33 (also available in African Writers Series).

grove, and she dies on the eve of the wedding. The handling of traditional religious belief is, though still exhaustively instructive, as close to plausibility as Nzekwu gets. But what might otherwise have become the unifying and saving grace of the last part of the novel is lost in dry as dust anthropology. As Peter sits by the body of his beloved Nneka during the funeral rites, there is no grief to affect his observant eye. Documentation does not simply remain unconvincing, but finally descends to the level of bad taste.

As the day grew hotter the corpse was beginning to decompose. But its odour was mitigated by the liberal sprinkling of strong-smelling scents and powder. The flies which hovered around increased every minute. The officiating priestess was given a strip of cloth which she wielded like a fly whisk in order to keep flies from the exposed face of the corpse. . . . Dancing groups began arriving at about three o'clock. . . . Lunch was served the women at around 4 p.m. Before the sharing was completed it was 4:30. . . . [The officiating priestess's] lot was a most unenviable one.

Sitting near the head of a corpse, sometimes a decomposing corpse, in the thick of the stench oozing from it despite the application of perfume, she ate as if she were in a London or American plush hotel. Flies buzzed and settled on the corpse, then shot up into the air and dived straight at her right hand coming up to her mouth with a lump of food. . . . She ate with one hand and kept away flies with the cloth fly whisk in the other.[13]

This grisly passage, given at some length from a considerably longer section in the novel, is an extreme example of the power of the informational motive, but clearly the African writer's artistic solution does not lie in this direction any more than it does in Conton's desperately Anglo–Saxon prose in *The African* (1960), at the same time a novel which in its idealism and Pan-Africanism indicates a turning from the past inward to the future of Africa. 'Don't worry about your ability to hold the fort, old boy. I am far too patriotic to take on a thing like this if I were not absolutely sure about you on this score.'[14]

Not all West African novels of this transitional kind produce such startling evidence of cultural unease. Flora Nwapa, in her otherwise uneven novel *Efuru* (1966), briefly approaches the integration of traditional belief and characterization. In the section dealing with Efuru's mystic dreams of being chosen by the 'lady of the lake' as one of her holy worshippers,[15] one gets a real sense of Efuru's essential difference from the ordinary folk around, a sort of passive moral isolation and strength.

[13] Ibid., p. 132.
[14] William Conton, *The African* [1960] (Heinemann, African Writers Series, London, 1964), p. 190.
[15] Flora Nwapa, *Efuru* (Heinemann, African Writers Series, London, 1966), pp. 182 ff.

Elechi Amadi, in his first novel *The Concubine* (1965), also achieved balance that requires notice, largely I think through his subjection of all other elements to the continuity and controlled irony of the narrative. Latterly in *The Great Ponds* (1969) there are times when he is very fine, as in the descriptions of Olumba's fear of the menacing uncertainties of the deity Ogunabali.[16]

In obvious ways Amadi is the heir of Achebe in *Things Fall Apart* (1958) or *Arrow of God* (1964). In language he is also his heir; especially in *The Great Ponds*, in the use of proverbs, allusions and songs from the oral tradition. Though he largely follows Achebe's example in handling the problems of linguistic and cultural transfer into English he can enjoy the legacy in avoiding to some degree a subjection to the mechanisms of transference, to which Achebe as the pioneer is frequently exposed. The special reception hut of the Ibo head of family, often painstakingly '*obi*, or hut' in Achebe, is simply 'reception hut' for Amadi. It was after Achebe that the relevances of types of transfer were most generally apparent, but Amadi's selectiveness goes a little further towards the reintegration of language in the West African novel.

The acceptance of a principle of language experiment reflects a deep dissatisfaction with the medium and a consciousness of the need to rework the internal relationships of the literary work of art. From the late eighteenth century onwards the African writer has differed from most others in that he has been to greater or lesser degree a bilingual writer. Even Equiano's dispossession maintained a precarious fingerhold on a few dimly recalled Ibo words, which though they were essentially scraps for the curious, are prophetic of later preoccupations in the literature. Christaller's introductory remarks on language in Reindorf's *History of the Asante* reveal a more purposeful approach to problems of expression already evident (Reindorf, Carl Christian, *History of the Gold Coast and Asante*, Basel, 1895) and Hayford was no longer able to avoid a glossary of words from African languages at the beginning of *Ethiopia Unbound*. It is this conscious movement towards the establishment of a new relationship with the medium of expression and the culture it carries that distinguishes African literature.

To some extent this is true of writers of African descent already established in literary traditions outside the continent. Charles Waddell Chesnutt's *The Conjure Woman* (1899) and his dialect stories sprang from an equally natural dissociation from the established medium, though he can also be seen in connection with a general American interest in dialect literature at the time. Concurrent with the increasing firmness of reattachment to African cultural traditions, the second quarter of the twentieth century saw with the more readily and generally available chance of literacy in English a correspondingly

[16] Elechi Amadi, *The Great Ponds* [1969] (Heinemann, African Writers Series, London, 1970), e.g. p. 146.

general bilingual balance in the community as a whole. If men such as Hayford had the scales of bilingualism tipped heavily on the side of English, the new writers, especially since the addition of more universities to Fourah Bay College following the Second World War, have come more and more to realize a balance between the mother tongue and English. Implicit in this balance is both a greater intimacy with the African languages and the fact that the modern writer's total day-to-day linguistic environment involves at least two languages, one or the other of which may be used in different situations: special cultural situations, more or less formal or intimate situations, and so on. It is almost twenty years since Charles Ferguson[17] pointed out the fairly common phenomenon of 'diglossia' in which different forms of a language, as in Modern Greek or Arabic, reflect a 'high' or 'low' style, varying according to formality, whether spoken or written, in ritual or in any number of culturally determined ways. The parallel within a single language with the idea of 'registers', or the habitual co-occurrence of certain forms of a language with certain situational features in its use, is obvious. The African writer's situation is even more complicated by his confrontation with a form of 'diglossia' which, conforming to no such distinction of high and low styles in any simple sense, cuts across not only the situational delimitations of forms of a language, whether in register or in two discrete linguistic codes, as in Arabic, but across the barriers of vastly dissimilar languages and cultures as well. In a direct linguistic sense the African writer using English has to convey literary experience in what is frequently less than half of his total linguistic and cultural experience. At least so it has seemed to the greatest number of modern African writers. On the evidence of the most successful recent writing from West Africa, this has perhaps proved to be only part of the truth.

At the risk of oversimplification, a convenient division can be proposed in the types of linguistic and cultural material the writer has to transfer into English; the non-deliberate, the involuntary drawing upon the immediate cultural and language environment; and the deliberate, or experimental, in which specific efforts are made to modify the medium. We cannot, of course, always be certain about the degree of deliberateness at any one time, though forms from the indigenous languages or English items peculiar to general usage in West Africa can be readily identified, such as the names of foods and clothing (garri, agbada, etc.), or recontextualization or compounding of elements already in the language (storey-building, mammy-wagon). Some degree of certainty, too, is possible in the determination of 'mistakes' in the selection of an English translation equivalent or an item of vocabulary or grammatical feature unacceptable to the reader of bilingual balance. One can also be sure about the deliberateness of the use of proverbs by writers such as Achebe, or the reorganization of syntax as in the work of Okara. One knows

[17] Charles Ferguson, 'Diglossia', *Word*, 15, no. 2, 1959, pp. 325–40.

that when a transferred item of vocabulary is attached to an explanatory tag (e.g. '*obi* or hut'), the explanation reveals a deliberate act of transfer aimed at at least part of the readership. It is a little more difficult to be certain of the degree of deliberateness involved in the effects of translation from the mother tongue resulting in forms not otherwise found in the use of English in West Africa or elsewhere, but some decision can be arrived at according to the degree of bilingual balance manifested by the writer, and frequently by his declared intentions in the matter. All these features, as well as others related to them at all levels of language (including 'mistakes', as Tutuola's eulogists have revealed), perform stylistic functions of one kind or another which distinguish African writing from that of any other part of the English-speaking world. At present I am concerned most with those forms that are clearly deliberate – not because they are necessarily more stylistically relevant, but because they reveal more clearly the African writer's search for the solution to the problems of creative expression.

In much the same way there can be said to be a worth-while distinction between cultural material transferred for specifically literary reasons and cultural information at the level of 'local colour'.

At some point almost every African writer has been committed to explanation, if not to information for its own sake. The most obvious problem of cultural and linguistic transfer is, of course, the fact that transfer does not automatically assure intelligibility throughout the complex readership, not only that outside Africa but that outside the writer's own region. Though the inward direction of more recent writers away from non-African readership has had far-reaching effects, the problem of communication across cultural and linguistic barriers exists within Africa and, indeed, usually within African nations. In other words, the African writer has been forced to attend to the medium, not at the exclusively literary level in a community where a certain reliability of response on the part of the reader can be expected, but at the pre-literary level of adaptation and establishment of criteria previous to response and criticism.

In a well-known statement, Achebe reflects the attitude of most West African writers in his general confidence that 'the English language will be able to carry the weight of [his] African experience', tempered by the knowledge that 'it will have to be a new English, still in full communion with its ancestral home but altered to suit its new African surroundings'.[18] The significant word here is perhaps 'altered', with its connotation of deliberation. Indeed, the problems of response to the medium have frequently given way to a concentration on its mechanisms.

Part of Achebe's attempt to fashion his language to 'its new African sur-

[18] Chinua Achebe, 'English and the African Writer', *Transition*, 18, 1965, pp. 27–30.

roundings' has depended on the form of adjustment to the communication of unfamiliar material, the paranthetical explanatory tag or 'cushioning'.[19] The commonest form of cushioning is the most obvious (*'obi*, or hut'; *'chi*, or personal god'; *'nno*, or welcome') and though Achebe never loses control, as Nzekwu does in the passage about the *ofo* staff quoted above, the total effect is one of distraction for writer and reader, an inhibition of syntax and fluency, that is no small contribution to the frequently remarked 'stilted' language of African novels. Achebe's particular gift is perhaps that he remains for the greater part of the time in sufficient control to avoid the stylistic tar-baby that so swiftly puts an end to the novels of Rattray and Nzekwu.

A more covert form of cushioning offers rather more encouraging results. This is the almost equally familiar resort to fashioning the immediate context of transferred material so that its meaning is made as clear as possible. Amadi, as well as Achebe, is a leading exponent of this device, and uses it freely in *The Concubine:* 'the okwos tore the air, the drums vibrated under expert hands and the igele beat out the tempo meticulously.'[20] The passage clearly refers to musical instruments, though the cushioning is by implication from the context: the 'okwo' might be a wind instrument, or possibly a relatively high-pitched, rapidly beaten percussion instrument such as the xylophone-like *ékwé*, and the 'igele' is certainly a percussion instrument, of whose function in the orchestra we also gain an idea. This method is, however, only superficially more liberating since it demands not simply brief tags of explanation but large 'areas' of immediate context to make it work. It is less obtrusive, but it still involves detail beyond the immediate requirements of expression.

The African writer walks a narrow path, and not all are as sure-footed as Achebe. Bernth Lindfors has pointed out the appropriateness of Achebe's transference into English of Ibo proverbs, varying from those of the rural setting of a novel such as *Arrow of God* to those of the urban *No Longer at Ease* and *A Man of the People*.[21] Indeed, it is precisely this control, and the integration of the material and expression, that singles out Achebe as far more than a pioneer of technique. But even here the inhibition of method over motive makes itself felt. A careful comparison of proverb translations in Achebe's novels with their Ibo sources reveals a very high degree of closeness to the originals, notably in attempts to preserve syntactical equivalence as far

[19] I have adopted this term after Howard Stone, 'Cushioned Loanwords', *Word*, 9, no. 1, 1953, pp. 12–15. Stone refers to the explanatory pairing of synonyms and the use of tags in Middle French medical texts, where an effort is made to avoid the use of unusual or obscure terms in translation.

[20] Elechi Amadi, *The Concubine* (Heinemann, African Writers Series, London, 1965), p. 35.

[21] Bernth Lindfors, 'The Palm Oil with which Achebe's Words are Eaten', *African Literature Today*, 1, 1968, pp. 2–18.

as possible. The two examples that follow, set out for comparison with Igbo
and word-for-word equivalents, are taken from *No Longer at Ease*.

if you want to eat a toad you should look for a fat and juicy one (pp. 5–6)
onye chọlụ ilī awọ̀ lii ṅke mālụ àbụ̀bà
who want to-eat toad eat that-of having fatness

the start of weeping is always hard (p. 97)
mbido akwā nà-àfịa ārụ
starting weeping (habitual) is-difficult (for the) body

The slightest breakdown in the writer's control of appropriateness, frequent
in writers other than Achebe and, most of the time, Amadi, results in an
isolation of the proverb in its surroundings that is potentially as restrictive as
the most blatant cushioning. Achebe himself, in his Foreword to Whiteley's
collection of traditional oral texts in the Oxford Library of African Literature,
has mentioned the difficulty of translating Ibo proverbs and riddles (*inu*)
because of the resulting isolation from the whole pattern of allusion and direct
cultural reference in the African language. The translation of proverbs in a
novel in English involves not only a transference from one language but also a
transference from one medium to another, from a spoken to a written culture.
In its source-language a proverb, or indeed a whole fable or myth, serves as the
point of reference for a whole complex of inventive allusion. As soon as the
proverb is written down in another language its flexibility is lost, and what has
been a signpost becomes a monument. It is Achebe's recognition of the need
to avoid this separation of a proverb from its environment in his careful main-
tenance of appropriateness that assures him of success. However, as a general
route to literary liberation it is precarious, for whereas the 'African vernacular'
he has compounded for himself shows flexibility in his hands, it remains a
solution to immediate artistic problems rather than a prognosis of a new
African medium in English.[22]

One sign of the limitations of the method is hinted at in the work of Achebe
himself. In *Arrow of God*, the third of his novels and the last before his

[22] Compare this view with, for example, E. D. Jones, 'Language and Theme
in *Things Fall Apart*', *A Review of English Literature*, V, 4, October 1964,
pp. 39–43; Ezekiel Mphahlele, 'The Language of African Literature', *Harvard
Educational Review*, 34, 2, 1964, pp. 298–305; G. Moore, 'English Words,
African Lives', *Présence Africaine*, XXVI, 54, 2nd quarterly 1965, pp. 90–101;
Bernth Lindfors, op. cit., and 'African Vernacular Styles in Nigerian Fiction',
CLA Journal, IX, 3, 1966, pp. 265–73. Or compare any or all of these views
to that of Obi Wali, who in 'Criteria other than linguistic' (Seminar paper,
Dept. of Adult Education and Extra-Mural Studies, University of Ibadan,
1965) finds Achebe's use of Ibo idioms studied, and failing to be 'psychologically
or dramatically appropriate'.

significant turning to satire in *A Man of the People* (1966), Achebe almost entirely discards the most obvious type of cushioning for the more covert type. This is in itself revealing. But, though *Arrow of God* is I think inferior in delicacy of craftsmanship to *Things Fall Apart* and the complementary irony of its sequel *No Longer at Ease*, Achebe achieves an integration of language and theme through means less exclusively concerned with the mechanisms of language. The effect is achieved even though this novel is the most deliberately didactic of the three, perhaps not least because in this final 'hymn to the past', directed primarily at his own people, Achebe can revert from a dependence upon the mechanism to a shared intimacy of response. The tragedy of Ezeulu, high priest of Ulu, depends upon the nature of the deity himself and on the realization that he is created by men in the image of the organic spirit of the clan. The interplay of the theme of culture conflict and the break-up of the organic society with the spiritual decline and eventual madness of Ezeulu equals anything in *Things Fall Apart*, where the tragedy, not essentially different in the dependence on cultural values for effect, is more mannered. The subjection of the medium to a point of greater balance in *Arrow of God* makes a fine piece of craftsmanship into a powerful novel.

Much the same point could be made about the plays of J. P. Clark. In *Song of a Goat* (1962), Clark is concerned with the adaptation of a western literary form to African values and responses. Mphahlele rightly remarked that we do not 'get anywhere if it is implied that because [critics] see the theme of . . . *Song of a Goat* as reminiscent of Greek tragedy (indeed it is!), then the reader or Clark is parroting Aristotlē'.[23] But we do need to remark the fact to feel the tragedy of Zifa's impotence. We get nowhere if we simply note the substitution of a kind of physical *hamartia*, unless we also understand the response of pity and fear to the implications of the disgrace of Ebiere his wife, the disaster of a marriage become barren, which is social and spiritual death. But moving though the play is, its concentration on one aspect of the tragic form prevents it from achieving real success. In *Things Fall Apart* Okonkwo's inability to allow for the clan's adaptability, and his exaggeration of its manliness without discrimination of its cruelty, make him a tragic anachronism. Though I feel the tragedies of Zifa and Okonkwo no less acutely than I do that of Ezeulu, there nevertheless remains a hesitation, a feeling that one is once again held in the surface tension rather than in the depths of the experience.

Clark's later play *Ozidi* (1966), is based on the Ịjọ saga of Ozidi, which he filmed and recorded over the seven days of its performance. The contrast with the earlier plays is remarkable. The saga is modified to fit the formalities of the five-act structure and scenes for theatrical production, but Clark restricts his modifications almost entirely to practicalities. The integration of music and

[23] Ezekiel Mphahlele, 'Polemics: The Dead End of African Literature', *Transition*, 11, 1963, p. 8.

dance into the action and expression of character is not the least of Clark's achievements. Ozidi fights Azezabife in a duel to the death as the drummers reflect the suspense in their playing of the combatants' personal tunes (III, vi) and at the close of the play the Story-teller symbolically merges with the music and dance as he is absorbed into the crowd. The language, too, with its fidelity to the changing moods of the living original, moves more freely than in the earlier plays.

The most concerted attempt to preserve the mother tongue through translation is Gabriel Okara's attempt in *The Voice* (1964) to transfer Ịjọ syntax and lexical rules into English. The closeness with which Okara does so can be determined by comparison with Ịjọ sources, and, as one would expect, he is unable to remain consistent in his method.[24] But the failure does not lie in this inconsistency, which would not wholly invalidate the method, or even simply in 'an annoying literary squint',[25] but in a fundamental misconception about the nature of language – that anything as complex as total meaning can be conveyed by preservation of very few of its parts. Syntax alone is not the vehicle of meaning, nor are a language's rules of collocation. It has been remarked that Okara is a much better poet than novelist and that *The Voice* is most successful in short lyrical passages.[26] Without wishing to beg the question of the incompatability of 'the language of poetry' and 'the language of prose', I think it quite possible that the fundamental weaknesses of meaning in *The Voice* are less apparent when subject to the firmer organization and control demanded by a verse-form. Indeed, there is a sense in which they are more acceptable, or at least accepted, there. However, the importance of Okara's work depends not on his success or failure but in the clearly conveyed realization that the artistic liberty of the African writer in English lies in the integration of expression and experience. By revealing one route to that end to be a cul-de-sac, *The Voice* remains a positive force in the development of the West African novel in English.

The same transitions can be followed equally closely in poetry and the drama. Examples of directly informational verse are numerous, and Adeboye Babalola's 'The Trouble-Lover' provides an extreme example.

> He is fond of marrying wives of other men,
> And so he often finds himself in hell at home.

[24] Cf. note 4 above, page 25.

[25] Sunday O. Anozie, 'The Theme of Alienation and Commitment in Okara's *The Voice*', *Bulletin of the Association of African Literature in English*, 3, November 1965, pp. 54–67.

[26] E.g. G. D. Killam, 'Recent African Fiction', *Bulletin of the Association of African Literature in English*, 2, 1964, pp. 1–10. Of *The Voice* Killam thought that 'the writing itself gives cause for genuine alarm'; he also missed the real significance of 'the curious syntax' (p. 3).

For sometimes his stolen wives are past-mistresses
In the art of domineering over husbands, of all kinds.
For instance, he once married Shango's wife,
That is, the God of Thunder's spouse,
But in his house she made him ill at ease
By belching fire from her mouth whene'er she spoke.[27]

A transitional form of the informational poem is that in which the description is enlivened into significance with a final bias of comment. Yetunde Esan's 'Ololu – an Egungun' is of this type. After the description of the *egungun* and the awe he traditionally inspires, the two last stanzas turn to a nostalgic sense of tradition and change.

I peeped out – a great crowd, all men,
I looked again – what did I see:
    A tall thin man,
    In plain pyjamas,
Barefooted, bareheaded, marks on his face.

And suddenly I wished I were back
In the good old days when Ololu was
    A semi-god,
    With seven skulls,
Not – no one in particular.[28]

For my part, I find this far more satisfactory as poetry than Babalola's poem, which may or may not be justified by its didacticism. But it remains at a wholly different level of experience than such poems as Soyinka's 'Abiku'[29] or the 'Dance of the Half-Child', dependent on the Yoruba idea of the *ibeji*, which concluded the 1960 Nigerian Independence production of *A Dance of the Forests*. Both these poems are still essentially 'transitional', and also illustrate the use of the complex concept of the Yoruba god Ogun, which provides a useful and convenient example of the development of the use of tradition in Soyinka's work as a whole.

Ogun is the Yoruba god of creation, of exploration, of war, of iron and

[27] In John Reed and Clive Wake (eds.), *A Book of African Verse* (Heinemann, African Writers Series, London, 1964), pp. 12–15.
[28] In Martin Banham (ed.), *Nigerian Student Verse, 1959* (Ibadan University Press, Ibadan, 1960), p. 26.
[29] 'Abiku' is to be found in *Idanre and Other Poems* (Methuen, London, 1967), pp. 28–30.

everything associated with iron, from the axe of the carver to the modern motor-road,[30] and his many characteristics and associations allow Soyinka the greatest freedom in literary interpretation. In *A Dance of the Forests* the immortality of Ogun is set against the mortality of Demoke, a carver, creative user of fire and metal, whom the god 'will not forget'. Demoke's mortal reflection of Ogun's aspect of creativity is brought out in Part One of the play in the discussion of the deaths by fire in the crashed lorries 'Chimney of Ereko' and 'Incinerator'. The acid humour in the cynicism of the lorries' names becomes doubly significant when in the discussion of what kind of death one or other of his companions would prefer Demoke recoils from death by fire and chooses what to them seems a no less frightful end. The lorries and the road are Ogun's, but the offence against creativity is not. The contradiction might also appear to exist within the deity of Ogun himself as the god of war. But Demoke's mortal circumscription in his comprehension of Ogun's infinite nature, which he instinctively honours, creates a tension between the complementary parts of the whole work, the significance of myth, the wisdom of traditional Yoruba belief and the cynical contradictions of the modern age. The 'topicality' of *A Dance of the Forests* is not simply in the 'Gathering of the Tribes' in the Federation at Independence (the play was first performed as part of the celebrations), but in the universal topicality of the re-fusion of total African experience. Soyinka refers obliquely to this wider significance when in his preface to *Idanre* he describes the poem in the light of tragic events in Nigeria following October 1965 'as part of a pattern of awareness which began when [he] wrote *A Dance of the Forests*'.[31] Indeed, the pattern is increasingly distinct in Soyinka's work until it finds its clearest resolution in *Idanre*.

In *The Road* (1960), as he remarks in his prefatory note for the producer, the *agemo* ('religious cult of flesh dissolution'), the festival of Ogun, and the symbolic expression of dance, are integrated by Soyinka in his exploration of the link between the mortal and the infinite.

The dance is the movement of transition; it is used in the play as a visual suspension of death – in much the same way as Murano, the mute, is a dramatic embodiment of this suspension. He functions as an arrest of time, or death, since it was in his 'agemo' phase that the lorry knocked him down. Agemo, the mere phase, includes the passage of transition from the human to the divine essence (as in the festival of Ogun in this play), as much as the

[30] In a paper on Soyinka given at the Conference on African Literature in English at the University of Ife in December 1968, Professor Eldred Jones makes a most interesting study of the significance of the road in the exploration of the 'essence of death' and, therefore, of life.

[31] *Idanre and Other Poems*, p. 58.

part psychic, part intellectual grope of Professor towards the essence of death.

And in *The Interpreters* (1965), itself the expression of complex past and present, the pattern is elaborated. In sharp contrast to his earlier externalized humour at the expense of modified Christianity (and its obvious analogy with the Nigerian political scene) in *The Trials of Brother Jero* (1963), the religion of Lazarus, as opposed to the muddled eclecticism of his congregation, is vested with mystical significance, which together with the theme of corruption and death and Kola's ever-changing and expanding painting of the Yoruba Pantheon sets up an unusually strong network of internal relations. But it is in *Idanre*, in the disciplines and liberations of poetry, that Soyinka achieves the full effects of his range.

In *Idanre* the Yoruba myth of the Creation, and especially Ogun's part in it, is the structuring force. Ogun is felt everywhere in the poem, a force as hard and terrible as the veined rock that in Man's first rebellion against an inexorable 'doom of repetition' Atunda rolled down to smash the god's 'fearsome nature' from the primal deity.

> Light, more
> Than human frame can bear
> Set flanges to a god, control had slipped
> Immortal grasp.

(III, st. 4–5)

In the following passage from the second section of the poem based on the postdiluvian phase of the creation myth, the awesomeness of the superhuman masculinity of the fashioning of the Earth after the first flood is set against the gentle Oya who adds grace to Ogun's hard power, and man moves closer to hope.

> Opalescent pythons oozed tar coils
> Hung from rafters thrashing loops of gelatine
> The world was choked in wet embrace
> Of serpent spawn, waiting Ajantala's rebel birth
> Monster child, wrestling pachyderms of myth,
>
> *And at the haven of a distant square*
> *Of light, hope's sliver from vile entombment*
> *She waited, caryatid at the door of sanctuary*
> *Her hands were groves of peace, Oya's forehead*
> *Dipped to pools and still hypnotic springs*

> *And now she is a dark sheath freed*
> *From Ogun's sword, her head of tapered plaits*
> *A casque of iron filigree, a strength*
> *Among sweet reeds and lemon bushes, palm*
> *And fragrances of rain*

Idanre is, in spite of everything, a poem of hope, of faith in the human spirit. Man can free himself from an apparently inevitable 'doom of repetition' in the world's eternal cycle of evil and corruption. Atunda's first revolt against the implacable power of the godhead shows man has a chance to leave the cycle, for in the very act of rebellion he creates a point of bias, 'a kink' as Soyinka calls it, from which evolution is possible. The 'self-devouring snake' of eternal recurrence is by rebellion modified from hopelessness to hope. As Soyinka remarks in a note: 'Even if the primal cycle were of good and innocence, the Atọọda [Atunda] of the world deserve praise for introducing the evolutionary "kink".'[32]

> Evolution of the self-devouring snake to spatials
> New in symbol, banked loop of 'Mobius Strip'
> And interlock of re-creative rings, one surface
> Yet full comb of angles, uni-plane, yet sensuous with
> Complexities of mind and motion.
>
> (VII, p. 83)

The modern world, as complex and contradictory as the nature of Ogun himself, may offer some hope of deliverance from the re-enactment of historical inevitability in the vision of 'Harvest', the earth's forgiveness, the transition from night to dawn and 'resorption in His alloy essence'.

It is not simply in the matter of intellectualism that in *Idanre* we have moved a long way from Babalola's 'Ojo, the Trouble-Lover'.

> He's frightful as the Iron god, for
> He sometimes runs about in the streets
> Holding high aggressively a glittering axe.

It is Soyinka, too, who among African writers has most liberated the English language from the more mechanistic preoccupations with style. He still uses the devices of cushioning, it is true, though his preference for glossaries and notes does something to avoid intrusion of information at the wrong moment. But above all, as with his use of the heritage of tradition, it is

[32] Ibid., p. 88; see also p. 87.

his reassertion of intuitive response to the linguistic environment as he finds it in all its complexity that assures him his success. It is this that makes his prefatory note on translation in *The Forest of a Thousand Daemons*, in which he asserts the 'sense' over the 'precise original', the most significant statement on the subject by an African writer to date, and that book as a whole the most successful attempt at continuous translation. The total linguistic environment is neither the mother tongue nor English. It is for him the leap from Yoruba, to English, to pidgin or to any number of shades of allusion and meaning between, the reflection of experience, whole as it is all these, or the best means at the best moment.

Soyinka's use of pidgin illustrates this freedom of multilingual balance in the joyous exploitation of the West African extension of diglossia. It is a technique he uses time and again: in the third scene of *Brother Jero*, when Chume's increasing excitement at conducting the service for the fleeing prophet is reflected in the transition from 'Church English' to deeper and deeper pidgin; in *The Interpreters*, when Lazarus's controlled preaching is superbly contrasted with the imperfectly understood and reproduced church rhetoric of the verse feeder, or when Egbo frantically questions the night-club waiter about Simi's giving him the slip, in a beautifully handled mixture of English, pidgin and Yoruba. The following speech is one of several of the kind by Samson in *The Road*.

A driver must have sensitive soles on his feet. Unlike his buttocks. His buttocks would be hard. Heavy-duty tyres. But not the feet you see. Because he does not walk so much, and he has to be able to judge the pressure on the pedals exactly right. I have such thick soles you see so I always revved the engine too much or too little. Then it was Fai! Fai! Fai! You think say I get petrol for waste? Take your foot commot for ancelerator! Small small! I say small small – you tink say dis one na football game. Fai fai fai! You dey press brake – Gi-am! – as if na stud you wan' give centre back. I say do am soft soft! Fai fai fai! All a waste of time. Every time I started the lorry it went like a railway – gbaga gbaga – like clinic for hiccup. Other times it would shoot off like sputnik – fiiiiom! That was when I got it worst of all – Fai fai fai fai! You wey no fit walka na fly you wan' fly? Ah, sometimes I wonder why I didn't go deaf. [*He stands for a while, trying to remember.*[33]]

This freedom of intuition over the scales of modern linguistic and cultural experience more than anything else sets Soyinka apart from his contemporaries. Significantly, too, his weaknesses as a writer can be ascribed to the same

[33] *The Road* [1960] (Oxford University Press, Three Crowns Books, 1965), Part Two, p. 64.

liberation of response where it lapses into an ensnaring verbal facility and mannered obscurities of expression, as it does occasionally in, for example, *The Interpreters,* or even *Idanre.* The balanced craftsmanship of the simpler plays such as *Brother Jero* or *The Lion and the Jewel* has an ease not possible in a play like *A Dance of the Forests,* which for all its apparent difficulty attempts a wider ranging through Soyinka's awareness. Nor is it inconsistent, though perhaps potentially misleading critically, to note his 'debts' to modern English poetry, notably that of T. S. Eliot, for these are no less part of his total pattern of awareness.

Soyinka's response to language and experience as elemental rather than mechanical truths represents the most advanced point on the long route which, historically and in microcosm, the African writer has had to travel towards using the English language and the heritage of tradition as what they have become, parts of the total modern experience rather than modifiable, separate conceptions. As a whole his work realizes the transition from the pre-literary preoccupations imposed by historical circumstance and a shrinking modern world to the natural literary starting point of self-possession which the African writer has so long been denied.

The transition in the handling of the oral tradition and the cultural heritage, if not exactly similar to the transitions in the history of eighteenth- and nineteenth-century English Romanticism, shares with Romanticism a development from surface to depth. The purely descriptive nature poetry that existed side by side with or gave way to the nature poetry of moral comment such as Dyer's 'Grongar Hill', or later extensions such as Cowper's 'God made the country, man made the town' passage in *The Task,* was as far from the 'soul of moral being' of *Tintern Abbey* as the two poems by Babalola and Yetunde Esan are from the novels of Achebe or from *Idanre.* The transition shares with romanticism, too, a profound faith in the wholeness of the human spirit and its place in the total scheme of things.

In language the progress has been similarly one of reintegration, following essentially pre-literary concern: the gradual assertion of painfully re-established response over induced attention to the means.

Christopher Okigbo expresses the triumph at the end of *Limits* ('Fragments out of the Deluge', IX and X) as he refers to the European intrusion.

> And the gods lie in state
> And the gods lie in state
>   without the long-drum.
>
> And the gods lie unsung
> And the gods lie
>   veiled only with mould,
> Behind the shrinehouse.

> Gods grow out,
>> abandoned;
> And so do they . . .

Until at last:

> The Sunbird sings again
> From the LIMITS of the dream,
> The Sunbird sings again
> Where the caress does not reach,
>
>> of Guernica,
> On whose canvas of blood,
> The newsprint-slits of his tongue
>> cling to glue . . .
>
> *& the cancelling out is complete.*

The African writer's spiritual and creative independence figured in Okigbo's lines has not become a withdrawal by rejection, as many would have had it, but one of gradually, often painfully, re-established harmony in the total pattern of his awareness. Professor Jones has remarked that for African literature to be 'universal' it must first be 'truly local'.[34] Indeed, this self-containment essential to the survival of the creative African consciousness, avoiding the simplistic solution of isolation, is ultimately of universal importance. Writing of E. M. Forster, in spite of *A Passage to India* a novelist apparently remote from the concerns of modern African literature, K. W. Gransden implies the full meaning and promise of the African writer's achievement to the world at large.

> The good place must be small enough to be known by heart. This insistence on the local, the truly known, seems especially valuable in our age of 'internationalism' in which the values of the great world, designed to appeal to all by meaning nothing to anyone, are gradually replacing felt values derived from specific traditions.[35]

From mere reminiscence and example for enlightened argument to protest and rejection, the African writer has worked out his relationship to the wider

[34] E. D. Jones, 'The Decolonization of African Literature', Paper given at the African–Scandinavian Writers' Conference, Stockholm, February 1967; a version also in *Topic*, 21, 1968, pp. 18–20.

[35] K. W. Gransden, *E. M. Forster*, Oliver and Boyd, Writers and Critics Series (Edinburgh, 1962; revised edition 1970), pp. 59–60.

world. Over two centuries he has sought to realize the reassertion of 'felt values' in the reconciliation of his own identity and literary integrity. Now, on his own terms, he offers it against 'the values of the great world'. It is a meaningful internationalism the West cannot afford to ignore.

Acknowledgement: I am most grateful to Dr Kay Williamson of the University of Ibadan and to Mr Kenneth Ofodile for the help they gave me in tracing and translating the Ibo proverbs given as examples in my discussion of Achebe.

3 Wole Soyinka: Critical Approaches

▼▼▼▼▼▼▼▼▼▼▼▼▼▼▼▼▼▼▼▼▼▼▼▼▼▼▼▼▼▼▼▼▼

ELDRED JONES

A CRITIC of Shakespeare needs to be able to use any selected critical method as a useful critical tool and yet remain essentially open-minded to discovery and to other possible approaches. The same care in adopting and applying known critical procedures to Soyinka's plays will help us to explore his meanings as well as his methods. An investigation of the cinematic 'flashback' device in the plays is an example. By using such an approach and by keeping comparative dramatic techniques in mind, the critic can look at Soyinka's drama in relation to the drama in general as well as for its distinctiveness. It is necessary also to look at the plays in performance and to understand how audiences react. The critic who stays in his library will miss a good deal, for Soyinka is looking for Nigerian roots and for a Nigerian audience, although thoroughly versed in modern dramatic theory and techniques, and well aware of a wider audience. An approach on the Aristotelian basis of serious matters considered in context (an undogmatic neo-Aristotelianism) is a useful way in which to begin an examination of Soyinka as a dramatist.

Eldred Durosimi Jones is editor of *African Literature Today*. He began his academic career as a Shakespearian specialist after research following graduation from Fourah Bay College, Sierra Leone, where he returned to teach and to become head of the department of English.

Coming to Wole Soyinka from Shakespearian criticism is excellent preparation if only because it puts us on our guard against trying to fit him into preconceived patterns. Shakespeare by his practice produced a personal poetic which demonstrates that drama cannot be circumscribed by rules, not even when those rules claim the authority of as observant a mind as Aristotle's. Anyone who approaches Shakespeare therefore with his mind made up comes away angry, confused, or just disappointed. Contrary to prescriptions, his clowns mingle with kings; he created soldiers who behave like blackguards and black men who speak like poets. His characters and his scenes put a girdle around Europe, and his five acts are as likely to span sixteen years as four hours. He used the romantic convention while undermining its mechanical concepts. Shakespearian criticism requires an informed but open mind.

The critic of Soyinka should approach him in a similar way; equipped, but open. His drama incorporates (more accurately, fuses) diverse elements from quite different traditions of thought and methods of presentation. The product of this fusion is often striking and novel, having transformed the original particularities from which it sprang. There are occasions when the result also becomes so complex as to be bewildering for the playgoer, while still holding rich rewards for the play-reader prepared to apply his mind in the study. Soyinka's plays thus have a secondary life as literature.

A study of Soyinka's use of one device, the flashback, could serve as a convenient starting point for a critical exploration of his plays, particularly as they demonstrate his fusion of various elements. The word flashback is a cinematic term, and it might save time if one quickly admitted that Soyinka may have been influenced by the cinema. His use of the technique however shows a flexible mind, which never merely copies, indeed this use is so varied that in no two plays does he exactly repeat himself.

One of the simplest uses of the flashback is seen in *The Swamp Dwellers*, where in fact the shift into the past is not enacted but is recreated through dialogue. (A contemporary cinematic director would not, however, miss the cue.) The scene is that in which Alu and Makuri, now old and sedentary recall the strange excitement of their wedding night. Alu stubbornly refuses to recall the strange consummation that she had instigated, and Makuri impishly jogs her memory:

MAKURI: You're a stubborn old hen . . . Won't you even tell how you dragged me from the house and we went across the swamps, though it was so dark that I could not see the whites of your eyes?

ALU (*stubbornly*): I do not remember.

MAKURI: And you took me to the point where the streams meet, and there you said . . . (*Pauses.*)

ALU (*shyly*): Well, it was my mother who used to say it.

MAKURI: Tell me just the same . . . just as you said it that night when I thought they were your own words.

ALU: My memory is not so good . . . but . . .

MAKURI: It will come. Think slowly.

ALU (*with a shy smile*): She said I had to say it on my bridal bed.

MAKURI: Just where we stood. Go on, say it again.

ALU: 'Where the rivers meet, there the marriage must begin. And the river bed itself is the perfect bridal bed.'

MAKURI (*thoughtfully*): Ay-ii ... The bed of the river itself ... the bed of the river ... (*Bursts suddenly into what appears to be illogical laughter.*)

ALU: Eh? Why? What are you laughing at now?

MAKURI (*futile effort to control himself*): Ay-ya-ya! The river bed ... (*Bursts out laughing again.*)

ALU: Are you well Makuri?

MAKURI: Ay-ii! You must be really old, Alu. If you don't remember this, you're too old to lie on another river-bed.

ALU: I don't ... What are you ...?

MAKURI: Think hard woman. Do you not remember? We did not know that the swamp came up as far as that part of the stream ... The ground ... gave ... way beneath us!

ALU (*beginning to laugh*): It is all beginning to come back ... yes, yes, so it did. So it did!

MAKURI: And can you remember that you were left kicking in the mire ... ha ha!

ALU (*no longer amused*): I was? I suppose you never even got your fingers muddy?

MAKURI: Well, I jumped up in time, didn't I? But you went down just as you were, flat on your back. And there I stood looking at you ...

ALU: Ay. Gawking and yelling your head off with laughter. I can remember now.

MAKURI: You'd have laughed too if you had stood where I did and seen what could be seen of you.

ALU: Call yourself a man? And all my ribs bruised because you stood on me trying to get me out.

MAKURI: If you hadn't been thrashing about so much, I'd have got you out much quicker ...

(*Alu has tightened her lips again. Bends rigidly over her work. Pause.*)

MAKURI: The whole village said that the twins were the very colour of the swamp ... eh ... Alu?

(*Alu remains deaf to him.*)[1]

In spite of the fact that the flashback is not enacted it adds a lively new dimension to the rather sad couple on the stage, but more importantly for the play as a whole, lays the foundation for one of its basic ironies. The twins conceived in such high spirits in the mire of the village, now grown up, had encountered each other in the city, and the one had become the embodiment of the city, which 'reared itself in the air, and with the strength of its legs of

[1] Wole Soyinka, *Five Plays* (Oxford University Press, 1964), pp. 164-6.

brass kicked the adventurer in the small of his back'. Soyinka's use of the flashback even in this comparatively simple way is no superimposed device, but something that is structurally integral to the play.

The flashback is used in other plays in different ways. In *The Lion and the Jewel*, again a not very complex play, Soyinka enacts his flashbacks through song, mime and dance. A London reviewer, Herbert Kretzner, wrote of this play:

> With its almost casual shifts into song, dance, and mime, this novel and entertaining Nigerian comedy achieves a cohesion that has so often eluded the makers of musical comedies on the stages of Broadway and the West End. There are no obvious, prepared cues for song, no sudden or inopportune dance numbers to show off the chorus. People in this show sing when they have to, dance when they must, deriving their motivation for these activities from the real life, rich with ritual of the African village in which the Nigerian playwright Wole Soyinka has set his little fable.[2]

It is clear that Mr Kretzner is judging Soyinka's 'show' by the standards of the 'musical', and he finds Soyinka's work more integrated, which it is. He has also noted that his easy and natural transition from spoken word to song and dance is connected with the natural environment of the play. Soyinka uses mime, song, and dance to make an easy transition from the present into recent history, and this device gives depth to the play. Thus the African village tradition is employed to give historical dimensions to this modern and sophisticated work.

One feature of Soyinka's use of the flashback in this play is noteworthy in that it predicts a much more complex use in *The Strong Breed*. In *The Lion and the Jewel*, the dance enacting the earlier visit of the photographer is in full swing and for the time being we are in the past. Then right on cue the chief, the Bale, comes in and interrupts the proceedings, momentarily returning the scene to the present. But when he orders the dance to continue, with himself as a participant, the scene returns to the past. Thus within a few moments the present is sandwiched between two slices of the past. (The dancing of course also puts the village belle, Sidi, squarely in the focus of the Bale, with interesting possibilities for the plot.) In *The Strong Breed*, the past and the present interact much more closely. Not only do we see the Eman of the present on stage observing himself in an earlier episode, but, just before he is sacrificed he is portrayed side by side with his father (long dead). He persists in following the figure of the old man as he carries in his symbolic canoe the evils of his village, and in the process he, the son, makes his own disinterested sacrifice for his adopted village, thus fulfilling the destiny of the strong breed to which he belongs.

[2] *Daily Express*, 13 December 1966.

By this juxtaposition of father and son, an earlier scene is recalled in which Eman had tried to escape his destiny. The irony of his father's words on that earlier occasion makes its full impact: 'Your own blood will betray you son, because you cannot hold it back. If you make it do less than this it will rush to your head and burst it open (*Five Plays*, p. 261).

Eman's death, which takes place off-stage, in a device which improves on the Greek method of narration, is portrayed through the symbolic effigy. A brief extract will illustrate the features of this device:

EMAN: But father!

    (*He makes to hold him. Instantly the old man breaks into a rapid trot. Eman hesitates, then follows, his strength nearly gone.*)

EMAN: Wait father. I am coming with you . . . wait . . . wait for me father . . .
    (*There is a sound of twigs breaking, of a sudden trembling in the branches. Then silence.*)

    (*The front of Eman's house. The effigy is hanging from the sheaves. Enter Sunma, still supported by Ifada, she stands transfixed as she sees the hanging figure. Ifada appears to go mad, rushes at the object and tears it down. Sunma, her last bit of will gone, crumbles against the wall.*)

(p. 274)

Eman's vision of his father is an externalization of his thoughts. The scene as we now have it is no flashback in the proper sense of the word, for it had never happened; nor is it really happening now. One thinks of Marlowe's externalization of the tussle in Dr Faustus' conscience by the good and bad angels, which he borrowed from medieval drama, but Soyinka's use here is a far more complex fusing of the present with the past; of reality with fantasy, all in one moment.

The function of the effigy is clear to the most unAfrican spectator. It suffices to say that effigies as substitutes for humans deeply underlie various social and religious customs in African life, a usage which Soyinka neatly borrows here to produce a pathos that would have been totally ruined by a realistic enactment of the death of Eman. Soyinka uses a similar substitution in the alternative ending which he wrote for *A Dance of the Forests* (*Five Plays*, pp. 87–9).

One last illustration of Soyinka's use of the flashback, in *A Dance of the Forests*, shows him using the technique as the vehicle for an ironic comment on human history. From the hubbub attending a contemporary celebration (a gathering of the tribes) in which we have been shown some rather unedifying human types, Soyinka, by the aid of Forest Head, transports the characters into the great African past, into the court of Mata Kharibu. We are led to expect splendour allied to noble conduct. The court is indeed a splendid one.

Mata Kharibu is a great warrior. Madam Tortoise sending men to their deaths
has a touch of Cleopatra. All the trappings that could give modern Africans a
warm glow of pride in their past are there. But soon it is clear that what is
enacted in this splendid setting is a petty scene of callous war-mongering,
greed, bribery, perversion of the truth, and simple cruelty. Madame Tortoise,
an embodiment of the destructive principle, boasts: 'I am the one who out-
lasts you all' (p. 64). The warrior who represents the voice of reason, of man
trying to save himself from the effects of his urge towards self-destruction,
bitterly predicts the fate of the human race, seemingly doomed to perish at its
own hands:

> Unborn generations will be cannibals, most worshipful physician. Unborn
> generations will, as we have done, eat one another.

(p. 55)

How do we assess Soyinka's use of the flashback? It is no simple transference of a well-known cinematic technique, any more than *The Lion and
the Jewel* is an African musical, however well integrated. The device has
sprung out of a mind steeped in tradition, familiar with extra-traditional
influences, and subtle enough to produce what the exigencies of the drama call
for at a given moment.

Soyinka's use of traditional elements in his plays is the subject of an article
by Oyin Ogumba.[3] What is even more interesting is to see how inexorably
fused these elements are with others from quite different origins. The critic is
as much obliged to inform himself on this aspect of the plays as it is necessary
for him to discover Shakespeare's debt to traditional elements like the medieval
drama, the masque, or the May Game. Soyinka's method is frequently to take
an idea in traditional belief and extend it into a framework for something
totally new and imaginative.

In both *A Dance of the Forests* and *The Road* Soyinka borrows from basic
Yoruba beliefs to produce an atmosphere in which at one and the same time we
are in contact with the living and the dead, the unearthly and the earthly
with the present, the past and the future. Belief in the continuity of life from
before birth to after death is common in Africa. It is a very strongly held
belief in Yoruba culture, which is Soyinka's primary culture. In *A Dance of
the Forests* Soyinka extends this idea and gives it physical reality. Quite simply
the play opens with a couple coming straight out of the earth without pro-
logue or apology, to walk among the living:

> An empty clearing in the forest. Suddenly the soil appears to be breaking
> and the head of the Dead Woman pushes its way up. Some distance from
> her, another head begins to appear, that of a man. They both come up

[3] 'The Traditional Content of the plays of Wole Soyinka', *African Literature
Today*, No. 4.

slowly. The man is fat and bloated, wears a dated warrior's outfit, now mouldy. The woman is pregnant. They come up, appear to listen.

(*Five Plays* p.3)

With this opening Soyinka ushers us into a fantastic folk-tale world in which the dead mingle with the living and the gods with men. As the play proceeds we are taken further and further into significant fantasy. The woman who starts the play already eight centuries pregnant gives birth towards the end, but only to a symbolic half-child, which features in a final pageant by which Soyinka peers into the future of mankind. By using this world of extended fantasy Soyinka liberates himself from a particular area of space and time and can look as it were at the whole universe and all mankind. This is the special liberating quality of the folk tradition.

This kind of tradition is not of course confined to Africa. Yeats mentions a similar background to other folk literatures:

All folk literature, and all literature that keeps the folk tradition, delights in unbounded and immortal things. The *Kalevala* delights in the seven hundred years that Luonaton wanders in the depths of the sea with Waina-moinen in her womb, and the Mahomedan king in the Song of Roland, pondering upon the greatness of Charlemagne, repeats over and over, 'He is three hundred years old, when will he weary of war?'[4]

There is a possibility that this sort of idea as a background for a play might be rejected outright by a certain type of audience. Anticipating this, Yeats rejected that type of audience. 'We must' (he urges his friends in the Irish Theatre movement) 'make a theatre for ourselves and our friends and for a few simple beings who understand from sheer simplicity what we understand from scholarship and thought.'[5] Yeats of course was being ironic. The folk tradition could produce sophisticated drama. Soyinka, particularly in *The Road, The Strong Breed*, and *A Dance of the Forests*, has used his own folk tradition as the basis of very sophisticated theatre.

As he himself explains in his note to the producer, *The Road* is set in the masque (*egungun*) idiom. One of the underlying beliefs of this tradition is that of possession. 'It is believed that the spirit of the deceased may be evoked to enter into the masquerader during the dance. At the height of the dance every true Egungun will enter into a state of possession, when he will speak with a new voice.'[6]

[4] W. B. Yeats, *The Idea of Good and Evil* (A. H. Bullen, London, 1903), p. 279.
[5] Ibid., p. 259.
[6] Ulli Beier, *A Year of Sacred Festivals in one Yoruba Town* (Lagos, 1959), p. 27.

Soyinka enlarges this basic belief to produce an indefinite suspension between life and death in the character Murano. He writes: 'Murano, the mute, is a dramatic embodiment of this suspension. He functions as an arrest of time, or death, since it was in his 'agemo' phase that the lorry knocked him down. Agemo, the mere phase, includes the passage of transition from the human to the divine essence ...' The author thus creates an enigmatic character who is in at least partial possession of the essence of death (for which Professor in the play gropes) but which he cannot reveal because he is mute. Soyinka further gives the idea physical form by giving Murano a limp. As Professor explains: 'When a man has one leg in each world, his legs are never the same. The big toe of Murano's foot – the left one of course – rests on the slumbering chrysalis of the Word.'[7] Soyinka is deep in Yoruba tradition (the left foot is chosen for its significance in folk augury), but he is also at his most imaginative. Murano is no carbon copy of anything else in any tradition. Reality and illusion are fused in him in a way that recalls Pirandello without suggesting derivation from him. The masque tradition and Soyinka's imagination have between them produced the extraordinary atmosphere in which *The Road* is set.

The two elements of realism and symbolism are present in even the simplest of Soyinka's plays, and in some – as for example the flashbacks in *The Lion and the Jewel* – at the same time. This play however is an obvious blend of the two elements. It is in *The Strong Breed*, *The Road*, and *A Dance of the Forests* that we see the two elements so fused as to give a double image at most moments of the play. In *A Dance of the Forests*, by giving the human characters double histories he releases them from the prison of particularity and makes them symbols of general humanity. This is how they function when they speak in their own persons, either in the present or in their earlier histories.

In the last section – the chorusing of the future – Soyinka introduces a very complex symbolism, so complex indeed that its meaning can only be fully grasped in the study. Even here, moreover, all is not plain sailing. (Margaret Laurence disagrees with both Ulli Beier's and Una Maclean's interpretation of the end of the play.[8]) In this section we have a general assembly of all the various kinds of characters in the play: humans who by this time have been shown in the present as well as the past, the 'guests of honour' who have come from the world of the dead, and the gods and spirits. In addition we have the purely symbolic figures – the spirits of the Palm, Darkness, Precious stones, Pachyderms, and so on. All these characters play out a scene through which, against the background of the present and of history, the playwright looks at

---

[7] *The Road* (Oxford University Press, Three Crowns Series 1965), p. 44.
[8] Margaret Laurence, *Long Drums and Cannons* (Macmillan, London, 1968) p. 43.

the future of mankind. Here his use of the human characters is ingenious. It is they who pronounce the dreadful words predicting the future as each of the symbolic spirits makes his appearance. The idiom is that of the *egungun* masque tradition. Soyinka puts his humans in a state of possession:

> *The Interpreter moves and masks the three protagonists. The mask motif is as their state of mind – resigned passivity. Once masked, each begins to move round in a slowly widening circle, but they stop to speak, and resume their sedate pace as they chorus the last words.*
>
> (*Five Plays* p. 73)

In this state of possession the humans present a double image. They are still the human characters whom we have seen cavorting in their folly, but now they are possessed of more than earthly wisdom; their voices are not their own; the doomed future that they predict for themselves therefore springs from a more than human vision and has a more than human authority:

> White skeins wove me, I, spirit of the Palm
> Now course I red.
> I who suckle blackened hearts, know
> Heads will fall down,
> Crimson in their bed!

or the Spirit of the Rivers:

> From Limpopo to the Nile coils but one snake
> On mudbanks, and sandy bed
> I who mock the deserts, shed a tear
> Of pity to form palm-ringed oases
> Stain my bowels red!
>
> (*Five Plays* pp. 73–5)

This, in the gnomic speech of the masque convention, only repeats the plainer words of the disgraced warrior to the Court Physician in Mata Kharibu's court:

> Unborn generations will be cannibals most worshipful Physician. Unborn generations will, as we have done, eat up one another.
>
> (*Five Plays* p. 55)

As this same soldier stands by watching the future being chorused, a hundred generations later, it becomes symbolically clear that nothing has changed, and that his earlier prediction is still valid. At that one moment, then, the whole of history as well as the future is invoked to present a pessimistic view of the human race.

This sort of analysis is perfectly possible in the study. How much of it will come out of a theatrical production is quite another matter. There is more than a possibility that a fairly intelligent audience unprepared by a previous careful reading of the play would only be mystified by this section, as well as by much of *The Road*. A study of the reactions of various types of audiences to Soyinka's more complex plays would be quite interesting. Would *A Dance of the Forests* or *The Road* be plain sailing to a Yoruba audience steeped in traditional practice but with no experience of western drama? This evidence is not available. We have however the reactions of a very different group: western critics who have no knowledge of Yoruba tradition. Their comments are worth examining, for they reveal quite fundamental differences in theatrical expectation.

One of the main objections that seem to emerge from the London notices of the Hampstead production of *The Lion and the Jewel* is that its pace was intolerably slow. Peter Lewis of *The Daily Mail*,[9] after praising some features of the play, commented: '. . . it's no use denying that Mr Soyinka takes more than his time to tell his story. We are not used to these leisurely ways. And the acting often seems grossly over acted, to us at least, although it may be quite realistic as a portrayal of the characters of a small Nigerian village . . .' The root of the problem for these critics is the dialogue and what they seem to expect of it. Milton Shulman of the *Evening Standard* wrote: 'Wole Soyinka's dialogue has a natural directness and simplicity that is often both pointed and comic. But there are obvious *longueurs* when one wishes that the action would be speeded up and the exchanges clipped to a more acceptable western pace.' Anthony Seymour of *The Yorkshire Post* isolated the proverbs: 'As full of proverbs as the speeches of Mr Kruschev, the writing tends to be too full blown. Several speeches run on to the edge of boredom, and there is much that is naïve rather than simple.'

All these criticisms are typical of a poetic arising out of a tradition of drama (of life even) that has been long separated from the oral tradition of literature. One wonders what an Irish country audience would have made of it. Judging from the remarks of Yeats, one feels that the Irish would not have noticed the *longueurs* provided they understood what was being said. One particular remark of Yeats suggests that outside Africa, Ireland would provide an ideal audience for Soyinka:

One has only to listen to a recitation of Raftery's *Argument with Death* at some country Feis to understand this. When Death makes a good point, the

[9] 13/12/66. Other notices quoted are also of this date.

audience applaud delightedly, and applaud not as a London audience would, some verbal dexterity, some piece of smartness, but the movements of a simple and fundamental comedy.[10]

In Africa, even modern Africa, the spoken word still has an extraordinary power. It is not considered time wasted for a character to spin out a thought in a string of proverbs. This earns independent applause in a way that one suspects a similar passage would have done in Elizabethan England. In an African production of *The Taming of the Shrew*, the audience waxed ecstatic at what for the majority was, and rightly, the climax of the play, Katharine's set piece on the place of a woman. This was as much because of the sentiment, which was approved, as for the fact that this sentiment is conveyed in a speech framed to sound like a succession of proverbs. A contemporary London audience tends to squirm at both the sentiment and what would no doubt be called the tediousness of the speech.

It would appear indeed that the very elements that induce *longueurs* in a smart western audience – the proverbs for example – are those that would earn special approbation from an African audience. The word could be a very good substitute for action.

Soyinka's plays reflect the elevated position, the almost magical status of words in the oral tradition. Agboreko's gnomic lines in *A Dance of the Forests* are straight out of the practice of the oral tradition, would be recognized as such, and would be duly applauded:

The eye that looks downwards will certainly see the nose. The hand that dips to the bottom of the pot will eat the biggest snail. The sky grows no grass but if the earth called her barren, it will drink no more milk. The foot of the snake is not split in two like a man's or in hundreds like the centi-pede's but if Agere could dance patiently like the snake, he will uncoil the chain that leads into the dead . . .

(*Five Plays* p. 38)

This passage is made up of translations of well-known proverbs. Soyinka indeed gives his own poetry a similar gnomic quality by the imitation of proverb-like statements:

> If you see the banana leaf
> Freshly fibrous like a woman's breasts
> If you see the banana leaf
> Shred itself, thread on thread
> Hang wet as the crêpe of grief

[10] W. B. Yeats, *Plays and Controversies* (Macmillan, London, 1923), p. 5.

Don't say it's the wind. Leave the dead
Some room to dance.

(Five Plays p. 39)

Soyinka's dream for Nigerian theatre is similar to that of Yeats for Irish theatre. It is to produce a theatre which has its roots in the Nigerian tradition and speaks to Nigeria and the world through that tradition. The playwright therefore has to find a way to induce the world to accept that tradition.

Plot, then, in the form of a story is perhaps not as important in Soyinka's writing as western critics expect it to be (though why they should expect this after Pinter, Albee, or Ionesco, it is difficult to understand). For long periods in *The Road* the story does not move. The appeal is mainly to the ear. (To glance at another African playwright, J. P. Clark, whose background includes familiarity with the long, slow-moving cyclic plays of the Ekine drama, has written a play, *The Raft*, which is almost entirely static. His *Ozidi* has more action, but even this is a boiled-down version of a much more leisurely cycle which took seven days to enact.)

Because of the importance of the ear in Soyinka's drama he pays careful attention to the language of his characters. One of the most difficult problems for African writers in English is to produce the right register in English for a character who (it is to be presumed) is in fact speaking an African language. Soyinka deals with this problem very well. A fair impression of his range of registers is seen in *The Trials of Brother Jero*. The burden of the dialogue is carried by a colloquial norm which varies according to character and situation. Amope, an ordinary housewife and trader, uses this language. As she is always either complaining or quarrelling, however, it takes on a sharp edge:

Listen, you bearded debtor. You owe me one pound, eight and nine. You promised you would pay me three months ago but of course you have been too busy doing the work of God. Well, let me tell you that you are not going anywhere until you do a bit of my own work.

(Five Plays p. 207)

While Jero also uses this norm for ordinary dialogue, his professional register is a highly rhetorical one, with injections of biblical idioms:

Yes, brother, we have met. I saw this country plunged into strife. I saw the mustering of men, gathered in the name of peace through strength. And at a desk, in a large gilt room, great men of the land awaited your decision. Emissaries of foreign nations hung on your word, and on the door leading into your office, I read the words, Minister for War ... It is a position of power. But are you of the Lord? Are you in fact worthy? Must I, when I have looked into your soul, as the Lord has commanded me to do, must I pray the Lord to remove this mantle from your shoulders and place it on a more God-fearing man?

(p. 230)

The M.P. is given a rather more vapid variation of this rhetorical style: 'Go and practise your fraudulences on another person of greater gullibility' (p. 229). Rhetoric of this kind in Soyinka's work usually betrays shallowness or insincerity.

Chume too uses the norm, but in moments of stress he lapses into pidgin. When for instance he suspects that his master Jero is not all that he makes himself out to be, he reasons with himself in pidgin:

What for ... why, why, why, why 'e do 'am? For two years 'e no let me beat that woman. Why? No because God no like 'am. That one no fool me any more. 'E no be man of God. 'E say 'in sleep for beach whether 'e rain or cold but that one too na big lie ...

(p. 230)

Soyinka makes similar distinctions between characters in poetry. There is in almost all of his poetry a certain gnomic quality. However within this general characteristic, variations can be seen. The Questioner in *A Dance of the Forests* uses what may be called the poetic norm – restrained, and informed with natural images:

> Three hundred rings have formed
> Three hundred rings within that bole
> Since Mulieru went away, was sold away
> And the tribe was scattered
> Three moultings of
> The womb-snake of the world
> And does the son return now
> Empty-handed?

(*Five Plays* p. 71)

Soyinka can vary this poetic norm to suggest glibness, or personal emotion, or the wisdom of the ages, or the voice of prophecy, as the case may be. In *A Dance*, whose poetic norm is elevated (in comparison with, say, that of *The Lion and the Jewel*), Eshuoro frenetically rages against Demoke, who has defiled him. The poetry is a modification of the style of the Questioner in the passage just quoted. It is more broken up, and although the same kind of image is used, the texture of the verse is much lighter.

Demoke, son and son to carvers, who taught you
How you impale me, abuse me! Scratching my shame
To the dwellers of hell, where
The womb-snake shudders and the world is set on fire.
Demoke, did you know? Mine is the tallest tree that grows
On land. Mine is the head that cows
The Messengers of heaven. Did you not know?
Demoke, did you not know?

(Five Plays p. 48)

For the dreadful prophecies of doom spoken by 'possessed' beings the poetry is given a gnomic obscurity:

Red is the pit of the sun's entrails, and I
Who light the crannies of the bole
Would speak, but shadows veil the eye
That pierces the thorn. I know the stole
That warms the shoulders of the moon.
But this is not its shadow. And I trace
No course that leaves a cloud. The sun cries noon
Whose hand is it that covers up his face.

(Five Plays p. 76)

In *The Lion and the Jewel*, pitched altogether in a lower register, all Lakunle's glibness is suggested as he reels off his facile ideas of progress, or hurls contempt at the 'uncivilized' villagers of Ilujinle:

Where is our school of Ballroom dancing?
Who here can throw a cocktail party?
We must be modern with the rest
Or live forgotten by the world
We must reject the palm wine habit
And take tea with milk and sugar.

(Five Plays p. 129)

Lakunle's end-stopped banalities are at the opposite poetic extreme from the language of the prophetic spirits in *A Dance of the Forests*. Such is the range of Soyinka's dramatic poetry.

Soyinka is a serious dramatist in the Aristotelian sense; his plays deal with things that matter; things that are worth troubling about. They are concerned eventually with the fate of man in his environment; the struggle for survival;

the cost of survival; the real meaning of progress; the necessity for sacrifice if man is to make any progress; the role of death – even the necessity for death in man's life. Certain plays like *The Trials of Brother Jero* and *The Lion and the Jewel* can be called pure comedies, but even here Soyinka's concern with serious questions is paramount. The rest of the corpus: *The Swamp Dwellers*, *The Strong Breed*, *A Dance of the Forests*, *The Road*, *Kongi's Harvest*, and *Madmen and Specialists*,[11] are all serious plays bordering on the tragic. They do not, however, conform to the rules of classical tragedy; indeed each play differs from the other in emphasis. An examination of the role of the hero in the serious plays would make the point clear.

In *The Swamp Dwellers*, Igwezu typifies man as the sufferer; as the victim of his environment. His life is one of total failure, a failure inexplicable in terms of his own conduct. His suffering is totally undeserved. He has been let down by life, by the land, by his brother, even by the god whom he had so meticulously sought to placate through his priest. There is no suggestion in the play that Igwezu is in any way at fault. His reaction to his total failure to make a success of any part of his life is therefore one of bewilderment tinged with anger. He looks for an answer to the Kadiye, the priest of the Serpent who is the god of the swamps.

> Perhaps he can explain. Perhaps he can give meaning to what seems dark and sour ... When I met with harshness in the city, I did not complain. When I felt the nakedness of its hostility, I accepted it. When I saw its knife sever the ties and the love of kinship, and turn brother against brother ...
> (*Five Plays* p. 186)

> Does it not suffice that in the end I said to myself ... I have a place, a home, and though it lies in the middle of the slough, I will go back to it ... I came back with hope, with consolation in my heart. I came back with the assurance of one who has lived with his land and tilled it faithfully ...
> (p. 188)

> It was never in my mind ... the thought that the farm could betray me so totally, that it could drive the final wedge into this growing loss of touch.
> (p. 188)

In the face of his own adversity, the obvious prosperity of the priest, fat with the offering of the villagers, nearly drives Igwezu to murder. For one tense moment, as he has the priest under his power in the barber's chair and with a razor in his hand, it looks as though despair would drive him to a bloody revenge. Soyinka avoids this neat tragic ending and heads on to a less final one. The Kadiye is let off, and Igwezu is still left with his problem of surviving, of

[11] For a discussion of this play see: E. D. Jones, *The Writing of Wole Soyinka*, Heinemann, London, 1973, pp. 90–5.

making a living, of producing some kind of meaning by which to live. There is no neat, easy solution.

> I know that the floods can come again. That the swamp will continue to laugh at our endeavours. I know that we can feed the Serpent of the Swamp and kiss the Kadiye's feet – but the vapours will still rise and corrupt the tassels of the corn.
>
> (p. 195)

In any case, having humiliated the powerful priest of the village, Igwezu has to return to the city, which had once before reared up and kicked him with its legs of brass, with no more prospect of success this second time. Unlike his brother, whose 'heart is more suited to the city', he is just as likely to fail again. So he departs, leaving his farm to be tended by a blind man. The irony here is typical, but the situation is not as absurd as it looks. The blind man, who ironically represents hope, is given qualities of persistence and endurance in the face of adversity to engender some hope, tempered, of course, by his serious disability. (In a similarly ironical piece of symbolism in *A Dance of the Forests*, Soyinka represents the hope of mankind as a half-child, who is furthermore an 'Abiku', doomed to die.)

Soyinka's *Swamp Dwellers* examines a situation in which the righteous is forsaken while the ungodly prospers. Igwezu fails because he does not have the ruthless commercialism that success in the city apparently demands, and he fails in the village from circumstances even further beyond his control. He is the victim of the elements or, in terms of the setting, the victim of the Serpent. This stern-eyed vision of the world recalls Blunden's lines, without the confidence which that poet finds in a divine presiding providence:

> I have been young, and now am not too old;
> And I have been the righteous forsaken,
> His health, his honour and his quality taken.
> This is not what we were formerly told.

Soyinka in his play displays a dramatic courage which does not flinch from the object of the tragic vision. At the end of a play like *The Swamp Dwellers* one is reminded of a remark of I. A. Richards, that 'Tragedy is only possible to a mind which is for the moment agnostic or Manichean. The least touch of any theology which has a compensating heaven to offer the tragic hero is fatal'.[12] Even though Soyinka is not trying to write classical tragedy, his vision of the world seems to be essentially tragic. Where the neo-Aristotelian poetic would have stipulated a hero with nobleness of status, Soyinka's hero is a man of

[12] *Principles of Literary Criticism* (1934), p. 246.

quite ordinary status, his tragedy arising from the dogged adversity of fortune in the face of total effort. The pathos of the play could not have been enhanced by an actual death. It is far more effective for ending as it does with this prospect of a possible repetition of the cycle of failure.

In *The Swamp Dwellers* we have a picture of man as victim; he suffers against his will because he can do nothing to avert suffering. In *The Strong Breed* we have a different kind of hero, who is impelled by something deep in his personality to take the hard road that leads to suffering. Soyinka uses the African idea of ritual cleansing through a victim in order to produce a vision of the kind of sacrifice through which society is saved.

Eman, the hero, is of the 'strong breed'; the family of men whose duty it is to carry away the evils of the village voluntarily to the river in an annual ritual. Although the victim does not die in the act, the task is onerous enough: 'Other men would rot and die doing this task year after year. It is strong medicine which only we can take. Our blood is strong like no other. Anything you do in life must be less than this, son.' (*Five Plays* pp. 260–1). The death of his wife is a sufficiently hard blow to make Eman seek to escape his role. But his father's words prove to be a prediction. So long as Eman takes himself along with him, he cannot escape his role, for the impulse is deep within him: 'Your own blood will betray you son, because you cannot hold it back. If you make it do less than this, it will rush to your head and burst it open' (p. 261).

Eman's work in his adopted village as teacher, amateur doctor, and general missionary leads him inexorably to offer himself as the willing victim in the place of his little idiot friend Ifada, in a sacrifice more terrible than his father's since his involves his own death. Eman becomes a symbol of human benevolence and love which sacrifices itself for others in the kind of sacrifice that seems futile, but in fact is the only hope for mankind. Here again Soyinka preaches no easy doctrine. There is only the merest sign at the end of *The Strong Breed* that Eman's sacrifice may have started something new in the village, which could grow. There is no suggestion that the redemption of the village is complete, and no calculation of how many more such sacrifices would have to be made before the task is complete. Indeed already the forces of reaction are at work. Jaguna, one of the elders who sees the old régime threatened by a new vision arising out of Eman's willing sacrifice, mutters: 'There are those who will pay for this night's work!' (*Five Plays* p. 276)

A Dance of the Forests presents Soyinka's most ambitious attempt to date at showing the plight of man in the totality of his experience: physical, spiritual, and in the context of the present, the past, and the future. (*The Road* for all its mysticism and its attempts to pierce the veil in search of 'the word' is essentially confined to the present.) For *A Dance*, Soyinka dispenses with the single hero. His human characters are all complementary parts, which together add up to a picture of man with all his capacity for creation and self-perpetuation, as well as his potential for destruction and self-elimination. In addition to the human characters there are the gods and spirits who represent the extra-human forces that influence human actions. Finally he introduces the figures of pure symbolism that predict the future of man.

Demoke (who in an earlier existence was Court Poet in the court of Mata Kharibu) represents the creative principle. He is the protégé of Ogun, the patron god of carvers. But the personality of Ogun is ambivalent. He is also the god of iron-made weapons, hence also of war and destruction. Elsewhere Soyinka explicitly notes this contradiction, which is fused into the nature of the god:

> Primogenitor of the artist as the creative human, Ogun is the antithesis of cowardice and Philistinism, yet within him is contained also the complement of the creative essence, a bloodthirsty destructiveness. Mixed up with the gestative inhibition of his nature, the destructive explosion of an incalculable energy. Contradictory as they are, it is necessary to experience these aspects of the god as a single comprehended essence.[12]

Demoke, the human protégé of the contradictory god, creates the magnificent totem which is the centre-piece of the gathering of the tribes, but exhibits the destructive principle, first by the very act of denuding the tree of its natural foliage, an act of desecration of which Eshuoro complains bitterly:

> But my body was stripped by the impious hands of Demoke, Ogun's favoured slave of the forge. My head was hacked off by his axe. Trampled, sweated on, bled on, my body's shame pointed at the sky by the adze of Demoke . . .
>
> (*Five Plays* pp. 47–8)

The more significant act of destruction is Demoke's murder of his own apprentice out of pique. His act of creation thus involved destruction, even the destruction of another human being. Nothing so dramatic happens in Demoke's previous existence in the court of Mata Kharibu, but the duality of his nature is exhibited there by his fulsome flattery of the powerful Madame Tortoise, whom he secretly despises:

> Your hair is the feathers my lady, and the breast of the canary – your forehead my lady – is the inspiration of your servant. Madame, you must not say you have lost your canary – (*aside*) unless it be your virtue, slut!
>
> (p. 52)

[13] 'And after the Narcissist?' *African Forum*, vol. I. no. 4, spring 1966, p. 59.

Madame Tortoise represents the destructive principle. The mother of the Half-child refers to her in language that removes her from the process of creation:

> I am certain she had no womb, but I think
> It was a woman ...

(p. 68)

Sophisticated, even majestic, her attraction is fatal. In both existences, she leaves a trail of dead admirers. Her callous reference to the death of a soldier on one of her trivial errands, even as she is about to dispatch the young novice on a similar errand, is typical:

> COURT POET: Did not a soldier fall to his death from the roof days ago lady?
> MADAME TORTOISE: That is so. I heard a disturbance, and I called the guard to find the cause. I thought it came from the roof and I directed him there. He was too eager and he fell.

(p. 53)

Her contemporary counterpart is equally indifferent to her trail of death. For her, the men who die as a result of their pursuit of her are only foolish investors. Indeed, when she is accused she turns round and by implication indicts society:

> When your business men ruin the lesser ones, do you go crying to them? I also have no pity for the one who invested foolishly. Investors, that is all they ever were – to me.

(p. 24)

In fact she is not to blame at all:

> I owe all that happened to my nature. I regret nothing.

(p. 23)

Soyinka's gaze is persistently fixed on human nature, which as it embodies both the destructive and the creative principle continues essentially unchanged throughout the centuries.

This conflict between the opposing forces is what is played out in the drama of the Half-child at the end of the play. The Half-child, representing the future of man, is constantly in danger. He is tricked into a game of *sesan* with the Figure in Red (Eshuoro in disguise) for a stake which turns out to be himself. He loses, and is thus in the power of Eshuoro, described by Soyinka as 'a wayward cult-spirit', and bent on giving men their head so that they can effect their own destruction: 'But if the humans, as always, wreak havoc on their own heads, who are we to stop them?' (p. 47). The Half-child hovers uncertainly between the protection of his mother and the more certain destruction that Eshuoro represents. The decisive step towards its mother is always interrupted at the critical point. (Soyinka keeps up the tension admirably here through mime and movement.)

The child then becomes the pawn in an even more perilous tussle for his possession. So demanding is the original script for this section of the play that Soyinka had to modify it in a substitute ending which he wrote for the 1960 production. The trick that is involved, while being exceptionally demanding on an ordinary actor, is one that is widely practised by professional acrobats in West Africa. The alternative ending is convenient for a stage production, but in that it mitigates the obvious physical danger of the live Half-child (the alternative ending substitutes an 'ibeji' carving) it is less satisfactory as a symbolic enactment of the precarious future of the human race.

The directions for the original ending read:

> When the Half-child is totally disarmed by the Jester, Eshuoro picks him up suddenly and throws him towards the Third Triplet who makes to catch him on the point of two knives as in the dance of the child acrobats. Rola screams, the Child is tossed up by the Third Triplet who again goes through the same motion . . . The Half-child is now tossed back to Eshuoro, and suddenly Demoke dashes forward to intercept. Eshuoro laughs, pretends to throw the child back, Demoke dashes off only to find that he still retains the child . . .
>
> (p. 81)

The peril of the Half-child is far more vividly portrayed here than in the alternative ending, whose import is, however, essentially the same. The game proceeds until Ogun outsmarts them, catches the Half-child and hands it to Demoke, who eventually hands it to its mother. The significance of this act has been variously interpreted.[14]

The crux seems to lie in Eshuoro's personality. He is a devilish trickster. All during this final section of the play he has been trying by various devices to influence the fate of the Half-child and hence of mankind as a whole. He first comes in disguised as the Questioner, and indicts the Dead Man, who represents an earlier generation of men:

[14] See Margaret Laurence, op. cit., p. 43.

> Three lives he boasted of, and each
> A certain waste, foolishly cast aside.
> Has he learnt the crime of laziness?
> What did he prove, from the first when,
> Power at his grasp, he easily
> Surrendered his manhood. It was surely
> The action of a fool. What did he prove?
> And does he come whining here for sleep?
> Let him wander a hundred further . . .

When his disguise is stripped off and he is revealed as the enemy of man, he is only temporarily discomfited, for he soon comes in in another disguise as the Figure in Red. It is in this disguise that he wins the Half-child. It turns out that even the Interpreter is Eshuoro's jester. It is clear from all this that Eshuoro will spare no pains in his battle for the Half-child. Yet when he is apparently outsmarted by Ogun and the Half-child is returned to the protection of his mother, instead of a gesture of defeat, 'Eshuoro gives a loud yell of triumph, rushes off-stage, accompanied by his jester.' He has in fact won. It would appear that Eshuoro had been involved in an elaborate game of pretence. He was all along confident that man left to his own devices would need no spirit to aid him in his own destruction. If perhaps some special divine aid had been offered as a protection to the Half-child, hence to humanity, Eshuoro would have been defeated. But man is left only to his own devices. Eshuoro had confidently declared earlier that he would do nothing *by his own hand* to hurt men:

> Not by my hand. But if the humans, as always, wreak havoc on their own heads, who are we to stop them? Don't they always decide their own lives?
> (p. 47)

At the end therefore he is content to let them have their freedom – this is enough. Forest Head, who knows the truth, is unhappy about the future of his creation. His decision not to interfere is in fact Eshuoro's triumph. Forest Head is in despair when he looks at his own creation. They will never learn. They will never change:

> The fooleries of beings whom I have fashioned closer to me weary and distress me. Yet I must persist, knowing that nothing is ever altered. My secret *is* my eternal burden – to pierce the encrustations of soul-deadening habit, and bare the mirror of original nakedness knowing full well, it is all futility. Yet I must do this alone, and no more, since to intervene is to be guilty of contradiction. . . .
> (p. 82)

The words of Forest Head sum up the basis of Soyinka's treatment of man in history; man, the victim of his freedom of action.

Soyinka's plays have the complexity of organization and of language that distinguishes literature from mere writing. The seriousness of their content make him a vital voice to his generation, but it is his art that sets him apart from a large number of well-meaning writers with a message. His work responds to serious criticism, and indeed needs it, for in the more serious plays there is a surface difficulty which has to be penetrated before the essence of the work of this important writer is fully revealed.

4 Cyprian Ekwensi: The Novelist and the Pressure of the City

▼▼▼▼▼▼▼▼▼▼▼▼▼▼▼▼▼▼▼▼▼▼▼▼▼▼▼▼▼▼▼▼▼

JOHN POVEY

ONE major need in evaluating art is to be aware of sociological and cultural contexts and then to consider their impact. Such considerations are directly relevant to critiques of African literature that concern themselves with questions of standards, and should be taken into account before the critic attempts to pass judgement. One has to begin with the fact that Ekwensi's work is usually held in relatively low critical esteem. There are major weaknesses in the novels and these weaknesses, both structural and stylistic, are serious enough to have inhibited Ekwensi from developing to the full a major talent for socio-political and urban satirical observation. Any serious study of Ekwensi must develop from an awareness of the relationship between social observation and popular or journalistic writing. External pressures contribute to what may be considered as the careless side of the popular novelist. But Ekwensi's professionalism also deserves recognition, nor can his major contribution to the development of the African novel be overlooked.

John Povey taught in South Africa before moving to the University of California at Los Angeles, where he is on the staff of the Department of English Language and Literature as well as having special interests in African studies. He is editor of *African Arts*.

Ekwensi has had a hard time from the critics. At first reviewers awarded him exaggerated accolades, such as that offered in the London *Daily Telegraph*, where he was called 'a Nigerian Defoe'. Then the serious critics took over: those who knew something about Africa and the significance of the phenomenom of African literature in English. The evaluation he has received at their hands has been harsh; perhaps excessively so.

Anyone attempting a re-evaluation has to begin by admitting that many of the condemnations made by these critics have been just. Yet to formulate a defence of Ekwensi one needs to go one stage further. Beyond the obvious inadequacies that present themselves there is a capable and seriously intentioned writer to be found deeply embedded in the palpable melodrama and covered by the purple passages of Ekwensi's sometimes lamentable prose.

This counter-attack to accepted critical comment can be legitimately mounted. The condemnation of the critics can be answered, and direct evidence can be set against the overall impression of shallow and shabby diction. Yet I feel most strongly that with such purely literary debate one has not reached the point where there is nothing further to say about the man as a writer and as a force in the contemporary literature of West Africa.

To make this kind of statement sets me, as an unrepentently rigorous literary critic, on awkward ground. One is beginning to tread that dangerously broad path towards the assertion that it is not the work of art but its content that is important; or that the writer's significance can only be perceived when set in the context of the social and political forces that have defined his assumptions.

Few academics in the field of literature would care to pursue that argument too far, for we know where it leads us . . . into reducing literature to a handmaiden of the social sciences: mere data at the mercy of the theories and themes of the historians and the sociologists. Yet I believe that this issue cannot be avoided in considering a certain type of African writing, which Ekwensi's work clearly exemplifies. There must be some concern for the sociological and cultural aspects of writing that would be of considerably less interest and significance when discussing more established literatures. This is in no way to say that standards of quality do not remain, as always, of paramount concern, but that the context of its creation and the intention of the writers are also important elements in any adequate comprehension of this literature and the direction that it takes.

It is this recognition that, to a large extent, makes the study of Ekwensi's writing of such general significance. For an understanding of the particular and peculiar elements of this new African writing there is no author so significant or revealing. This is not to say that any novel of Ekwensi matches the profundity and authority of Achebe's *Arrow of God*, for example, or that any of his work shows the skill and genius of Wole Soyinka's writing. But simply because this is so obvious, and because it has been so often stated, it has blinded us to the valid qualities that are to be found in Ekwensi's work. In arguing that he isn't Achebe, that he does not match the solid qualities of the transhipped Victorian novel, we cannot at this point dismiss the man's work. That would be to fall into the dangerous trap that awaits critics who accuse a writer of not doing what he never intended to do and belabour him for the lack of those qualities that he quite deliberately avoided. One must consider

Ekwensi in terms of what he creates and what he attempts, and from that standpoint there are many important and influential qualities to be found in his work. Ekwensi creates the image of a particular kind of social truth; presenting his morality through the mirror of his novels and their plots. These books cannot be dismissed as unworthy of our consideration because of the banality of some of their most obvious features.

In thinking of Ekwensi I am reminded of a young American working on his doctoral thesis. He was a mid-west American, well read in English literature, but he had not been to Britain. His thesis was to have some such title as 'The Caricatures of Charles Dickens'. He had judged from his readings of the novels that Dickens, because of the exaggerations and the artificial tricks and mannerisms he employed, was unable to create a realistic and human character. The theatrical simplicity of his people contradicted in this scholar's estimation the complexity and subtlety truly realistic portrayal requires. As part of his research he travelled to London. He came back awed and astounded, saying to me: 'There they were, all walking about as large as life. The British people really are just as Dickens draws them.' I hope he found a good new thesis title, such as 'Dickens, Master of Character', as a result of his discovery. He wasn't exactly right in his perception, of course, but it is a warning to us all to beware of our own prejudgements. *People of the City* is melodrama, and no doubt vulgar and crude, but nevertheless, the book *is* about the people of the city, and those who know Lagos will begin to wonder at the accusations of gross exaggeration that have been thrown at the author, for the people Ekwensi portrays do walk about the streets of Lagos, themselves a little larger than life.

The key to any general appreciation of Ekwensi comes surely in his assertion that he regards himself as a writer for the masses. He does not, that is, write for intellectuals. In passing one notes the significance of the fact that his characters are rarely university people and 'been-tos'. He thinks of himself as a popular writer, and a popular writer in English. It needs little knowledge of modern Africa to see how significant that position will be. The difficulty in making an exact assessment of Ekwensi's position arises precisely because he is an African. Transpose the geography and we would have no difficulty in fixing his position in American letters. He would range somewhere between popular paperbacks and the middlebrow book-of-the-month. Such a character as Jagua Nana would clearly indicate the hope for a lucrative film contract.

It is well known that Ekwensi's first book was one of those legendary, ephemeral, popular romances sold in the market and called 'Onitsha novels'. Its title was typically romantic, *When Love Whispers*. Comment on this early writing has assumed this to be a mere novelty, of interest only as a curiosity. It is, I think, rather, evidence of a decided direction in the writer from his earliest attempts at his craft. This is the first link in a demonstrably continuing chain of professional entertaining. Major aspects of Ekwensi's work derive from this beginning. It is this that explains Ekwensi's tone. His writing often seems sentimental, vulgar, melodramatic and trivial; lacking in all that Matthew Arnold meant by 'high seriousness'. But might there not also be a 'low seriousness', unencompassed by Arnold's solemn dictates? In this sense Ekwensi's lowness is not necessarily evidence of his own lack of serious preoccupation with his subject. It has more in common with associations of high and low, as Northrop Frye employs these concepts in his *Anatomy of Criticism*.

For all the qualifications one has to make from a purely literary standpoint, Ekwensi remains an important figure in African writing because his concerns are so determinedly with modern Nigeria; with the tension of politics in the crowded new cities. He does not safely insulate himself in the past problems of the colonial bush, but with Lagos now, its slums and violence. This is in many ways a difficult task. It is certainly a very necessary one, which for a long time only Ekwensi attempted to meet head on. It is significant that the better novels of more recent authors have selected this field for their themes.

Ekwensi's first major book was *People of the City* (London 1954).[1] The story concerns the adventures of Amusa Sango, who, brought to Lagos by the city's alluring promise, has become a crime reporter with the *West African Sensation*, and a part-time jazz-band leader. Before the novel concludes with his facing the dawning future hand-in-hand with his true love, a series of dramatic incidents have been presented. Amusa has affairs with several women, who get stripped in the street, slugged into a miscarriage, have cayenne pepper rubbed into their private parts, and die of venereal disease. Love is also the cause of his best friend's being shot in the stomach. Sango's journalistic activities allow descriptions of what Ekwensi would no doubt call the seamy side of life: murder, suicide, strikes and riots.

This surfeit of adventures, enough for any three normal novels, distorts what might have been a serious examination of modern Nigerian city life into a tale that is largely melodrama. Ekwensi wants to be taken seriously, but covering the bones of his no doubt honest intention is a plot and a use of language both of which demonstrate lack of judgement and restraint. Somewhere between the African vision and the ensuing European publication a distortion has occurred, and this distortion seems to have come from outside, not indigenous sources; from the influence of Ekwensi's unselective reading, not from the quality of Ekwensi's original experience.

This is a very significant fact, for it raises the whole question of the origins of the assumptions made by the African contemporary novelist. The novel is

[1] *People of the City* (Heinemann, African Writers Series, London, 1963). Page numbers for quotations refer to this edition. The paperback edition (Fawcett, New York, 1969) has been somewhat revised.

a genre that has no African antecedent. Its form, no matter how modified by particular cultural circumstance, is necessarily derived from the writers' own expectations of structure established by the background reading. In Ekwensi's case he has apparently given excessive attention to the more trivial styles of the novel that appear to constitute his assessment of acceptable form. Somewhere he has obtained an entirely false and corrupt view of what a novel has to be, as if a promising young African painter saw only the meretricious copies of magazine illustrations and took these as a reasonable model. Ekwensi's presentation is warped because he presents his experience using only the tired and crude tools of the American hack. But that American hack fairly consciously, even cynically, prostitutes his writing to achieve a certain market. Ekwensi seems incapable of distinguishing true style from rubbish; his intention is serious, but he seems unable to see how his intentions are blighted by the literary means he employs.

Sango could have been an ideal character to demonstrate conditions in modern Lagos. As a journalist and a musician he is articulate and sophisticated, yet without the posing and narrowness that separates the 'been-tos' with their new cars and European-level government quarters from 'the people of the city'. This lack of a university degree in itself importantly distinguishes this character from the protagonists of the majority of such novels. The social milieu in which Sango lives is a world far removed from traditional village life or civil-service existence, those extremes of experience that more usually bracket the lives of many other characters and, one might observe, of their creators. Yet Sango's experience is a thousand times more commonplace and familiar in contemporary Africa. The *élite*, by definition, represent a minute proportion of Ibadan or Lagos people.

Sango's job gives him freedom of access and income. Journalism makes him a convenient eye for Ekwensi's intended criticism of crooked politics and the misery of Lagos slum life. The jazz band brings him into contact with the frivolous gaiety, the dangerous transient lure of the city that Ekwensi will condemn. This is most promising, for it suggests that a fresh extension of situation is in the offing.

Unfortunately the freshness of the characters' background is in no way matched by any originality of event, unless one argues that stock situations must always have some novelty value on being exported into a new geographic context. Common American stereotypes stand like shadows behind many incidents and set Sango largely beyond Ekwensi's control. Sango as a man becomes masked by our recognition that his experiences have been encountered in a thousand previous versions: the clichés of the American B movie. Behind the young African journalist lurk those late-night movie repetitions of the mercifully outdated image of the editor in green eye-shade and the reporter always cramming on his hat to follow up a hot tip. Consider the following incident. It is surely American in origin except for the African names.

> The phone rang. Sango went over.
> 'West African Sensation.'
> 'May I speak to the editor, please?'
> The voice was tinny, strained, very excited. . . .
> 'Who's speaking, please?'
> 'Never mind who I am. If you want something for your paper, come out to Magamu bush, and you'll get it. . . .'
> 'Where are you speaking from? Hello. . . . Hello. . . . Hello! Oh! He's hung up. . . .'
> He reached for his hat. As he left the office the typewriters were clattering again . . .
>
> (p. 50)

It is a friend who later reminds us of the source of such scenes. He takes the words out of our mouths in remarking 'I thought such things only happened in films' (p. 29). In other places the derivation is from commonplace fiction. The diction recalls the enticing 'come-on' selection inside the cover of a 35p cheap paperback.

> While those who as yet had found no man, would twist their hips alluringly before admiring eyes, tempting, tantalizing, . . . promising much but giving little, basking in the vanity of being desired.
>
> (p. 11)

It is not only in creating character that Ekwensi finds problems. There is the difficulty of transmitting serious emotion through such unsuitable words that his intention is lost in diction that conflicts with the tone he seeks. If one were not seriously concerned about Ekwensi's writing, it might be merely amusing to point out the influences upon him. There is the curiously eighteenth-century subtitle to part one: 'How the city attracts all types and how the unwary must suffer from ignorance of its ways.' When Aina, abandoned by Sango, is in the dock accused of theft, we are treated to this raging stream of consciousness:

> What would happen now? O, my mother! O Lord, what made me do this mad thing? Why did I plead guilty? They have fooled me; they have deceived me because I am so ignorant.
> 'Three months!' said the magistrate.
> 'Next case. . .!'

'O my mother! My mother, come and save me! O Lord, I'm dead!'

But the stalwart men had been handpicked and she might just as well have saved her breath.

'Ha, ha! . . . Your mother . . . go on call her! Call her to come and save you! Ha, ha!'

(p. 44)

We know where we are here: a century later somewhere between Dickens at his lachrymose worst and nineteenth-century melodrama with the mustachioed villain who cries 'ha ha!' all over the place. At other times Ekwensi derives his style from more modern sources, favouring the bad prose of advertising jargon and aping purple passages from novelettes: 'This is a city of bubbles. You see men riding shining cars and taking glittering women to restaurants . . .' (p. 63).

Invent any incident and Ekwensi is capable of driving it into the ground with hideously borrowed diction. There is a hospital scene. 'Dr Kildare' scriptwriters could do no worse than Ekwensi, which is only a way of saying that they both approach the hospital with sentimental reverence, which precludes honest intention. The following lines are in stock form, without any redeeming quality:

[The doctor's] deft fingers handling the instruments with cold efficiency . . . the swift application of the swabs . . . the eyes half-cocked at the racing clock on the theatre wall . . . the tension of the anaesthetist . . . the sterilized instruments being handed over with automatic precision.

(p. 226)

And as the operation continues, Sango indulges in the worst type of declamation:

What a narrow margin there was between life and death! In that thin borderline when the body loses all sensations of pain, the daring doctor stood his ground, challenging death with no more weapon than his sword of knowledge.

(p. 226)

Perhaps the climax of this sort of thing comes in the arrest of two thieves (naturally called 'robbers'). How many clichés from Sherlock Holmes stories can one find in the following passage? 'The game was up. The robbers were challenged. Handcuffs glinted in the moonlight, snapped on their wrists as they were led away' (p. 156). In the same vein we have the police capturing their man with the splendid cliché, 'We've had our eye on him for some time. He hasn't escaped us this time' (p. 156).

The scenes where Ekwensi tries hardest are the mining strike and the funeral of the great patriot, de Periera. But when he attempts to describe the suffering of the miners, which undoubtedly moves him with considerable concern, there is the same fatal diction that deflates his honest emotion by reducing pathos to bathos: 'Sango stood among the miners and made the descent into the bowels of the earth to those dripping ozonated crevices where man, crouching, hacks away at the fuel of life . . .' (p. 126).

At the funeral Sango's sincerity at 'seeing a new city: not just a collection of landlords and tenants, but something with spirit and feeling' (p. 165) is soon overlaid by his discovery of a woman in the crowd. The book concludes with his marriage to this woman, who accepts him in an odd reversion to eighteenth-century style'. She affirmed her desire that her life be with Sango's with no further delay' (p. 234). And the final lines as he embraces her are, 'God bless you . . . and us' (p. 237). It's quite like Tiny Tim!

One can argue that the kind of criticism above is deliberately partial, though not incorrect as far as it goes. In order to find the quality that makes this novel of interest one has to turn back to the title, *People of the City*. The words deliberately avoid imposing any single event as the central context. It even avoids a single name. The focus is in fact on the city itself, which in the words of Ekwensi's opening subtitle, 'attracts all types', where 'the unwary must suffer from ignorance of its ways'. We do see this suffering of the unwary and the types (that word too is revealing) who seek their liberation within the city with its threatening but tempting excitement. The vision is an old one. Though particularly popular in American nineteenth-century fiction, the idea of the city as simultaneously exciting and alluring yet morally dangerous and corrupting to the young is as old as the first time a young man left his farm in any society. It is implicit in much medieval and early Elizabethan poetic and dramatic sermonizing.

Ekwensi's morality, although obvious and pronounced, does derive, as moralizing should to be effective, from within the actions and the context of the plot. His judgement is both obvious and true, only a little less penetrating for its exaggeration. The awkward ending indicates the impossibility of effective resolution of the dilemma, both moral and economic, that he propounds for his characters.

It is worth observing that by legitimately criticizing the secondhand nature of Ekwensi's work, we are making judgements based on an external experience, not on that of Ekwensi or his African audience. What we are saying is that the reaction we obtain is the result of a plethora of prior readings and viewings. We who have seen too many B features, we who turn off the television when the Dr Kildare show is screened, we who make low camp humour out of what we take for Victorian baroque novels and plays, are conditioned to our culture judgements. It is necessary to mention in passing that in the context the question of the cliché is important though to pursue this issue thoroughly would require an entire critical essay. Its apparent tiredness derives from its over-use. But if there is a social context in which it has never been used, can it be seen to have its original freshness? Think how a child delights in discovering a simile like 'as cool as a cucumber'. Its effectiveness makes its original impact considerable. Banality is in the eye of the beholder. The critic's essential duty is to develop his judgement to the level where banality can be recognized and legitimately condemned. Yet an etiolated taste has its own potential excess too. Where do we seek the middle ground of judgement for African prose?

With *Jagua Nana*,[2] Ekwensi's second major novel published in 1961, many of the same doubts apply. If one can point out some effective and serious incidents one is driven to admit that Jagua herself is that cliché of all clichés, the prostitute with the heart of gold dogged by misfortune; a Nigerian Sadie Thompson. She is more sinned against than sinning, and the siren voice of Lagos must take much of the blame for bringing her to this position. The novel is rather more coherent than *People of the City*. Except for that exotic trip to Bagana, where warring tribes are reconciled by one passionate squeeze to her ample bosom, the plot centres firmly round the co-ordinating force of this woman's character. *People of the City* only appeared to centre around Sango; in fact it did so in a merely picaresque way – things happened to him and he was often the mere spectator. Jagua causes the situations to happen.

If one is going to try to suggest that certain elements in this novel show a marked advance, one has to begin by admitting that there is only too much of the previous inadequacy. The spelling of the heroine's name is important. She is *Jagua*. When she is really girded up she is *Jagwa*, and *in extremis* may even be called *Jaagwa*! To one's dismay the novel begins with Jagua dressing after a bath, and there are breasts, sensuous arcs, armpits and a 'provocatively' exposed pink brassière (p. 7). She has come to Lagos to escape from a husband who is not adequately 'jagwaful', and is living with Freddie, a teacher and hopeful correspondence student of law. Freddie constantly upbraids Jagua about her way of life, but manages to avoid the admission of his own pimping position by emphasizing what Jagua calls euphemistically 'love' and Freddie protests is a dark infatuation.

One thing we have to accept in this novel is that the major characters use pidgin English. If this device allows Ekwensi to escape from the worst examples of stilted English conversation, he substitutes a no less awkward effect. Even if one is not capable of assessing its literal accuracy one can judge the literary ineffectiveness of 'We mus' show our skin and let de sun-shine kiss our body. Is nothin' bad in de sun kissin' your woman body' (p. 8). Ekwensi defends his choice with the interesting suggestion that although both Jagua

[2] *Jagua Nana* (Hutchinson, London, 1961). Page numbers refer to the paperback edition (Fawcett, New York, 1969).

and Freddie are Ibo-speaking, they use pidgin in Lagos because 'They did not want too many embarrassing reminders of clan or custom' (p. 6). This is hardly likely. It rather expresses the desperate search of an African writer for some diction to render the local idiom more effectively into English. This is a valid and necessary task that preoccupies all African writers: in Ekwensi's case with only irregular success.

The central situation of this book is the weakest part and the one most redolent of clichés, stretching back to *Manon Lescaut* and beyond. Jagua claims to love a man who cannot afford to support her in the luxuries that her heart craves. She seeks this luxury in the local nightclub, 'Tropicana'. The scene is set very characteristically.

> All the women wore dresses which were definitely undersize, so that buttocks and breasts jutted grotesquely above the general contours of the bodies. At the same time midriffs shrunk to suffocation. A dress succeeded if it made man's eyes ogle hungrily in this modern super sex market.
>
> (p. 14)

'Modern super sex-market' or 'modern sex super-market'? Ekwensi is getting a little confused here. A page later his prose returns to an almost eighteenth-century rhythm. 'Each girl had the national characteristic that appealed to some male, and each man saw in his type of woman a quality which inspired his gallantry' (p. 15). That last is an odd choice of word for their intention.

Poor Freddie finds it difficult to accept the moral position inherent in the fact that 'She loved Freddie well, but his whole salary would not buy that dress. He must understand that taking money from the Syrian did not mean that she loved him less' (p. 22). He turns for consolation to the neighbour's young daughter, Nancy, and his passion knows no limits of diction: 'her sweet breath beat warmly against his lips. The hard slim bust strained closer to his shirt' (p. 18).

When Freddie is taken in the disgusting act of discovering that 'firm and elastic' is more attractive than 'flabby and soggy' (p. 40), it is Nancy who stands up to Jagua's righteous wrath. This moment of passion becomes a perfect example of the way in which Ekwensi can totally destroy his effects at times where he wishes to be most impressively impassioned. Where does Ekwensi get such phrases as, 'Freddie wanted to raise her by the arm and shout "Champion"' (p. 43) or the description of Jagua in the fire of her rage as 'Like a fighter when the "seconds-out" bell has just been rung?' (p. 45). I have observed such effects in P. G. Wodehouse, but at least he is being intentionally facetious.

The book is fleshed out with two other incidents. Jagua goes to visit the chief of a warring tribe and settles the battle by exciting violent lust, described in prose compounded of a mixture of Oscar Wilde and a cheap magazine: 'he became a man lusting after her; her temper made him her slave, willing to obey her maddest whims merely to restore the smile to her lips' (p. 108). Jagua also meets with a young thief, which gives Ekwensi yet another opportunity to indulge in his description of passion: a subject that he should above all avoid. When Jagua sees his eyes, 'like two hot loaves of coal from a black-smith's forge' (p. 122), she obligingly suggests that as Freddie is in England, 'You can taste what 'e use to chop every night before he come back an' marry me proper' (p. 122). With sentences like that echoing through one's mind, one asks helplessly how one can take such unspeakable writing seriously, and what possible redemption there could be for such scenes. In *People of the City* I suggested that the successful scenes were those that touched upon the literal truth of real experience and perceptive descriptions of Lagos life. Ekwensi's major successes in this book, too, are the political incidents, which demonstrate knowledge, bitterness, and more valuably, artistic restraint.

Jagua meets Uncle Taiwo, the secretary of a major political party. Taiwo is Ekwensi's most successful character, perhaps because he is so obviously developed from life, not from rehashed cheap fiction. Taiwo is large, gross, confident. His false laugh booms out unhumorously on all occasions. With his crass appetites, his shameless and ruthless bargaining for votes, he becomes the epitome of all vicious power-hungry politicians. In the Falstaffian sense he is larger than life, yet he becomes, not a caricature, but an appalling archetype of human greed. There are some antecedents to this Huey Long-type figure in American novels, but Taiwo is no copy; he is grandly and grossly African – an African who has chosen to absorb and use all that is worst in European ways. When at last the Tropicana gets indigenous dancers, his dismissal is contemptuous, and yet it has a raw power and evidences an open allegiance to his own vulgar principles, debased as they are.

> Uncle Taiwo yawned, 'Music! give us *real* music!'
> 'You jus' heard real music,' Jagua told him. . . .
> 'Is bushman dancing!' said Uncle Taiwo. He roared with laughter.
>   (pp. 141–2)

Uncle Taiwo is irresistible. For all his coarseness, Jagua finds his powerful confidence, his assured rhetoric holds her to him. He miscalculates in having his opponent beaten up, and public opinion swings the votes against him. His party will not forgive failure, and has him murdered. His death is recorded with a restraint unusual in Ekwensi. It is the more powerful for that.

> Lagos was in a state of chaos that day. It seemed as if the ghost of that corpse had gone abroad among them. The body was lying there twisted and

swollen; one knee was drawn up against the chest, the arms were clutching at the breast like a statue. . . . In Africa you see these things.

(pp. 199–200)

There are many strong and competent moments set within the shallowness of this novel. The very name, Jagua Nana, makes a significant hybrid. Nana is the ultimate European prostitute, from Zola. Jagua is not, as one might assume, a reference to the sleek jungle cat. The metaphor is more materialistic. 'Because of her good looks and stunning jungle fashions they said she was Jagua after the famous British prestige car' (p. 5). That unexpected comparison gives considerable power to one of the extraordinarily revealing perceptions of Nigerian life that Ekwensi can at times so casually and yet skilfully capture. In a single simile he has indicated much about the essential values of this society. Its materialism is more marked than its somewhat haphazard sexual depravity. I am reminded of those extraordinary graffiti recorded by Armah in a much later urban novel, *The Beautyful Ones are Not Yet Born.*[3] On the lavatory wall someone has crudely scribed 'Vagina Sweet'. Underneath a more cynical or more rational commentator has scratched: 'Money sweet pass all.'

This is the assumption, in a crucial sense, of Jagua Nana too. For if the talk is constantly of love and passion and such sexual activity as approximates to those emotions, the core concerns the 'serious' things, money and power. It is this emotional priority that Ekwensi catches so fiercely. There is an immense certainty in the manner with which he accomplishes the description of his inherited contemporary world. He knows this world of bars and politics, of shabby shared rooms around sordid courtyards. With a writer's skill he exemplifies every part of their context. There is a real authority in these sections. Also there is a far greater strength of characterization in this book. Jagua Nana and Uncle Taiwo are impressive and in an important sense convincing. Of course they are larger than life, but this is not a novel of simple understated reality; this is, to revert, the style of Dickens, in which men are simultaneously exaggerated and real; extreme and yet exemplifying the most ordinary motivations that possess and drive them.

Perhaps the diction affords the most crucial clues to which of the sections are significant and which are merely shallow rhetoric. Invariably the language is the key to the conviction that Ekwensi can bring to a scene. The conversation quoted earlier when Uncle Taiwo dismisses the 'real music' of the African tradition with the violent condemnation of 'bushman dancing' remains in the memory. Its impact will not be argued away by any subsequent rationalistic assertion that the story has only glib and exaggerated life.

[3] Ayi Kwei Armah, *The Beautyful Ones are not Yet Born* (Houghton Mifflin, Boston and Heinemann, African Writers Series, London 1969).

Ekwensi is still at the mercy of his false assumption of what the novel ought to be and his style can be simply bad. In fact he doesn't seem able to assess which are the bad parts of his writing. But there are moments of character and effectiveness. Significantly, these occur in scenes and episodes with realistic Nigerian settings.

Ekwensi's next novel, *Burning Grass* (1962), is outside the concerns of modern Nigeria. His subsequent novel, *Beautiful Feathers* was published in England in 1963.[4] In this book Ekwensi often displays his exasperating dualism; for the work ranges between art and rubbish; between real skill and unmitigated trash. Yet there is considerable competence in this novel. There are lapses in style and diction, but they are rare and obvious, separable from the finer aspects of the book. One way in which this novel is superior is that the plot is virtually single and tightly drawn. We are grateful to lose what has been stupidly praised as Ekwensi's fecundity of invention because we also lose the twisting meanderings of inadequately organized sub-plots.

The story of *Beautiful Feathers* again touches on urban politics, which is at the heart of all of Ekwensi's work and perhaps, at a deeper level, at the heart of all the contemporary Nigerian experience since independence. It concerns Wilson Iyari, druggist and part-time politician. His gradual success as a politician is set against his increasing failure as a husband to Yaniya and father to his revolutionary band of children, Lumumba, Jomo, and Pandhit. Each development of the plot balances these two aspects of his life in a way that is both perceptive and technically sophisticated. There is confidence in his description that shows even in the opening scenes at the bus stop. The new simplicity can occasionally slide, as when the simple druggist's act of 'checking the poisons and dangerous drugs' becomes 'supervising the mixing of magic liquids that brought health to thousands' (p. 11). But these have become isolated, and are not the very fabric of the book. When he is approaching the heart of his theme, his touch is more sure.

The members of his new party for African solidarity meet at Wilson's home. He harangues them with power and authority, and then Ekwensi sets up one of the most effective dramatic moments in his novels. His wife chooses this moment to go out, clearly to meet her lover.

'Solidarity is imperative. We don't care how difficult it is. . . .' As he mentioned the word 'solidarity' Wilson saw the door of the bedroom open. His wife, resplendent, came out, passed through the sitting-room, and before they could rise to greet her, she was outside, leaving a bewitching trail of Balmain.

(p. 48)

4 *Beautiful Feathers* (Hutchinson, London, 1963 and Heinemann, African Writers Series, London 1971). Page numbers refer to this edition.

D

Nothing more; there is no need. Just that perfect confrontation that tells all without straining diction.

Just as effective are the scenes of marital antagonism between Wilson and his wife. Ekwensi records exactly the bitterness, the cold mixture of anger and frustrated despair of a marriage that is destroying itself. There is no echo here of any previous scene of Ekwensi's; nothing in the ardent knock-down battles with which Jagua exposes her wrath prepares one for the shrewd sad study of this pair.

Wilson is finally provoked into asking for a divorce, and there is no fight, no rich anger to purge the cold spite; one feels instinctively that this is the true spirit of the moment when such decisions are made. 'In the early days of their marriage, Wilson would have struck her' (p. 42). Now there is not that much passion between them, and there is an infinite defeat and pathos as Wilson cries out, 'Say what you like. Behave to me as you like. The fact remains; to the world outside I am something' (p. 43). When he tells her to leave, Ekwensi describes the scene without sensationalism; without excess.

> She did not say a word. He waited for her to say something before he plunged deeper into the mess he had now made. She opened her mouth like one struck, and closed it. But there were no words. He turned and walked slowly to his room. There was a book at his bedside. He opened it and lay back on his bed to read. The print swam before his eyes.
>
> (p. 43)

End of chapter. Nothing more said or needed, but how effectively Ekwensi has handled that incident; accurate in characterization; subtle in diction.

It is the calibre of such scenes that make Ekwensi's relapses all the harder to accept. Yet it is important to see that these inferior sections are invariably the over-emotional scenes of passion. When the wife goes into her lover's arms we are treated to this poeticism:

> Like a lover, the drizzle had crept upon the night quietly fertilizing the earth. . . . The langorous arms of Yaniya, female, supple as the twining plant, clung round her lover's neck. Her wet lips mumbled obscenities. . . .
>
> (p. 52)

It reminds one of the worst excesses of *Peyton Place*. This particular incident is immediately sterilized by the next scene, where Yaniya returns home from her adultery and there is no triumph, only the feeble whimpering of her baby. Illusion is changed into reality, and recorded with sharp honesty:

As she put [her clothes] away it seemed to her that all the furtive and tiring joy she had gone out to buy was being shed away for the reality which now confronted her; pissing children, the wrath of the outraged husband. She touched little Jomo's napkin and found that it was wet. She took it to the sink and changed it.

(p. 40)

In the political scenes Ekwensi's touch is even more certain. It is this topic that again permits us to glimpse the shrewd understanding that is the basis for Ekwensi's serious political satire. Wilson's sponging brother-in-law, Jacob, is well drawn as a corrupt, petty, local demagogue who could 'assemble masses of people quickly and effectively and convert three votes to a thousand – for a consideration' (p. 13). Jacob is like Uncle Taiwo in his sharp greed, his surface sophistication, his taste for fat-buttocked girls. But he lacks Taiwo's vastness, his dangerous geniality. Jacob is only mean; a petty hyena, rather than a corrupt lion.

Another more openly comic satire is the character of the Minister of Consolation. The very department sounds like Evelyn Waugh at his most inventive, and the portrait is worthy of that comparison. The minister, when not goading his British secretary, spends his time searching his mirror for the most effective poses. At press interviews, 'He showed his teeth in the manner which the mirror had told him was most flattering ... The minister manoeuvred the reporter till he was farthest from the camera' (p. 78). Hugely comic and ominous, the minister, with his constant group of toadying leeches, dominates this section of the book.

These political elements are powerful and skilful, leading us again to an essential social truth. They become the revelation of the political disasters that constitute the system. Ekwensi establishes that particular kind of truth which a work of art can provide. It is a truth that is very closely linked with the reality of the situation that provides its data. Yet it is not record, not mirror. It is art that alchemizes event into philosophical statement. It is the skill of the novelist that takes the individual character and sets him into that context which makes him expose the universal of the human experience. We cannot know an Uncle Taiwo. One could argue whether such a character as the Minister of Consolation could, let alone did, exist. Yet we recognize truth at a much deeper level. Here is the essence of a certain kind of vice. This is political wickedness raised to its highest motivation. Through such people and the scenes in which character is so exactly displayed Ekwensi touches upon that truth that is the deep nature of art.

The same skill can be found in other African writers. Achebe is an obvious example. In *Arrow of God* we gain some understanding of the eternal and essential tragedy in the recognition that Ezeulu brings to his personal disaster,

Ekwensi has had to approach the more difficult task of finding tragic significance in contemporary events which are assumed to contain as much low comedy as high tragedy, in our literary judgement of things. Wilson, after all, is the ultimate traditional butt of comedy, the cuckolded, henpecked husband, utterly unable to control his beautiful wife. Here it simply isn't funny. The human revelation is of agony. There is skilful balance in the way in which the parallel paradox of political success and emotional incompetence is handled. Wilson ceases to be a puppet; he is in fact quite understated in the subtlety of his development. His characterization touches chords of experience in a reader, revealing deeper levels of perception than the political devices that motivate him.

Even now Ekwensi is not always able to decide what is drama and what is sensation. There is the false incident when Wilson's friend attempts to return to his native country in spite of being a political exile. After a sentimental arrangement with the priest to have a mass said for his soul, he crosses the border and is melodramatically shot down in a scene by Graham Greene out of Hemingway. The explanatory phrase 'like something out of a movie' (p. 147), is a disagreeable reminder to us that at this intense moment Ekwensi has reverted to his old sources. In fact, the whole book from this point degenerates in a series of regrettable indulgences in the sentimental, as Ekwensi perseveringly attempts to twist his plot into a happy ending. There is the intolerable incident when Wilson's wife, in a mood of self-sacrifice, throws herself into the path of the assassin's knife-thrust intended for her husband. With nauseating self-abasement she insists that he should marry a far worthier woman. 'It is good like this, I am so happy . . . Wilson. I am no use to you any longer. I told you . . .' (p. 156).

There is a hideously sharp distinction between the sophisticated certainty of the earlier scenes and the sloppy and crude winding up of the plot. Again there is the feeling that Ekwensi is so bemused in his assumption of what a novel is supposed to be, how its plot ought to be organized and justified, that he cannot allow the story line to establish its own reality. Such reality of form would permit the consequences to derive inherently from within the inevitability of its own structure, not be caused by gross and open manipulation. Happy endings and simple solutions invariably run counter to that adult sense of the truth by which all works of art are measured. The last sentence is horrible, like Dickens at his unctuous worst.

They had truly come together now. It could be said of him that he was famous outside and that at home he had the backing of a family united by bonds of love. Wilson's beautiful feathers had ceased to be superficial and had become a substantial asset.

(p. 160)

That is a dreadful tone for Ekwensi to conclude upon. Perhaps after it one should go back and re-read one of the earlier scenes to take the taste away. The beautiful and tender farewell of Chini and her English lover, with its touching dignity, is a fitting antidote. Scenes like that are a measure of Ekwensi's capacity as a writer, and they are to be found in *Beautiful Feathers*.

Unfortunately *Iska*[5] is not much of an advance over *Beautiful Feathers*. The elements are there, but the urgency to make a moral condemnation of the destructive and divisive tribalism which was to lead to the Nigerian Civil War brings some of that same strained overwriting that marks Ekwensi's over-emotional approach to individual passion. The sharp observations set within incidents that require skill and above all detachment, are exchanged for lugubrious moralizing on the level of: 'What I want you to remember is this. People are only human. There is no tribe which is all bad . . .' (p. 39). The same pessimistic and cynical assumptions are revealed in more subtle ways in *Jagua Nana* and *Beautiful Feathers*, but they are now openly declared and therefore paradoxically less affecting for a reader. 'Both [i.e. Hausa and Ibo] had lived peacefully together for a hundred years. Then came politics – the vulture's foot that spoils the stew' (p. 14).

The story concerns an inter-tribal love between Filia and 'Dan Kayabi, her man' (p. 13). There are the usual series of excitements: the dashing of ambulances and the scenes of high tension in the hospitals. But there are interesting if not entirely convincing aspects that are revealing of the direction Ekwensi's writing is taking. The girl herself is intriguingly upgraded in appearance, background and implicit sexuality. Not in this book the earthy, somewhat grimy, embraces awarded to Jagua's well-paying customers. There is still the inevitable 'high proud bosom' that is so essential in such description. (One might comment that this is presumably imported from the breast-complex society of America!) After all 'When a girl is big breasted . . . the men in the Ministries gaze at her' (p. 16). But there are now revealing changes of attitude. If Jagua Nana in some compulsively materialistic way set her heart on moving upwards from slum to riches, it was with a very crude and utterly understandable determination to achieve wealth and comfort. Yet for her there can be comfort, security, and an essential ease in the return home. She has village roots as a base to which she retires. Filia has a more compli-cated problem, which must afflict many 'been-tos'. 'She felt too sophisticated now to live in mud walls and pan roof. This was the college girl feeling, she knew . . .' (p. 18). Unfortunately Ekwensi does not pursue this very important and characteristic dilemma of modern Africa at this point. There are family antagonisms to her style of living, her mother is ready to condemn: 'You would not wear robes and sandals, only English dress. You speak English all

---

[5] *Iska* (Hutchinson, London, 1966). Page numbers refer to this edition.

the time. You associate with other tribes' (p. 30). There is great political significance in the obvious crescendo in this series of accusations. Their complexity will not be argued away by such banalities as Dan's answer to his father. 'Things are changing' (p. 30).

Just as Filia's taste in clothes and living standards is more sophisticated, complex and aware than Jagua's, equally so is her taste in men. In comparison Jagua seeks very superficial qualities of power and wealth. Filia wants 'men who are elegant and civilized, not just those who think their money can buy me' (p. 65). Jagua would be most happy to be bought if the price were sufficiently high. Filia is equally ambitious on her own account. 'Mama, I want to be famous. I want to appear on the stage, in newspapers, on television. And when I marry it must be a man who is known, a man with something. Lagos is the place I'll go' (p. 70). The magnetic attraction of the metropolis remains for both; the expectations have been developed through several degrees and, one might comment in advance, in this novel they are reached. This is the tale, at one level, of triumph rather than defeat in the city. This supports the dream expectations of the country people in the way that legendary stories of Las Vegas winnings fill the gambling halls with those who irrationally expect the mathematical odds to abdicate temporarily in their favour so that they will gain a fortune. One might, in philosophical terms, argue whether Filia's position is in fact more moral than Jagua's almost innocently vehement use of her sexuality for wealth and advancement. Filia's ambition is more idealistic, more optimistic, but considerably less believable.

The lure of the big city is the one consistent element in all Ekwensi's novels, and it is described here with exceptional fervour. 'There are people who cannot leave Lagos for one night. They cannot leave the highlife, and the noise, the island club and the races, the ceremonial parades and the sirens, the business meetings and the pretty girls. It's a great place' (p. 84). But its hardships are even more specifically recounted as a warning. Remi's experiences of Lagos are considerably more depressing than Filia's. 'I walked from one office to another, searching for work. I never even got the jobs. . . . I lived with one pick-up after the other. Then I got V.D., it nearly killed me' (p. 96). But such dangers and disasters will never keep people away from the city, with its exotic and beckoning vision: 'Lagos glittered with a million street lights and the chrome on passing cars . . .' (p. 103).

As if prose were not enough, one character, Dapo, admits 'I once wrote a poem about the girls of Lagos.' He proceeds to recite forty lines of drivelling verse, of which a typical passage is:

> Who can sit back and ignore
> light skin girl along the street
> all make-up from wig to nail paint,

> head held high and bosom taut,
> rear end wiggling, calculating, tantalizing,
> eyes afire with dare-me challenge.

(p. 188)

To Dapo's dismay, at the end of his recitation Filia is heard to be snoring. I wish I could believe that this was Ekwensi's deliberately comic condemnation of the verse, but I think it is merely a device to further the plot, so that the reader may learn that she is tired!

Yet beyond all the hospitals and melodrama there is a surer hand when it comes to the political element. Nothing here, alas, is as good as the earlier books, for there is no major character around which the political incidents can focus. There tends to be more debate and comment than observable action to establish the correct response of the reader. Nevertheless there is still a firm and sardonic hand detectable in some situations. Setting aside the crude moralizing recounted earlier, Ekwensi has his grip firmly on the responses of average individuals who make up the proletariat of this new town. Some sections read much like Achebe. There is little difference of tone between *A Man of the People* and lines such as these:

> The generation of today; a generation that was in a hurry to live, to make progress, to accumulate wealth, to bed girls, to eat, drink, be promoted to fill fat salaried posts, to be in power only to line one's pockets.

(p. 73)

But what is different is the sure awareness of the underlying resentment and bitterness of the poor, which is a powerful quality of Ekwensi's perception and plays little part in the novels of the intellectuals. The following dialogue has the ring of authenticity in its surly illiterate anger.

> 'Why do you wreck people's cars?'
> 'Is the instruction.'
> 'Why?'
> 'People have done nothing for us, that's why. We have independence. They just leave us to suffer and they get all the big money and everything.'

(p. 108)

There is a similar cynicism at a less basic level of physical destructiveness in an awareness of the manipulations that mark the skills of the political organizers. The resentment is expressed in terms of a simple definition. 'My business is to capitalize – on anything, any situation. That's politics' (p. 182).

Even that view isn't so simple. Ekwensi slips in a sharp reminder of the necessary dualism of the political act and the direction which such manoeuvres take. If politicians are now seen as despicable nuisances, they did create the pressure that ended colonialism in West Africa. One notes the counter-argument: 'It's the politicians who bring all the trouble. It was also the politicians who brought national pride and freedom' (p. 173). This is an obvious fact that is part of the oblique perception that must be brought to the complexities of the contemporary African situation; a vision that is lost in simplicities of condemnation.

There are good moments in this book. The description of the argument over the cost of potatoes culminating in an incensed battle between Ibo and Hausa groups is confidently handled. 'Not one of them tried to find out what was wrong. . . . They joined their own man' (p. 23). Following this event the description of the exodus from the North is aware and touching, its details reminding us of the painful truth. 'Thousands of people were cramming in. . . . Women with children strapped to their backs held other children by the hands while the sweat beaded the tips of their noses' (p. 26).

Alas, these moments are rare, largely because Ekwensi has not created a major political figure in this novel. There is Filia as a sophisticated and moral Jagua, and her lovers have the same wet blandness of Freddie. No figure stays relentlessly in the mind in this slender bitter-sweet love-tale. Politics becomes merely a backdrop to the events. Dapo's wife leaves him and falls in love with a space research scientist – an intriguing modernization. Yet happily for once the book does not peter out in a series of emotional platitudes. This is because Ekwensi holds to his concern with Africa, with Nigeria, not to the simplistic emotions of his amorous pairs.

There is a real political awareness in his dismissal of patronizing European judgements through the speculations of Dapo, when he questions whether 'Everything had to be measured against the morality of the western countries in which, according to her, there was no corruption, no political instability . . . a society in which things never went wrong as opposed to Africa' (p. 221). This is a legitimate question indeed.

The novel concludes on a note of emotional dedication that does not seem unduly exaggerated or silly, though one admits that it is not much more than a prose statement. Dapo in personal despair affirms 'his love for Nigeria, his belief in Africa, his frustration with the endless dissipation all about him of the useful energy, talent and human power'. At least, in a daring gesture, we are spared a 'happy' ending. Although the unhappy conclusion is in fact not necessarily more than a reversal of the original cliché, and has equal potential to become banal even in the 'adult' way that films would claim, it does destroy one line of convention. Once the single rut is escaped from, any other change of direction can be made, even if the initial decisions are not substantial improvements on earlier ventures.

If one calculates things statistically Ekwensi may not fare very well. A few lines of perceptive political observations, a pair of powerful, if stagey characters are the best things among all the dross of four novels. Yet this is not the final evidence upon which our judgement of Ekwensi must stand. The most significant thing is that Ekwensi is a professional writer. Not for him those one-shot 'first' novels, the thinly disguised autobiography in which the turns of the plot most precisely match the biographical information proffered on the dust-jacket. There has been regular assertion that the second novel is crucial in that it is likely to be the first book that does not present undisguised experience in the form of a tale told by an omniscient author.

Ekwensi has written many books, several more than the four I have chosen to discuss here. In this very professionalism there is for him a distinct trap. He may set his sights low, be willing to accept the meretricious rather than the superior, to find his pre-chosen audience. There is a disagreeable feeling that in Ekwensi's work his finer pieces are like coke, a by-product of some other activity. More important is the feeling that this end-result sometimes verges on the accidental.

Perhaps a fairer way of putting that statement would be that in his pursuit of a particular kind of popular novel he may be undermining a more significant and substantial talent. An important question would be the degree to which this is a deliberate decision. If a writer truly intends to create a popular love-novel, shoddy and discreditable as that determination might be, it is obviously his prerogative. Who are we to set other targets for him? Yet there is a feeling, which may represent nothing more than further evidence of that supreme arrogance of critics that has maddened artists throughout history, that we know better; that we could direct Ekwensi to pursue those elements of his writing that have in our estimation the most significance and impact.

Such a thought brings us back to more fundamental questions. If the critic has a legitimate function, and none of us would deny our bread and butter by heretically questioning such a thing, it is to direct the attention of both reader and writer to what we deem to be the excellent and significant, and to point out the lapses that indicate sloppiness of presentation, both stylistic and structural. When one does this with Ekwensi it is tempting to have a heyday. But like some of his characters, Ekwensi will not be argued away quite so readily by accusation of mediocrity. Just as his characters remain in the mind long after rational explanation has deemed them stagey and extreme, moments in his novels rise to convince us of his talent long after the shabby scenes have ceased to grate upon the sensibility.

Ekwensi has potential. I realize perfectly well how pompous and pretentious such a remark may sound, applied to a professional writer who has written more to date than any other African contemporary writer, yet it is meant at a very serious level. In his work there is recognition and skill, the dual elements by which a writer first perceives his experience and then translates it into the events and words of a novel. At present, too often a vulgarly emotional note intrudes, but the evidence of skill remains. It is upon this that one bases an assertion that the future may still offer the prospect of a major novel from Ekwensi.

Reading this through one is possessed anew by a sense of the pompous; that there has been too much condemnation and the sort of grudging and partial praise that is deplorable. The condemnation is essential, in that unless critical analysis is brought to bear upon such work there is no valid basis upon which any judgement, positive or negative, can be based. But even an analysis such as I have here attempted, although it emphasizes weaknesses, also allows distinguished qualities in this writer's work; any too ready and sweeping condemnation of Ekwensi must appear as shallow as the faults such critics presume to find in his work.

There is an important general point to be made here. That it is a truism makes it none the less true in restatement. The quality of a writer depends upon the authenticity of the creativity he brings to the experience. Too often in Ekwensi's case there is tiresome evidence of the intrusion of ideas and activities that derive from worlds far removed from his own immediate experience. More damaging under the circumstances is the fact that the source of these borrowings is so totally foreign. Deliberately pilfered clichés from the western popular novel and film are paraded for the reader in preference to that more direct vision that Ekwensi could offer from his own Nigeria. The ability to draw upon an environment with accuracy and awareness is a major quality of good writing, in Africa as elsewhere. This skill occurs only intermittently in Ekwensi. In his work the reader has the disconcerting sense that he is passing with bewildering speed from moments of illuminating truth into events of staggering melodramatic banality, and then taken equally suddenly back into a section that requires intelligent reaction because of its sensitivity and alert observation. At these latter moments, and only then, Ekwensi's novels contain an important and valid vision of the Nigerian situation; dispassionate and truthful. Only at such moments may Ekwensi be argued to have those qualities of skill and judgement that make a writer significant. This, as observed earlier, if taken quantitively may not seem much, yet that there are these important moments is definite and unarguable. They remain to make Ekwensi a writer who will never readily be shaken from that position in contemporary African letters that he is destined to maintain. Those who are dismissing him now as too popular for serious critical consideration are disregarding a phenomenon in African writing that may produce results considerably less trivial than now appear.

5 Themes and Development in the Novels of Ngugi

W. J. HOWARD

NGUGI'S vision is a personal one, and although influences from other writers, English or African, can be discussed, such comparisons do not help much in getting at his main ideas. A more fruitful approach is by narrowing the frame of reference to the stylistic development that occurs; this can then be related to the increasing power and maturity of Ngugi's themes and ideas as he becomes more and more occupied with a few major issues. These are to do with how a character responds to the cultural and political world he has to inhabit, to matters of belief, politics and society as well as to personal emotions. With each work there is a noticeable change in the use of narrative technique, structure and imagery; internal evidence suggests that there is also a shift from a semi-autobiographical to a complex yet impersonal point of view. Ngugi's methods have their weaknesses, but his strengths are what is important, and the examination of his techniques is the way to reveal them. The evidence produced by this study should be sufficient to accomplish this task.

W. J. Howard is an eighteenth-century specialist now teaching at Scarborough College, University of Toronto, Canada. He has published articles on Caribbean and African literature and now teaches a special course on it.

Ngugi has published a play, books of plays, short stories and essays and three novels. By far the most interesting of his works are the novels. *The Black Hermit*, a play, is best passed over in silence; the only justification for its having been published is to swell the volume of African publications as a mode of encouragement for other aspiring authors.[1] Several of his old and new stories are being put together in a collection called *Secret Lives*, and the earlier

[1] *The Black Hermit* was first performed in Kampala in 1962 but not published until 1968 (Heinemann, African Writers Series, London) in a much revised version with an explanatory note by Ngugi.

stories are not without merit; even though three of the stories are studies which were later reworked into novels. The fourth, 'The Fig Tree', dramatizes the relationship between the ritual cosmos and the individual, and we shall examine this briefly before moving on to the novels themselves, which still remain the most interesting of Ngugi's works.

'The Fig Tree' is the story of a young wife, Mukami, who, because of what seems to be her unfortunate sterility, leaves her husband. During the night she spends at the sacred grove, Mukami realizes that she is in fact pregnant, and returns home. Written into the story is an attitude of the author that is exceptionally helpful for a consideration of his later novels. Mukami is struggling against a ritual social order that is threatening to kill her, to 'crush her soul', and flight seems to be the only answer. Through her recollections the reader discovers that Mukami has always been rather a-social in her attitudes. After her initiation, she insisted on violating the customs of her people. Contrary to expectation, she rejected suitors of her own age and chose a much older and more successful man who already possessed four wives. Action of this nature led to 'scorn and resentment', to the judgement that she was bewitched, to enlisting the sympathy of the whole village against her, and to sentiments of jealousy. The point worth noticing is that these human emotions and accusations are transformed; they undergo a ritual and cosmic metamorphosis. The night becomes lone and savage. Even though Mukami is fighting for survival, the magic that pervades the cosmos is threatening, unseeing, unfeeling and in mute condemnation of her action. It is pervaded with the judgement of silent and pitying contempt, because she has not accepted *her rightful place*. Death nearly destroys her, the overreaching woman in her barrenness, because she is caught in an all-too-human, ritually structured cosmos; she should have submitted to the beatings of her husband, not because of the barrenness but because of the social judgement against her former pride; she should have submitted to the fatal punishment, the shame of which would have vindicated the village judgement against her and restored a levelling order to all. Against her effort to assert her individuality, the elements conspire to implement the judgement of her society; their cold and lifeless touch seeming to push her as if 'by many invisible hands' (p. 5) into the land of ghosts.

The author, however, is obviously on the side of individual assertion in the face of social pressure, and through a mystical experience Mukami realizes that Mumbi, the mother of the tribe, has touched her, has blessed her with a pregnancy; in fact, has blessed her with the realization that she 'has been pregnant for some time'. Since she is vindicated, an imposed order is restored. She returns to her rightful place beside her husband.

'The Fig Tree', then, touches several questions not explored by authors of recent English fiction, Golding's *The Inheritors* being a possible exception, and which might be grouped under the general heading of the genesis of ritual. As one reads the story one becomes vividly aware of an *imposed* order, not necessarily sympathetic towards the aspirations of the exceptional individual, but rather ritualizing in a sacred, not a secular sense the judgements and condemnations of the village community. Communal judgements and condemnations are projected into a hardened divine order that is unalterable, within which one is either vindicated or condemned, depending on one's degree of conformity to that rigid sacred-from-profane cosmos. Conformity to an ordered cosmos is the final impression of 'The Fig Tree', not the mystical experience of the sacred grove, in spite of the quotation from D. H. Lawrence that introduces the action; and as such, conformity to a sacred-social cosmos becomes an excellent starting point for an investigation of Ngugi's novels, whether it be in the challenged ritualistic setting of *The River Between*, the oppressively secular historical setting of *Weep Not, Child*, or the changed and more comfortably humane cosmos of *A Grain of Wheat*.

I wrote 'The River Between' first. I had come from a missionary school and I was deeply Christian. . . . In school I was concerned with trying to remove the central Christian doctrine from the dress of western culture, and seeing how this might be grafted on to the central beliefs of our people. 'The River Between' was concerned with this process.[2]

The difference one notices immediately between *The River Between* and *Weep Not, Child* is a formal and technical one. *The River Between* is more aesthetically shaped and united by image patterns than is the latter. From the beginning, *The River Between* deals quite simply with a structure dependent on several sets of image patterns, all of which cluster about one major theme, the land, and it is presented with the simplicity and directness of any creation myth. 'The two ridges lay side by side. One was Kameno, the other was Makuyu. Between them was a valley. It was called the valley of life.'[3] Although the author never falls into the trap of simple allegory, the struggle between Kameno and Makuyu is quite naturally, from time to time, extended to include all of Kenya. 'Behind Kameno and Makuyu were many more valleys and ridges . . . sleeping lions which never woke. They just slept, the big deep sleep of their Creator' (p. 1). The full first paragraph, then, presents a microcosm of the book's structure – the tribal geography of the land giving rise to conflict which is embroiling all of Kenya.

However, the author is quick to point out that the conflict he explores is not a conflict based on difference, but on a variation from a common background.

[2] *Union News*, Leeds University, 18 November 1966.
[3] *The River Between* (Heinemann, African Writers Series, London, 1965), p. 1. All further page references are to this edition.

'A river flowed through the valley of life. . . . Honia [the river] was the soul of Kameno and Makuyu. . . . When you stood in the valley, the two ridges ceased to be sleeping lions united by their common source of life. They became antagonists' (p. 1) The antagonism that Ngugi sets out to explore is no simple conflict of opposites, but rather something much subtler and much deeper, it is a conflict arising because of variations from the commonly understood, ordered, social and religious cosmos, which leads to 'a life and death struggle for the leadership' (p. 1). The struggle for leadership, arising from a common experience and interest but leading to serious and tragic division, is the content of the image patterns created in *The River Between*, while the river Honia embodies the symbol of the longed-for dream of harmony between antagonisms, giving rise to joy. If for a moment one presupposes the world of *A River Between* to have been the rigid religious and socially ordered world of 'The Fig Tree', where the unique individual must, of necessity, even with divine help, conform to be successful, then the social and religious variations from that norm are indeed cosmic and socially shattering to the people of Kameno and Makuyu, and are to be challenged very seriously.

Ngugi elevated his basic preoccupation to a cosmic level, and emphasized its tragic nature by blending two separate religious myths – Gikuyu and Christian. The first myth introduced is the peopling of the country according to the Gikuyu cosmos: 'Gikuyu and Mumbi sojourned there (in Makuyu) with Murungu on their way to Mukuruwe-wa-Gathanga' (p. 2). The struggle between the two ridges is presented in the context of the Gikuyu cosmos: each ridge claiming a divine mandate to rule, each claiming to have received the injunction 'this land I give to you, O man and woman. It is yours to rule and till, you and your posterity' (p. 2). These words echoing from the past once again become the source of a tragic antagonism, while the image of the sleeping lions recurs throughout the book, representing the dangers of the awakening awareness of the ridges. History and genealogy are also invoked to support Kameno's claims against the Christianized Makuyu, because they are a linear cause-and-effect explanation for the present situation – a subsidiary theme that is never far below the surface in any of Ngugi's writings. History and cosmic mythology are presented as ossified early in the novel – each ridge imposing a ritual cosmic order on the past in an effort to support its claim to exclusive loyalty from the Gikuyu people. The hills were the heart and soul of the land: 'They kept the tribes' magic and rituals, pure and intact' (p. 3). When rigid cosmos provides the framework for rivalry, tragedy is bound to ensue, especially for one who tries to vary his thought and actions from the established pattern during a period of radical change. Even before the central action begins, Cerge sees Kabonyi's conversion to Christianity as a betrayal of the tribal religion, and the authority for this judgement is attributed to tribal gods.

Quite simply, the narrative line is a young man's story. Waiyaki, a natural leader from a family of natural leaders, slowly develops, because of his father's foresight in giving him education, into one of the leading educationalists of the area. His achievements, however, are short-lived because he tries to end antagonism and restore unity to the peoples of the ridges. Political jealousy, tribal rivalry, human love and malice, as Waiyaki recognizes all too late, combine with his own strength and weakness to destroy his work and himself. Certain lesser threads complicate the action: his love for Nyambura, Joshua's daughter; the rivalry between the old man Kabonyi, the leader of the Kiama, and Waiyaki the enlightened teacher; the hatred between Kabonyi as leader of tribal interests and Joshua, the Christian leader. Ngugi's interests, then, are dramatized in the public forum, although everything, all activity and motivation, depends on the land and its ritualized geography.

The Gikuyu cosmos and the land combine to form a functional geography in which the action takes place. After the introduction a youthful Waiyaki appears on the plain, once a field of battle but now the neutral territory where he first begins to manifest his leadership. Like Moses he demonstrates his future messianic claim by attempting to establish harmony between Kamau and Kinuthia. But the traditional rituals form a continual counterpoint to the narrative action. The author points out that Waiyaki had not been through his ritualistic second birth or initiation into the tribe, the only path to success, while his father 'knew, more than any other person, the ways of the land and the hidden things of the tribe. He knew the meaning of every ritual and every sign. So, he was at the head of every important ceremony' (p. 8). Some people had 'abandoned the ways of the ridges and followed the new faith' (p. 9). Or again, the author warns: 'The white man cannot speak the language of the hills . . . who from the outside can make his way into the hills?' (p. 9). The rigidity of the social structure threatens the future. Even as a child at play Waiyaki is forced to see the importance of the ritual order; because he is not circumcised he feels small, and the only ways of happiness are ways of ritual conformity:

Waiyaki wanted to be happy, very happy. Was he not going to learn the ways of the land? Was he not going to drink the magic ritual of being born again? He knew he wanted to be like his father, knowing all the ways of the land from Agu and Agu, long ago.

(p. 13)

Ordered progress with the full sanction of social history bears down on the young hero – second birth, circumcision, manhood, and 'the spirits of the dead and the living would be invoked to join in the ritual' (p. 14). Conformity to a social and ritualized pattern is juxtaposed to the theme which closes the third chapter and portends things to come. 'This was not what usually happened' (p. 15). He who is different prepares for the social test.

The texture of *The River Between* is permeated with ritualism. Chege, Waiyaki's father, takes his usual place by the pole, the symbol of contact with the divine. Initiation reveals the masculine cult-secrets of the tribe, the 'hidden things of the hills . . .' Sacred places and sacred patterns – against these Waiyaki must struggle. Waiyaki sees his father undergo a transfiguration; he receives the gospel of the ridges, both old and new testament; he hears that he is of the line of religious leaders; then he is faced with the prophecy of the future: with 'Salvation shall come from the hills. From the blood that flows in me, I say from the same tree, a son shall rise. And his duty shall be to lead and save the people!' (p. 24). The moment Waiyaki is experiencing the rigidity of an ordered cosmos in its most impressive ritual manifestation, he is also designated to begin the violation of that cosmos – he is the one who varies from it and challenges it – the son who learns another religious order, another structured, ordered cosmos with the full weight of divinity behind it: 'learn all the wisdom and all the secrets of the white man . . . salvation shall come from the hills . . .' (p. 24). Gikuyu myth and Judaic Old Testament touch, and in the touching the established order of each is threatened.

After the initial Moses allusion, Ngugi continues to refer to the 'central Christian doctrine'; allusions to the saviour myth are frequent and direct. 'Waiyaki was not aware of anything strange in his eyes, although sometimes he felt something burn in him, urging him to say and do daring things' (p. 13). He is born again into the tribe. The prophecy that his father reveals to him recalls the Messiah prophecy of Jeremiah. 'Salvation shall come from the hills. From the blood that flows in me, I say from the same tree, a son shall arise. And his duty shall be to lead and save his people!' (p. 24). Variation is played on the theme by conjoining the two modes of salvation – Christian and tribal. 'Preparations for initiations went on, while Joshua and his followers prepared for the birth of a saviour' (p. 37).

Opposing tribal religion and cosmic structure is Christianity – equally as biased, equally as ordered, and equally as necessitated by the psychological dispositions of the people who espouse it. Variation from Christian order creates its own form of guilt in the daughters of Joshua. Circumcision, a necessary tribal ritual, is anti-Christian, wrong and sinful, a pagan rite against which, time and time again, the white missionaries had warned Joshua. For one who is saved from sin, circumcision is not a ritual fulfilment but a defection, and Muthoni is caught by the rigidity of both systems and their demands to choose either completely.

Christianity is a solidification, the ritualization of all too human psychological motivations into a cosmic order. While most people of the ridges 'remained conservative, loyal to the ways of the land' (p. 33), Joshua sought the power and knowledge of the white man; he found a sanctuary in the white man's ritual, as opposed to the ignorance of his people and the darkness in which they lived. Valid psychological reasons continually motivate the actions and reactions between characters, not infrequently stemming from pride and the desire to lead the ridges. About Joshua the author writes:

> Joshua himself was strict and observed the word to the letter. Religious uniformity in his own home was binding. He meant to be an example to all, a bright light that would show the way, a rock on which the weak would step on their way to Christ.
>
> (p. 34)

This is an obvious example of pride, and is presented as such. Muthoni's disobedience to Joshua causes shock to the village, because as Joshua's wife recognizes, obedience to him is an expression of faith, of belief in his way of life. Muthoni's 'betrayal' is Joshua's personal disgrace ritualized into a cosmic damnation and blamed on God.

> From that day Muthoni ceased to exist for him, in his heart. She had brought an everlasting disgrace to him and his house, which he had meant to be an example of what a Christian home should grow into.
>
> All right. Let her go back to Egypt. Yes. Let her go back. He, Joshua, would travel, on, on to the new Jerusalem.
>
> (p. 42)

If one of the author's main concerns in the novel was, as earlier stated, 'to remove the central Christian doctrine from the dress of Western culture and see how it might be grafted on to the central beliefs of our people', it has been quickly overlaid by a concern about rigid obedience to sacred ritual patterns and the male, public forum of tribal leadership. Nevertheless, a second theme is established from the beginning and symbolized by the river Honia: a theme of union based on love, one more radically at the basis of the central Christian doctrine. 'The importance of Honia could never be overestimated. Cattle, goats and people drew their water from there. Perhaps that was why it was called "Cure" and the valley, the valley of life; that is what it was, a valley of life' (p. 26).

Every aspect of this theme is introduced and initially explored in the story of Muthoni – the beautiful, tragic daughter of Joshua, who is caught between the positive values of Christianity ('No one will understand. I say I am a Christian and my father and mother have followed the new faith. I have not run away from that' [p. 50]), and the tribe ('I want to be a woman made beautiful in the tribe; a husband for my bed; children to play around the

hearth' [p. 51]). In her attempt to reconcile the positive values of both traditions she is destroyed, and the destruction is neither sympathetically understood nor intellectually appreciated by either side – Christian or tribal. In fact,
Muthoni's death leads to further strife.

Quite deliberately, the first dramatic episodes explored at any length
involve Muthoni and her variation from demanded loyalties towards incorporating into her life the good and the beautiful from both religiously
ritualized cosmic structures. Muthoni challenges Waiyaki because he was
unthinkingly loyal to an ordered tribal structure; her challenge is clearly in
terms of a social rebellion. 'Was he himself capable of such a rebellion? But
he reflected that it was only proper to obey one's father. Perhaps Muthoni
had been wrong to disobey' (p. 57).

After her death, her attempted reconciliation is seen to represent a threat
which each cosmic order must face. Each solidifies and reinforces itself; each
determines to overcome the other completely. Reconciliation would destroy
both. 'Joshua was determined to triumph, to walk . . . with his eyes on the
cross. Muthoni had been an outcast. Anything cursed here on earth would also
be cursed in heaven. Let that be a warning to those who rebelled against their
parents and the laws of God' (p. 62). For Chege, the representative of tribal
thinking, 'This was a punishment to Joshua. It was also a punishment to the
hills. It was a warning to all, to stick to the ways of the ridges, to the ancient
wisdom of the land, to its ritual and song' (p. 62). But the author has his own
view: 'nobody knew for sure what the death portended' (p. 63). Variation
from ritual loyalty, ritual obedience, is a threat to a social order. As an insert
within the novel, Muthoni's tragedy is a perfect piece. No effort is made on
her part at justification – her story is merely presented with simplicity and
completeness. Nevertheless, the dream, the symbolism, the question, the
desire for discovering a way to unity through love and thus to life is reintro-
duced again and again later. The river imagery is re-echoed. Waiyaki meets
Nyambura at the river. The crisis of unity, because of Ngugi's functional
geography, appears again and again at the river. Finally, Waiyaki's tragedy
and failure in his effort at reconciliation takes place at the river. But to what
purpose?

After Muthoni's death things seem to become more complicated. No
further exploration of the reconciliation theme or its deeper implications is
presented through the story line, other than a continued lamentation at its
tragic absence. Ngugi might counter, as he has elsewhere: 'I am very suspicious about writing about universal values. If there are universal values, they
are always contained in the framework of social realities',[4] and this statement
is well taken; fidelity to a history of sorts may be a valid answer for an author,
and the last section of the novel has been described as being a dramatization

[4] *Union News*, Leeds University, 18 November 1966.

of the reasons for lack of unity between opposing ideas, e.g., education, tribal loyalty, Christianity, human rivalry. If this is so, then the reader is justified in asking why there should be the elaborate functional geography, the introduction of the double symbolic mythology, the large unifying cosmic image patterns? The novelist gives every indication by his introduction of elaborate image patterns that the content of the novel justifies the imagery – that the problems introduced match in their significance the way they are treated. But the key to the value of various image patterns is to be found not solely in the saviour imagery, but in the masculine/feminine use of saviour imagery. By juxtaposing two forms of salvation, Waiyaki emerges as the new tribal saviour. Waiyaki undertakes the leadership of the independent-school movement; he sees himself more as a saviour even to the point of preaching reconciliation. Allusions multiply: the continual reference to him as 'teacher', or 'the man to lead the people', the occasional parallels to the crucifixion narrative as Waiyaki's fate draws in upon him, for instance the Christ – Peter parallel in Kinuthia's protestation of fidelity: '"I will never leave you!" he cried "Whatever the others do, I will be with you all the way"' (p. 160). Christian allusions function as a pattern which supports one obvious movement of the plot – the tragedy of the rejected leader – to which is conjoined accurate human psychology. But before looking at the particular psychological development, one further general point must be made.

The appearance of the white man with his oppressive land-grabbing and taxation is a much more serious threat to ritual order, which education and politics try to combat – in a word the sacred gives way to the profane. Even though the values change, the content remains the same; both the schools and the Kiama try to maintain the loyalties of the people. Waiyaki pursues education with the determination that Chege himself gave him early in his life. He also pursues it with single-mindedness, simplifying the complexities of a whole society into one solution: 'the new drive in education. Perhaps this was the answer to a people's longings and hopes. For a moment he became lost in his contemplation of education and the plans he had in mind . . .' (p. 75). Waiyaki became too obsessed with schools, and loses 'contact with the people that can only come through taking part together in a ritual' (p. 128).

Kabonyi on the other hand is the self-constituted representative of the secular polarity to education; once again an ossifying process can be detected – the desire to lead the ridges combines with a hatred for a rival, in this case Waiyaki, and results in a deliberate exclusiveness demanding total loyalty. 'Kabonyi had led the breakaway movement . . . he had laboured for the tribe . . . He feared Waiyaki might be the sent one . . . And he hated this' (p. 106). The new secular variations are also ritualized into cosmic imperatives. The relation between Kabonyi and Waiyaki is the natural result of an old man's ill will and hatred.

Kabonyi did not like it [Waiyaki's leadership]. He himself had laboured for the tribe. He had led the breakaway movement and was responsible for the starting of the people's own schools. And was he not a leader in every field? Kabonyi saw Waiyaki as an upstart, a good-for-nothing fellow, a boy with rather silly ideas.

(p. 106)

After Kabonyi's public defeat at Waiyaki's hands during the school debate, his feeling sharpens considerably and becomes, as is so often the case, based on principle.

And he hated Waiyaki intensely and identified this hatred with the wrath of the tribe against impurity and betrayal. To him then, this was not a personal struggle, it was the continuation of that struggle that had always existed between Makuyu and Kameno.

(p. 166)

Since Waiyaki is himself the innocent saviour he is freed of these more serious faults; however, it is pointed out that he continually misses the significance of events because he is blinded by his educational dream. After the crucial school confrontation he muses:

He even wanted Joshua and his followers to come and join hands with him. Education was life. Let it come. And with a fleeting feeling of guilt he remembered that he had forgotten to preach reconciliation.

(p. 112)

And he had been training himself for this mission: end the Kameno-Makuyu feud and bring back the unity of the tribe. Yet when the appropriate moment came he had failed. He had become intoxicated with wonder, anger and surprise and had lost himself. The moment had come. The moment had passed. Had he remained calm he would have spoken outright for reconciliation.

(p. 115)

After a hut is destroyed Waiyaki comes to another realization all too late:

Waiyaki could not tell why, but he connected the incident with the Kiama. Was Kabonyi determined to destroy all that stood against him and the tribe? The realization came to him as a shock. He instantly thought that he should not have resigned from the Kiama. Its power and influence was there, everywhere.

(p. 129)

A realization, too late, that he has been outmanoeuvred combines with the outlawed love he has for Nyambura the Christian, and produces a typical young man's reaction – bitterness and revolt, which in turn leads to the tragedy of the people's putting the final judgement of Waiyaki's fate in the hands of the Kiama. In this 'life and death struggle for leadership' the young saviour quite understandably fails because he does not read the implications of the events deeply enough.

Ngugi's selection of the saviour pattern for the hero of the book holds a twofold implication for his writing: first, because the saviour is one whom the reader admires and sympathizes with because of both his appeal and his failure. The double attraction to Waiyaki ensures to some extent the success of the characterization and the story of his fate. This has been a long-recognized characteristic of Aristotelian tragedy. Secondly, however, and more importantly, the saviour pattern must possess the built-in element of failure, which an author consciously or unconsciously develops so that the reader also engages his critical faculty and, while appreciating the value of a character sympathetically, still understands his defeat intellectually; otherwise fatalistic hopelessness is the only result. What Ngugi's precise attitude to Waiyaki is in *The River Between* may be uncertain, but his ideas about the 'saviour' myth undergo considerable development.

Although the saviour imagery is used with many variations, it has one predominant function – to support the nobility and futility of varying from any ritually ossified, social or religious structure imposed on others by communal order. The saviour pattern operated in the cosmos of Chege, a sympathetic representative of tribal beliefs; he was wrong. It was taken up by Kabonyi as leader of the secular and political Kiami; he was wrong. It was expounded in the Christian context by Joshua, who blamed everything on loyalty to God; he too was wrong. It was suffered and tested by Waiyaki in his educational leadership; he was most tragically wrong. But the image pattern is also employed to test something far greater, and its major use is reserved for the cumulative metaphorical statement of the book. The saviour myth reinforces most consistently the theme of variation from biased social pressures, and includes more female than male characters, as opposed to the Jesus complex, if you like, which permeates the male characters of the novel. When Muthoni attains harmony within her own life, she thinks in saviour patterns; when Waiyaki tries to span the polarization between education and the Kiama, he thinks in saviour patterns; when Nyambura recognizes Waiyaki's attempt to reconcile tribal and Christian biases she thinks in saviour patterns; and most important, the author himself, when championing the individual's right to vary from demanded behavioural impositions, also creates in terms of saviour patterns.

Honia is introduced in terms of the metaphorical geography as the source of reconciliation and harmony (see pp. 50, 56, 61, etc.), and as the issue of reconciliation becomes more important, the saviour theme becomes more encompassing for the author, based on the deep-seated drive for harmony in all humanity, irrespective of biases. The river and the saviour join in Muthoni, a woman. She is the first real incarnation of the myth. When Waiyaki meets Nyambura at the river he muses: 'Something passes between them as two human beings, untainted with religion, social conventions or any tradition' (p. 88), the conjoining of the river and another woman. Later Waiyaki recognizes that even he is in danger of becoming a slave to the tribe (p. 84). He succumbs to a Jesus role through education: 'all he wanted was to concentrate his attention and energy on the mission he had undertaken. The Kiama could look to the purity of the tribe' (p. 116). He rejects this temptation when he recognizes a value in 'Action now'. Nevertheless, the author reserves the synthesizing speech not for Waiyaki but Nyambura – it is she that frees the saviour image from tribal, Christian, educational or political biases and projects it into the humane sphere of free response. This happens during the scene when Waiyaki attempts to warn the Christians of the Kiama:

> A religion of love and forgiveness stood between them. No! It could never be a religion of love. Never, never. The religion of love was in the heart. The other was Joshua's own religion, which ran counter to her spirit and violated love. If the faith of Joshua and Livingstone came to separate, why, it was not good. If it came to stand between a father and his daughter so that her death did not move him, then it was inhuman.
>
> (pp. 154–5)

The saviour theme represents those who react or diverge from the accepted pressures of ordered groups, and the hero and heroine discover the courage to free themselves from the forces that control them socially – religion, politics, or parents (cf. p. 163). Through Nyambura Waiyaki realizes that 'not all of the ways of the white man were bad. Even his religion was not essentially bad. Some good, some truth shone through it. But the religion, the Faith, needed washing, cleaning away all the dirt, leaving only the eternal' (p. 162). Ritual order is broken and the action of the novel is supported by a much deeper use of the saviour myth – Kinuthia delivers the protestation of Peter to his saviour Christ that I quoted earlier. He subsequently betrays Waiyaki through weakness:

> And Kinuthia thought of moving forward and giving a warning to Waiyaki, but a big fear settled on him, weakening his knees so that he did not move from where he sat. Instead he sought to hide himself in the crowd as if he did not want to be identified with the Teacher.
>
> (p. 172)

Lip-service to the Jesus myth progresses from words of biased interests into the metaphor of the plot, through the saviour myth; the hero and heroine freely take up the crucifixion so that the record of history may read 'Waiyaki and Nyambura would be placed in the hands of the Kiama, who would judge them and decide what to do' (p. 174). Free, independent efforts at unbiased social reconciliation even in the face of ossified ritual may lead to the death of the religious, educated or political person. But it also encourages the life of the transcending human spirit. That many important themes are introduced (communal leadership, the conflicts arising from the legacy of history, religion, custom, human aspirations) is an admirable beginning. Moreover, *The River Between* shows great formal potential, with important material content introduced and controlled to a significant degree. And I feel the reason for this success is not difficult to discover. The author began the work under one impetus, which has already been discussed. As he progressed, larger problems were uncovered and integrated into the artistic structure, not as fictionalized history, but as human experience. As for the original impetus that motivated the novel, Ngugi has explained that himself. 'But it was not that I woke up one day and decided that I was no longer a Christian. It just gradually lost its appeal to me as I began to see what it stood for.' This change of feeling is recorded in *The River Between* in the dichotomy between formal structure and verbal protestation.

In my second book, 'Weep Not, Child', I was primarily interested in evoking what a simple village community felt, caught between forces which they could not quite understand. I lived through the period myself....[5]

Stylistically *Weep Not, Child* differs considerably from *The River Between*, and nowhere can the difference be seen more clearly than in a comparison of the openings of the two novels. While *The River Between* began cosmically and symbolically, *Weep Not, Child* is swift, straightforward narration:

Nyokabi called him. She was a small, black woman, with a bold but grave face. One could tell by her small eyes full of life and warmth that she had once been beautiful. But time and bad conditions do not favour beauty. All the same Nyokabi had retained her full smile – a smile that lit up her dark face.

'Would you like to go to school?'

'O, Mother!' Njoroge gasped. He half feared that the woman might withdraw her words.[6]

[5] Op. cit.
[6] *Weep Not, Child* (Heinemann, African Writers Series, London, 1964), p. 3. All further page references are to this edition.

The ritual order is gone, and with it have departed the image patterns that rendered the content of *The River Between* significant. *Weep Not Child* is by choice contained within a cosmos of secular history, and presents a whole set of new problems for Ngugi, which are immediately reflected in the novelist's craft. Swift straightforward dramatically narrative prose characterizes the opening; obvious aesthetic patterning is gone. Stylistically Ngugi has opted for a progressive historical realism, which gives evidence of a completely different view of history, hinted at but never completely espoused in *The River Between*, and in this instance it has the family as its centre.

Basically, *Weep Not, Child* is Njoroge's story. A young boy from the ridges is offered education and the seemingly limitless opportunities that education implies. He begins his studies, but the tangle of history swiftly overtakes him as he sees his brothers take to the forest to fight, the terrors of the Mau Mau visited on his people and families he has known, the establishment of the home rule with its harsh retaliatory measures, the destruction of his own family caught up in the tragedy of Kenya, and the collapse of all his dreams. Njoroge's story is the story of many a young Kenyan youth during recent decades, and it is swiftly and simply controlled to an effective conclusion. Within this narrower scope Ngugi works quite effectively, and the ability he showed earlier for psychological characterization, although uncertain, develops considerably.

The limits also have their drawbacks. The point of view in the novel is Njoroge's. All the dramatic events are presented through his eyes. It is to the credit of the author that he can catch the psychology of a young boy so accurately while facing such shatteringly crushing historical events. And once again he develops Njoroge very much along the saviour pattern, motivated by an innocent pride. But the saviour vision has dwindled in vitality, and in *Weep Not, Child* is without much significance. From the beginning the 'saviour' motif is the product of an idealistic daydream, and is pictured without sympathy. Njoroge as saviour is consistently naïve. Education is seen by the young lad as leading to all kinds of expectations:

> He knew that for him education would be a fulfilment of a wider and more significant vision – a vision that embraced the demand made on him, not only by his father, but also by his mother, his brothers and even the village. He saw himself destined for something big, and this made his heart glow.
>
> (p. 44)

This view of himself develops as his education expands: 'He liked the stories in the Old Testament. He loved and admired David, often identifying himself with this hero' (p. 55). As the emergency becomes more confusing and the wreckage of his own family becomes more evident, Njoroge sees himself as a saviour.

> And the difficulties of time seemed to have sharpened his appetite. Only education could make something out of this wreckage ... When these moments caught him, he actually saw himself as a possible saviour of the whole of God's country. Just let him get learning.
>
> (p. 93)

Towards the end of the novel the author intrudes more frequently to pass judgement on Njoroge and to reveal a weakness that should have been dramatized during the unfolding of the events. He writes quite abruptly: 'Njoroge had always been a dreamer, a visionary who consoled himself faced by the difficulties of the moment by a look at a better day to come' (p. 135). 'That day for the first time, he wept with fear and guilt. And he did not pray' (p. 137). The death of the saviour vision also ushers in the death of all that Njoroge held important. Once his idealistic world is destroyed, all positive values are lost as he himself comes to realize: 'But why did he call on God? God meant little to him now. For Njoroge had now lost faith in all the things he had earlier believed in, like wealth, power, education, religion. Even love, his last hope, had fled from him' (p. 152).

Often the omniscient author intrudes to explain motivation or analyse characters where it would be impossible for the boy Njoroge to do so. Early in the story he describes his mother in these terms:

> Nyokabi was proud of having a son in school. It made her soul happy and light-hearted whenever she saw him bending double over a slate ... She felt elated when she ordered her son to go and do some reading or some sums. ... She tried to imagine what the Howlands woman must have felt to have a daughter and a son in school. ...
>
> (p. 18)

But even when the author intrudes, only to a limited extent does he manage to convey the anguish of a family torn by tragic events, even less of 'a village', which was his expressed intent. An early authorial intrusion is presented this way: 'There was something strange in Ngotho's eyes. He looked as if he had forgotten all about those who were present ... it was as if he was telling a secret for the first time, but to himself' (p. 28). The scene presents a certain atmosphere, but fails to convey any deep feeling of a father, or of older brothers.

The only successful penetration of Ngotho's character is presented by Ngugi in Chapter Three, where he manages to communicate Ngotho's deep,

almost sacred love for the land, as well as the confusion caused by his uncertainty about its future. Understatement conveys the dilemma at the time of
the strike.

> He could not quite make up his mind about the strike. He doubted if the
> strike would be a success. If it failed, then he would lose a job and that
> would keep him away from the lands of his ancestors. This was wrong, for
> the land was his. None could tend it as he could.
>
> (p. 59)

Nevertheless, on the debit side, motivation surrounding the Jacobo incident
remains unclear, and Ngotho's relationship with his sons is never deeply
developed. What the reader experiences is a description of a man who is
growing more uncertain about his position of family leadership and his own
manhood. Even during the refusal to take the Mau Mau oath at Boro's hands
the only glimpse we get into this father-and-son relationship is one of external
description – Boro scorns his father, and Ngotho, although uncertain, resists
his son. Gradually the father is broken:

> He felt like crying, but the humiliation and pain he felt had a stunning effect
> Was he a man any longer, he who had watched his wife and son taken
> away ... Was this cowardice? It was cowardice, cowardice of the worst
> sort ... He now knew that even that waiting had been a form of cowardice
> a putting off of action.
>
> (p. 91)

The scene in which he is completely broken after admitting Jacobo's murder
and is once again faced by Boro is badly underwritten. The reader sees no
aspect of Boro other than that of a repentant child facing the situation too late
Further penetration is deliberately avoided, as if the author could not depict
the complexities of reconciling oneself to having fought in the forest. To the
extent, then, that *Weep Not, Child* is successful, it is so because it manages to
convey emotionally the experiences of Njoroge and externally describes the
emotional reactions of others, but without penetrating them or making them
intelligible. And although external description played a major part in *The
River Between* as well, the aesthetic patterning also interpreted the history
making it more universally significant. *Weep Not, Child* seems to lack this
extra dimension.

   A further and more serious criticism must be levelled at Ngugi's creation of
character, however – his handling of Mr Howlands. The first two appearances
of Howlands are well done for a light, quick, background character. His love
of his farm, his fear and bluff, which result in threats of dismissing any

strikers, are all quite believable. All the more reason why his third appearance seems to be exaggerated to the point of sensationalism. Even if certain men are capable of the cruelty described, pincers and all, that 'the red beard and grey eyes laughed derisively' (p. 128) when Howlands walked out after torturing Njoroge seems bordering on grade B Hollywood theatrics, and is unworthy of Ngugi. It is the gesture of a villain of melodrama and should have been edited.

The last appearance of Mr Howlands is much more difficult to deal with because, for reasons known only to the author, we have a completely new picture of Howlands. The character who had formerly been presented quite simply as loving the land and worried about the strike has become a child-beater and castrator, haunted by Njoroge's eyes, a drunk, consumed with hatred for Ngotho because Ngotho loves and protects his sons, dim-witted (only slowly does he realize Boro's involvement), a satyr with black women (although he doesn't know why he misses his wife), cringingly clinging to life. Ngugi should have employed the art of understatement here instead of over-writing; it might have saved this near-final scene both from the poor judgement and the clichés that abound. 'He cursed horribly' – really?

Ngugi is still faced with the formidable problems that his material presents. In *Weep Not, Child*, by narrowing his ambitions he has by judicious selectivity and the admirable creation of Njoroge's point of view found a working formula for creating a flawed but moderately successful novel of a much narrower scope than that of *A River Between*; and of course, this is an author's prerogative. He has achieved a formal heterocosm a 'world' in which the material and the considerations it provokes are (with one serious reservation) handled adequately, but only because more important implications are filtered out by Njoroge's point of view, or externally described by an omniscient author. *Weep Not, Child*, for all its formal and material success, still remains a young man's novel, a novel that has given in to the complexities of history and seems to end in despair. Because he narrowed his scope considerably and more or less filtered all his action and reaction through the consciousness of a young boy, or the author's comment on him, Ngugi has been able to control his material with some accuracy; however, in doing so he has confined himself to a much less ambitious purpose than his words quoted at the beginning of this section would indicate. Admirable as the character of Njoroge is, it is fairly limited. The youthful idealist, full of belief, slowly confronts history or has it forced upon him, then gives in to extreme disillusion and despair, relieved by a glimmer of hope. Njoroge obviously cannot influence the events about him, nor can he react to them as an adult (not necessarily educated but certainly more complex). He cannot even cope with or interpret the crushing history of his own family. The combination of a youthful point of view and a progressive historical realism leads to some fairly predictable yet well presented results.

Although the author himself seems to have suffered through the events *Weep Not, Child* describes, in the novel he has isolated himself and the reader against a full and mature consideration of the implications that those historical events provoke; he has given in to the temptation to rise above the events. Once again the problems posed by the novelist are not made adequately intelligible. Ngugi has succumbed to the inherent weakness of nineteenth- and early twentieth-century historical fiction, which needed to do more than successfully dramatize history. Very good historical prose fiction has always included an interpretation or a reading of the history as part of its significant form (as in Patrick White, Joseph Conrad or Chinua Achebe). This creative coming to terms with historical fact is absent in *Weep Not, Child*.

One possible alternative might be suggested that would mitigate the criticism I have just levelled at the novel. The author may have meant the purpose of the history to be summed up in the title and conclusion of the book – that is coming to terms with cowardice, and a future defined by service. In other words, following the ideas of Frantz Fanon in *Black Skin, White Masks* Njoroge should not weep because no matter what history has perpetuated, the individual who recognizes he is an active participant in and not a passive terminus of a relationship, even a relationship to his own history, always has the free choice to recognize what must be done and do it (see Fanon, chapter 7 ff.). Incidentally, a knowledge of Fanon would also explain, but not justify, the transformation in Howlands' character as well. Nevertheless, to come to terms creatively with one's own cowardice so that it is possible to continue life of active service is a difficult and tortuously complex problem. Nowhere in the novel is the reader shown how Njoroge is prepared for the slight glimmer of wisdom dramatized at the end of the novel when he opens the door for his mother. That Njoroge chooses to live with his cowardice through service is real step forward in Ngugi's vision, but it leaves far too many questions unanswered about the character he has created in this novel. It is more an unmotivated authorial manipulation (and here I am willing to go out on a limb and say that it was imposed after the novel was completed or at most as it was drawing to a conclusion) than an act stemming from the character himself within his fictionalized world. In the context of the novel the act can only be justified if considered motivated by the same unthinking rashness that Njoroge displays throughout the book. The conclusion, then, has no real meaning other than 'that's the way it was' – unsuccessfully modified by the title and the last page something less than good historical fiction usually offers.

In *A Grain of Wheat*, I look at the people who fought for independence – see them falling into various groups. There were those who thought the white man was supreme. They saw no point in opposing that which was divinely willed ... there were others who supported the independence movement and who took the oath. Of these some fought to the last but others, when it came to the test, did not live up to their faith and ideals. They gave in. Finally there were those who we might call neutrals – you know, the uncommitted. But these soon find that in a given social crisis they can never be uncommitted ...[7]

I am not sure at what point Ngugi became familiar with the works of Frantz Fanon, but in *A Grain of Wheat* the thought of that social philosopher can be seen shaping the presentation of the characters as well as the movement of the main theme. That he was familiar with Fanon's work while writing the novel and that it did influence the shape of the work was admitted by him in his interview at Leeds. And without insisting on the point, it will suffice to say that I feel Fanon's influence may be seen in the treatment of each of the major characters. While earlier Ngugi began with either a tribal hero (Waiyaki) or a simple character who aspired to be a people's saviour (Njoroge), in *A Grain of Wheat* the alliance of the author is downward, away from the saving hero to the people of the village themselves.[8]

By the time Ngugi wrote *A Grain of Wheat*, the 'living with cowardice' theme, which was introduced but not entirely worked out in *Weep Not, Child*, received full examination; the vision of the saviour, as tragic and destroyed, or as disillusioned and defeated, has receded from interest. That is not to say that *A Grain of Wheat* is not without its saviour; in fact, the novel has two characters through which the pattern is still present. Kihika is the most obvious example and Mugo is a variation on the theme; but the author's attitude toward the saviour theme has altered considerably. The centre of interest for Ngugi in *A Grain of Wheat* is the living with cowardice among the little people – the average villagers.

The overall structure of *A Grain of Wheat* follows more closely the pattern explored in *Weep Not, Child*. It is closely dependent on historical progressive realism, and once again the author is caught by the particular method he has selected, even though the circular structure of the novel is much more ambitious than that of *Weep Not, Child*. It is as if each major character of this novel is a variation on the psychological realization to which the author brought Njoroge.

Each major character develops through a real personal failure occasioned by the Emergency to a process of reconciliation with that failure in an attempt to continue a valued life. Each figure, after experiencing the tragedy of personal

---

[7] *Union News*, Leeds University, 18 November 1966.
[8] *A Grain of Wheat* (Heinemann, African Writers Series, London, 1968). All page references are to this edition.

cowardice and personal failure, is forced by the present to choose his futur course. Through a series of flashbacks Mugo, Gikonyo, Mumbi and Karanj examine their youth, the personal failure he or she has suffered, and with th hard-won wisdom of the present each has deliberately attempted to live wit their failure, on one way or another. It is as if the author, exploring the cul-de sac of the saviour theme, has begun to concentrate on the corollary of tha theme, those in need of saving, a theme which is much more interesting.

In so far as the novel has a villain, Karanja is he. Driven by his rejected lov for Mumbi, he compromises too much. The reader meets him cringing befor the presence and power of the white colonials, and little by little one discover the reasons for this posture. To begin with, Karanja takes no active part in th Emergency because of a misguided love for Mumbi. In fact he compromise his manhood and self-respect because of love for a woman, a Gikuyu ide which at another historical moment might have been admirable. Remainin near by to protect her, little by little, he joins the home guard and the becomes its local leader after the removal of his predecessor. If there is a non heroic 'all-for-love theme', Karanja embodies it and thereby gains for himse the contempt if not the hatred of all who suffered for the cause of indepen dence. Although Karanja is presented with great psychological understandin Ngugi nevertheless dismisses him as a man who must go nameless into a ne society to live as best he can with himself. Karanja's tragic failure, then, is t place the positive value of human love above the independence movement at historical moment when more was being demanded of him.

Mugo, the orphaned villager, alone in the world, did not want to be a pa of the Emergency; he wanted to be left alone to farm his land. To emphasiz the values in question from the beginning of the novel, Ngugi places the ult mate value of Mugo's life in his love for the land and his desire to farm it; simple desire which in other historical periods would have been admirabl and a theme which had been sympathetically explored in _Weep Not, Chil_ This second important ideal of Gikuyu society is the ultimate value to whic he wishes to sacrifice everything, but cannot. The activities of Mau Mau the person of Kihika draw him into the national struggle, and his own pe sonal betrayal. Initially his secret betrayal of Kihika becomes a source of publi strength, as if social need and social acceptance are all that are required f leadership. After his return to his village, in an effort to save his self-respe and sanity, as well as in response to the role that his fellow villagers have force upon him, Mugo justifies his former failure by recognizing that the villager need a saviour. However, response to role or self-justification are found wan ing in _A Grain of Wheat_ – the book is about those who need salvation, n about the saviours; as the title indicates, those who will bear fruit are thos who have truly died to the old world. The ultimate judgements on Mugo methods of self-reconciliation are given by Mumbi and other villagers. '"Pe haps I could have saved him. Perhaps I could if I had gone into his hut that night," Mumbi lamented . . . "There was nothing to save," Wambui said slowly. "Hear me? Nobody could have saved him . . . because . . . there was nothing to save"' (p. 274).

Although sympathetically presented, the author's judgement on Mugo is fairly complete – 'There was nothing to save.' Nevertheless for Gikonyo the thought of Mugo's confession does act as a form of salvation and gives him the self-knowledge and wisdom to rejoin active society and once again accept the flawed Mumbi as his wife. Mugo's story also demonstrates the presence of Frantz Fanon's influence upon Ngugi, especially in his directive that the Black personality has to face itself psychologically at a certain point in history, not in an abstract situation devoid of historical implications. The content of Fanon's *Black Skin, White Masks* is tragically fictionalized in the character of Mugo.

Mumbi's story is much more complex, and shows a transformed return to the use of symbolism with which Ngugi began *The River Between*. On the surface Mumbi's story is that of any attractive young bride caught in the events of the Emergency. For most of the Emergency she struggles to remain independent and untouched, motivated by a love for her husband. She is, however, aided in the struggle for survival by Kihika, who manifests his unwanted affections through gifts of food. When Mumbi learns of Gikonyo's return she inexplicably gives herself to Kihika; later she gives birth to his child, a situation which Gikonyo cannot accept after his return. Psychologically Gikonyo's refusal to compromise with Mumbi's betrayal and her child is well done; moreover, the situation is gradually transformed into one of symbolic meaning. In the world of Ngugi's fiction, specifically in *A River Between*, Ngugi's genesis story, Mumbi and Gikuyu are the parents of the tribe. Throughout *A Grain of Wheat*, while depicting the psychological torture which Mumbi suffers, Ngugi gradually suggests that Mumbi's suffering creates a far richer person: a person who can sympathize with Kihika and try to prevent his useless slaughter; a person who tries to save Mugo from himself and laments the fact that she does not succeed; a person who through her acceptance of her weakness, her success at creating a new life, and the assertion of her own independence as a person, helps her husband to accept the changed situation of the village life. The final page of the novel presents the psychologically changed, strong woman who has come to terms with her situation, who can say to her husband:

No, Gikonyo. People try to rub out things, but they cannot. Things are not so easy. What has passed between us is too much to be passed over in a sentence. We need to talk, to open our hearts to one another, examine them, and then together plan the future we want . . . He [Gikonyo] knew, at once, that in the future he would reckon with her feelings, her thoughts, he desires – a new Mumbi.

At the end of *A Grain of Wheat* Ngugi has created a new mother of the tribe with real psychological and historical claims to that title, and married to th man who has been simultaneously transformed into her equal.

Gikonyo embodies the motives of love for village and family. Throughou his story he is presented in this light. When the novel opens, the autho describes him as a successful business man who has also become an importan spokesman within the village. Little by little we learn that Gikonyo ha changed because of the Emergency, and that before the trouble and detentio he had been quite a happy although socially awkward wood-carver who love Mumbi. The description of Gikonyo's carving of the podo-wood panga fo Mumbi is one of the best descriptions of work to be found in current literature The real joy of wood-carving is caught and transmitted to the reader in muc the same way that Camara Laye has achieved it in *The Dark Child* in describ ing the moulding of gold. In a very low-keyed and traditional way Ngugi i establishing Gikonyo as a new type of hero – more African and more artisan he is the traditional carver, the interpreter of the gods (qualified by th thought of Fanon).

But the Emergency has transformed him. Having suffered through deten tion, having managed to survive, Gikonyo returns home, one who loves hi traditional heritage, ready to take it up again and develop it. That the autho has a tremendously deep appreciation for Gikonyo is further supported by very successful short story first published in *Penpoint* and republished i *Origin East Africa*, entitled 'The Return'; for the hero of this short story is a earlier study of Gikonyo. Although the lesser characters and situations var slightly, the hero of the story returns to his village to find that his wife has gon off with another man. In the short story, all too quickly done, the young man' love for his countryside and its river heal his wound and restore him to hi family. No such simple solution exists for Gikonyo, however, although he i described as having the same love for the land, the hills, and the river as th hero of 'The Return'. Gikonyo must adjust, not to an absent wife, but to on who has given birth to another man's child. Much like the hero of 'Th Return', Gikonyo not only takes up his life in the new, post-Emergenc village but he also becomes a hero, a model for other members of the com munity.

And in the manner of a fictionalized Fanon hero Gikonyo turns from th former trade of artisan to that of merchant. Recognizing the problem of th village to be economic rather than historical, racial, or personal, Gikony plunges into the post-emergency economics of Kenya, begins a prosperou business of trading and amassing wealth, and becomes a new leader in a ne society in spite of the faults and legacy of the past. Once again, following Fanon's lead, Ngugi transfers a previous cultural hero from his former position to that of the new cultural hero based on post-Emergency values. This activity is presented as being neither healthy nor necessarily admirable. Ngugi does, however, try to indicate that Gikonyo has admirable qualities and that he is, in so far as any of the little people are, the hero of the book. Nevertheless, Gikonyo's romantic vision of wife and home have been betrayed by the Emergency; upon his return he finds a failure to which he reacts totally and deeply. He cannot accept Mumbi his wife because she has been flawed during her own efforts at survival. The author manages to create the sense of pain, time, and a great deal of mental suffering until an answer is hammered out.

Like the traditional wood-carver who through his skill interpreted the person of the gods, so Gikonyo's role is to put failure in its perspective. Recalling Kerinyaga (the legendary sacred mountain) in a reverie, he contemplates carving a stool (the traditional symbol and explanation of power and authority) for Mumbi (the new mother of the tribe), and the carving would, as is traditionally true, indicate the explanation for her power or authority. 'The seat would rest on three legs curved into three grim-faced figures, sweating under a weight. On the seat he would bead a pattern representing a river and a canal. A jembe or a spade would lie beside the canal' (pp. 277–8). But the carving keeps changing as it evolves in the mind of Gikonyo.

> He changed the figures. He would now carve a thin man, with hard lines on the face, shoulders and head bent, supporting the weight. His right hand would stretch to link with that of a woman, also with hard lines on the face. The third figure would be that of a child on whose head or shoulders the other two hands of the man and woman would meet.
>
> (p. 279)

One final change completes the gift for the new Mumbi. 'I'll change the woman's figure. I shall curve [*sic*] a woman big – big with child' (p. 280).

As a conclusion to *A Grain of Wheat*, the traditional symbol of the carved stool interprets much of the action of the novel. The seat of authority shifts in Gikonyo's mind (himself no saviour, and a failure) from the 'three grim-faced figures, sweating under a weight', that is, the men of the detention and the tragedies of the Emergency, to the thin, hard, lined survivors of the Emergency willing to take up a flawed existence (the illegitimate child is one independent figure) based on the hope of the future, the pregnancy.

Not the characters, but the stool becomes the ultimate statement of the novel. This makes more convincing the way in which the characters presented

E

as being caught up in and explored in the crush of historical progressive realism, resolve themselves into a hope for the future. The cause-and-effect of history no longer gives rise to despair and death for the saviour figure, but to hope for a whole flawed and humble society that has suffered, in which each member has been forced to come to terms with himself and make a deliberate choice for the future. This solution is much more satisfactory, though the author is still tied to a progressive historical realism. *A Grain of Wheat* is a well-written historical novel with good psychological analysis, and the characters and events once again begin to transcend a particular time and place through the traditional African symbol of the stool.

Without carping, I think it is safe to claim that *A Grain of Wheat* has two major flaws: the first the treatment of the colonials, especially Margery; and the second, the excessive amount of historical fact included in the novel. To deal with the second first, for anyone who is remotely familiar with any East African history it seems that Ngugi has included far too much of it for no purpose. Perhaps he meant to present background for the reader unfamiliar with the situation; if so, the interest of the reader is taxed on occasion, and the longer historical passages might well have been edited for the sake of his art.

Once again the treatment of the colonials must be faulted. Either to present the colonial world as a peripheral one which occasionally impinges on the main characters, or conversely to present a fuller background of the colonial world to give the novel more solidity, is an author's decision, and it seems that either method would be defensible. That the author has given the reader a rather full background for some of the colonials may be justified on the basis that he is expanding the compass of the novel to include all of Kenya. To defend the presence of the colonials' history on the basis that these things might happen or have happened – now I am particularly thinking of Dr Lynd's story or the affair between Thompson's wife and Dr Dyke – is once again to confuse history and fiction. The two episodes that have no function in the novel are precisely the two that include Margery, Thompson's wife, and Dr Lynd; both deal with the sexual adventures of the two women. Neither has an aesthetic purpose in the novel, and neither is necessary for the development of the central theme, or of any particular episode in the book for that matter. One is then prompted to ask why they are included. Since any possible answer would merely serve to point out a further weakness in Ngugi's writing, I shall merely let the question stand.

In conclusion, then, the more interesting writings of Ngugi, the novels, have a good deal of merit in their own right, even though each in its own way gives evidence of the author's uncertainty in his use of the novel form. The particular history of Kenya or the personal history of individuals of that country may be interesting in themselves. But as the history of fictional writing has proved more than once, the art of the novel differs considerably from the ability to tell an interesting or unusual story. Even within the very recent history of the African novel, a good number of semi-fictionalized educational stories have been published, and justly ignored. Ngugi's writing demands much more attention than these deservedly forgotten works, and I do not mean to equate his writing with them. Nevertheless, his work does evidence the presence of a confusion between fiction and history. Where the author is true to himself, although his writing is uneven and his style has not yet fully developed, his work succeeds very well; where the personally involved historian is not edited or the history is not transformed, the writing fails; through either uncertainty or obvious bad judgement. But *A Grain of Wheat* indicates that Ngugi is shaping his talent towards the thought, the imagery and the needs of a new Kenya; on occasion this imagery becomes universalized as he moves deeper into the human problems of all men rather than the immediate historical problems of some.

CHRONOLOGICAL TABLE OF THE WORK OF CHRISTOPHER OKIGBO

The dates of composition are those given by the poet himself. The poems discussed are mainly from the collection *Labyrinths with Path of Thunder*, published by Heinemann with Mbari, 1971. References to this volume are abbreviated as *LP*.

Full bibliographical references for other volumes are given in the footnotes.

POEM	DATE OF COMPOSITION		DATE OF FIRST PUBLICATION	DATES OF REVISED PUBLICATIONS
'Four Can-zones'	Song of the Forest Debtor's Lane Lament of the Flutes Lament of the Lavender Mist	1957 1959 1960 1961	*Black Orpheus* no. 11 (1962?)	—

Heavensgate	Idoto
	   I Passage
	   II Initiation
	   III Watermaid
	   IV Lustra
	   V Newcomer
		
		1961
		1960/61
		1961
		1960/61
		1961
			1962 by Mbari, Ibadan	*LP*, Heinemann, 1971

Limits	Pt 1: Siren Limits I–IV Pt 2: Fragments out of the Deluge V–X	1961 1961/62	Pt 1: *Transition* no. 5, 30 July– 29 Aug. 1962 Pt 2: *Transition* nos. 6 and 7, Oct. 1962	(*a*) 1964 by Mbari, Ibadan (*b*) *LP*, 1971
'Silences'	Pt 1: Lament of the Silent Sisters Pt 2: Lament of the Drums I–V	1962 1964	Pt 1: *Transition* no. 8, 1963 Pt 2: *Transition* no. 18, 1965	Pt 2: *Black Orpheus* no. 17, June 1965. Parts 1 and 2 *LP*, 1971
'Distances'	I–VI	1964	*Transition* no. 16, 1964	*LP*, 1971
'Lament of the Masks'	I–IV	1965	*W. B. Yeats 1865–1965* ed. Maxwell and Bushrui, 1965	—
'Dance of the Painted Maidens'			*Verse & Voice*, 1965, ed. D. Cleverdon	—
'Path of Thunder'	Thunder can Break Elegy of the Wind Come Thunder Hurrah for Thunder Elegy for Slit Drum Elegy for Alto	May 1966 Dec. 1965 17.1.66 May 1966 May 1966	Feb. 1968 in *Black Orpheus* vol. 2 no. 1	unrevised, *LP*, 1971

6 From Reality to the Dream: the Poetry of Christopher Okigbo

▼▼▼▼▼▼▼▼▼▼▼▼▼▼▼▼▼▼▼▼▼▼▼▼▼▼▼▼▼▼▼▼▼▼

DAN IZEVBAYE

THE most convenient means of interpreting poetry with a mythological framework is to treat the figures as variations of well-known images and symbols. However, when a poem is obscure because of a lack of continuity between the poet's system and the traditional ideas of his audience or his society, this method becomes inadequate since the personal associations of the images are more important than their usual significance for the poet's audience. It is in cases like this that the poet's sources become a valuable means of re-creating the experience of the poem by helping the reader to go through some of those selections from experience which the poet has used for his poems. The poet himself can provide the sources, as Okigbo does in *Labyrinths*. But because the poet's use of these sources often transforms the material and even changes some of the significance which it had in its original context, it is necessary to approach the poem as a coherent unit, a world in its own right, even though it refers back to the actual world by being a reconstruction of what that world is or might be. The reading which follows takes this verbal context of the poem as the basic requirement for understanding and response; but it also refers to the other 'contexts' of the poem – other poems by the same poet, as well as the cultural and biographical contexts which provided the raw material for the poem.

Okigbo, like certain other poets who have created a system of symbols, can be difficult to read. The causes of difficulty include some degree of alienation from his society (as with Blake), the absence of many shared beliefs and concepts, and his revival and use of concepts and myths from his own society that are now little known or forgotten (as in the practice of Yeats). Perhaps the most important reason is his purpose of keeping the reader at a distance, partly in the hope of frustrating attempts to find misleading social or personal connections with parts of the poem, partly to give the experience a general and archetypal, rather than a particular quality.

Daniel Izevbaye was born of Bini parents in the northern part of Nigeria, where he spent his youth. He was taught in schools in the North and in the West. He read English at the University of Ibadan, where he also took a doctorate. He has taught courses in English, African, and American literature at the University of Lagos. He is at present a lecturer in literature at the University of Ibadan. He is married with three children.

> A poet must . . . divest himself of the prejudices of his age or country . . . he must disregard present laws and opinions, . . . he must therefore content himself with the slow progress of his name; condemn the applause of his own time . . .
>   Samuel Johnson

In discussing a topic like the rift between a poet and his audience, it is almost unfair to choose one's illustration from a thoroughbred neo-classical critic, when there are abundant illustrations to be had from thoroughgoing romantics. But to be able to induce support from such quarters is itself sufficient indication that poets who seek freedom from social conventions may be motivated not by mere desire for a literary independence on Crusoe's island, but by the necessity to free themselves from the pressures of time and place.

As the literary medium most receptive to private emotion, poetry is the most effective means by which an artist may express his independence of society. For many critics poetry has proved the most rewarding form for verifying the autonomy of art. Some begin by asking whether or not communication is a property of literature, and conclude with attempts to outlaw as critical fallacies all evidence of the social attachments of art – like communication, intention and *affection*. Such positions have not been so popular in Africa because of the urgent cultural needs of the continent. A number of critics are now increasingly showing concern not so much with the literary character of a work, as with its cultural or political significance.

Against this background it is not surprising that one occasionally comes across a view that is not particularly favourable to the impersonal poetry of Okigbo because it assumes that the poems can only be discussed without reference to society. It is however possible – even with the most impersonal poetry – for criticism to be a bridge between literature and society without forgetting that the literary character of a work should be kept at the centre of discussion. Even the most autonomous literary work can be located in a context of relationships linking the literary work, its audience, the artist and his society. When there are problems of acceptance for a poet like Okigbo the problem can usually be traced to social sources.

Although there did not seem to be any problem with recognition when *Heavensgate* was first published,[1] the question of acceptance has occasionally arisen – a problem that is given poetic expression in *Limits* II. The difficulty of accepting the poetry in spite of the willingness to concede its merits comes from an objection to two of its features: its obscurity, and the poet's apparent pursuit of the strange gods of Europe. The clearest articulation of this objection is Professor Mazrui's article on Okigbo's abstract verse.[2] 'Abstract verse' is defined as verse which is unintelligible because it is imagistic and musical rather than 'conversational'. It is therefore untranslatable. 'To put it bluntly, Africa cannot afford too many Okigbos. She cannot afford too many versifiers whose poems are untranslatable, and whose genius lies in imagery and music rather than conversational meaning.'[3]

Perhaps the problem of communication should be traced not to the limitations peculiar to a poet's personal genius, but to deeper social causes. An approach to the problem should therefore begin by examining the traditions within which a poet is or is not writing. According to Eliot in his seminal essay 'Tradition and the Individual Talent' (1919), tradition involves the assertion in a poet's work of the immortality of the dead poets, his ancestors. In a later attempt to develop this idea Eliot defined tradition as 'the inherited wisdom of the race' and heresy as deviations from tradition. His description of the fight against heresy in his time would have suited a similar African struggle in our time. The struggle, he writes, is 'to concentrate, not to dissipate; to renew our association with traditional wisdom; to re-establish a vital connection between the individual and the race.'[4]

This struggle was a central concern in Okigbo. Some of his critics have been impatient mainly because of his unorthodox way of tackling the problem, just as Eliot decried what he called the literary heresy of his times. Eliot himself described how such a pursuit of strange gods begins: 'where there is no custom to determine what the task of literature is, every writer will range as far afield as possible'.[5] The modern world with its expanding frontiers of knowledge seems particularly suitable for such enterprise, giving rise to what I. A. Richards defined as 'the use of responses not available without special experience, which more than anything else narrows the

---

[1] Reviews by S. O. Anozie, 'Okigbo's *Heavensgate*, a study of Art as Ritual', *Ibadan*, no. 15, March 1963, p. 11; and Ulli Beier, 'Three Mbari Poets', *Black Orpheus* (Mbari, Ibadan), no. 12, (n.d., 1962?), pp. 46–7.

[2] Ali A. Mazrui, 'Meaning Versus Imagery in African Poetry', *Présence Africaine*, no. 66, 2nd quarterly 1968, pp. 49–57.

[3] Ibid., p. 57.

[4] T. S. Eliot, *After Strange Gods: a primer of modern heresy* (Faber, London, 1934), p. 48.

[5] Ibid., p. 32.

range of the artist's communication and creates the gulf between expert and popular taste.'[6]

These two accounts of the 'twenties seem an appropriate explanation for Okigbo's almost unique combination of material from the oral tradition with the apparently extraneous material from other cultures. The pursuit of strange gods is a response to a situation that requires the poet to fashion a literary tradition for himself. The allusiveness is the result of inevitable contact with different cultures, ancient and modern. It demands of the reader an unusual range of knowledge, whether it be of the archaeological excavations of Egypt, or the uncovering of the Gilgamesh tablets, or African oral traditions. The allusiveness suggests, in fact, that the relationship between literature and society is not ideal. There would be no problem of communication between critic and poet in an ideal period. When a poet seems to lapse into obscure symbolism this is usually a direct response to a cultural situation, and the duty of criticism is to stand as far back as possible from the great debate between the artist and society in order to see more clearly the lines of tension distorting the ideal balance between art and society. Okigbo seems to be working within that convention in which the artist seeks the integrity of his art not by denying social claims, but by seeking to enshrine poetry's fundamental right to exist according to the peculiar constitution of literary art. That is, the artist claims for his art only a relative independence from, or primacy above, other social products, although peculiar social situations may force him into what *appears* to be a retreat from reality. For all his preoccupation with form and symbol he does not in fact seek to lose sight of the reality behind the work of art, realizing that literature can never really exist in isolation from the reality that encompasses it.

Because of this social factor it is necessary to discard an inadequate term like 'abstract art' and try to understand the poetry on its own terms. This can be done by placing it within or near a tradition from which it derives or to which it is similar. Okigbo's poetry has obvious affinities with the type of poetry written by Eliot and the Symbolists. The relationships are obvious enough. There is the fact of direct influence: Okigbo's 'Debtor's Lane' was modelled on 'The Hollow Men', and the first version of 'Silent Sisters' (see chronological table) carries an epigraph from Mallarmé's 'Hérodiade' – an implied tribute to the French poet. The synthesis of a medley of experience as a basis for poetic composition comes straight from Eliot. But there are more basic similarities which suggest that the conception of poetry held by Okigbo is similar to that of Eliot and the Symbolists. For example, it is mainly within the symbolist tradition that we encounter the odd combination

[6] I. A. Richards, *Principles of Literary Criticism* (Faber, London, 1924/63) p. 215.

of irrational poetic intuition and coldly calculated craftsmanship; that is, the imposition of formal control over an essentially romantic emotion. In both Eliot and Okigbo we find the evocation of childhood memory as a means of creating poetry; both have a similar interpretation of time; both make references to river or sea in connection with childhood memories; in both there is an awareness that tradition should include the past – one's ancestors or poets of the past. An example is provided in the hero of *Heavensgate*, whose longing to fashion a tradition by searching in the past is determined not by a romantic nature but by necessity. In the Canzones and in *Heavensgate* the present society is unbearable because the poet-hero has suffered the unpleasantness of initiation into an alien culture, symbolized in *Heavensgate* by the religious figure of the tyrant Leidan. Memory and dream are therefore his means of seeking his salvation. His memory recalls an experience which is no longer an immediate reality because, having become initiated into the world of strangers, he has become technically a prodigal to his own. Hence his dream of reunion with mother *Idoto*, which is almost like the longing for mother Africa of the not-too-distant past, a longing for a creative return to tradition.

As with his hero, Okigbo's sense of tradition extends to the oral tradition even in his early poems, although then he did not exploit this exhaustively except at a thematic level as a means of working out the cultural dilemma of his hero. Oral poetry appeared at first as a thematic adaptation rather than a formal one, although there is an awareness of the potentialities of the oral tradition – as in the directions for traditional instrumental accompaniment in the Four Canzones,[7] or the rendering in the 'Initiation' section of *Heavensgate* of 'a lewd Ibo song about the testicles of a ram'.[8] Although this additional influence of the oral tradition later became strong enough to inform his view of poetry, there is no real clash with the symbolist view, as will be discussed later.

The three features of symbolist theory that are relevant to this discussion are a rejection of 'meaning' or 'communication' in the ordinary sense, an emphasis on the poet's unity of being, and thirdly, an attempt to preserve the integrity of art by an aesthetic withdrawal, which is not an escape from reality because the poet has never rejected reality; he has only refined it as a means of deriving the symbols by which reality may be interpreted. That is why, for example, a poet like Eliot can speak of the autonomy of art as well as its social function at the same time.

A dream-like state often marks the point of departure from reality into art. The appropriate setting for the creative act is usually a half-waking state.

[7] 'Four Canzones (1957–61)', *Black Orpheus*, no. 11, pp. 5–9.
[8] O. R. Dathorne, 'Ritual and Ceremony in Okigbo's Poetry', *Journal of Commonwealth Literature*, no. 5, July 1968, p. 81.

In *Limits*, dream is important because poetry comes unbidden, and only in moments of intense semi-consciousness, a privilege denied waking moments, when poetic intuition inevitably evaporates:

> And the dream wakes
>   the voice fades
> In the damp half light
>   like a shadow,
>
> Not leaving a mark.
>
> (Limits III; LP p. 26)

According to Yeats, 'in the making and in the understanding of a work of art, and the more easily if it is full of patterns and symbols and music, we are lured to the threshold of sleep'.[9]

Music is essential to this conception of poetry. A poet may turn to a non-rational equivalent like music because he believes that words are by themselves inadequate for transmitting a true poetic experience. Thus Okigbo describes 'The Silent Sisters' as an exploration of 'the possibility of poetic metaphor in an attempt to elicit the music to which all imperishable cries must aspire';[10] words which recall Debussy's 'music begins where words are powerless to express'. When Okigbo described himself as being influenced by composers like Debussy[11] or as being primarily a composer of sounds, it is important not to take him too literally. To deny that he ever intended to communicate meaning is not the same thing as denying the presence of meaning in his poems. He himself admitted that a close reading of his poems would yield a meaning.[12] Sense often lurks behind the sound of the music of poetry. Ordinarily one expects nouns like 'kite' and 'eagles' to be accompanied by verbs like 'fly'. So in phrases like 'the kite flows' and 'the eagles flow' the idea of flight is still an implied part of the meaning, the context. The delight in verbal skill in the following lines does not prevent the poet from also creating an image to suggest the ease with which birds glide over their prey:

[9] W. B. Yeats, 'The Symbolism of Poetry' in *Ideas of Good and Evil* (Macmillan, London, 1903), p. 249.

[10] Introduction to *Labyrinths*, p. XII.

[11] Answer to Transition Writers' Conference Questionnaire, *Transition* no. 5 1962, p. 12: 'My HEAVENSGATE ... was influenced by the Impressionis Composers ... I wrote several parts ... under the spell of Debussy, Césa Franck and Ravel. My LIMITS ... was influenced by everything and everybody. But this is not surprising, because the LIMITS were the limits of dream.'

[12] 'Death of Christopher Okigbo', *Transition*, no. 33, October/Novembe 1967, p. 18.

(1) And who says it matters
Which way the kite flows,
Provided the movement is
Around the burning market –

(*Limits* VII; *LP* p. 30)

(2) The eagles flow
over man-mountains,
Steep walls of voices,
horizons;
The eagles furrow
dazzling over the voices

(*Limits* VIII; *LP* p. 31)

An inevitable result of the use of suggestion by analogy is the primacy of the image or metaphor, a basic method of composition in Okigbo's work. But the poetry does not remain 'a mere pattern of little pictures'.[13] What brings the different images together in unity is the power to make free associations, which enables the poet to organize the images into metaphors for his emotion. If the description of the method here sounds like Eliot's account of the image of feeling, it is a logical response to the nature of the work under discussion, as will be shown by a similar description in a London interview between Okigbo and Robert Serumaga:

In his poems, the traditional African ritual, the Babylonian gods, heroes of Roman mythology and twentieth century scientific mythology are all *commandeered to form the cavalcade of vehicles for the poet's feelings*. Lesser souls, drawing on more limited experiences might feel, as they read his poetry, like outsiders eavesdropping on a private conversation or intruding into a secret ritual. [italics mine][14]

The distinction between 'lesser souls' and the poet is similarly made by Eliot in his description of the poet as one who is 'engaged in the task of trying to find the verbal equivalent for states of mind and feeling':

When a poet's mind is perfectly equipped for its work, it is constantly amalgamating disparate experience; the ordinary man's experience is chaotic, irregular, fragmentary. The latter falls in love, or reads Spinoza, and these two experiences have nothing to do with each other, or with the

[13] Mazrui, op. cit., p. 50.
[14] *Cultural Events in Africa*, no. 8, July 1965, Supplement.

noise of the typewriter or the smell of cooking; in the mind of the poet these experiences are always forming new wholes.[15]

The reference to 'the ordinary man's experience' may perhaps explain one important source of obscurity in Okigbo's poetry – the unusual collocation of images. This unusual power to form connections between images is used for creating a context for the main experience of the poem. This is what happens in *Limits* V where the theme of rebirth or resurgence, which is associated with the appearance of the giant fennel branch and the new branch in Enkidu, is set in a mood of freshness and glory:

> Smoke of ultramarine and amber
> Floats above the fields after
> Moonlit rains, from tree unto tree
> Distils the radiance of a king . . .

(LP p. 28)

There is also the pathetic fallacy which follows upon this peaceful scene when violence breaks in *Limits* X:

> And dawn-gust grumbled,
> Fanning the grove

(LP p. 33)

The linking of these images often suggests the type of structure in which the significance of certain motifs is determined by the pattern of their recurrence. Just as in music a melody becomes identified with certain emotions by constant association, so in Okigbo the structure is a means of redefining the meaning of certain words and giving them new meanings of the poet's own. This method has been defined as

the art of handling complex ideas in simple language, by the constant re-arrangement of a selected group of words and symbols. Okigbo re-handles such words as laughter, dream, light, presence, voice, blood, exactly as Eliot teases out all the possible meanings of beginning, middle and end in *East Coker*.[16]

The words take on meanings which are not always made clear by normal usage, and it becomes necessary to be familiar with the other contexts of Okigbo's work in which they have occurred.

[15] T. S. Eliot, *Selected Essays* (Faber, London, 1963), p. 287.
[16] Gerald Moore, *The Chosen Tongue* (Longmans, London, 1969), p. 176.

One obvious requirement for understanding such poetry is a knowledge of other poems by the poet, since these provide the context that helps to define the meaning of his words. In the context theory, which receives its most systematic definition in I. A. Richards' 'theory of how words mean', outlined in *The Philosophy of Rhetoric* (1936), meaning is defined as 'the interanimation of words'. Following Richards's argument, context here will be taken at three levels:

(1) The original context from which a poet borrows a word. This is usually made less important by the fact that in the process of creating a coherent world of his own, a poet like Okigbo usually re-defines the words he borrows from their everyday contexts.

(2) The immediate context of the words. The words in a poem are affected by other words in the same poem in which they occur. This means that it is not enough to discuss a passage from a poem without reference to the other parts of the poem. One may recall here Samuel Johnson's analogy of the landlord 'who, when he offered his house to sale, carried a brick in his pocket as specimen'.

(3) The larger context of a poet's works taken as a group. The assumption here is that the whole of a poet's work helps one to understand his individual poems. In most cases the creation of a poem is a process of exploration, and a poet discovers his meaning only in the process of using words.

The way in which the larger context defines words in Okigbo's poems may be demonstrated by taking two examples of words at first seemingly used in their ordinary sense, but gathering deeper significance with subsequent poems. The words *wind* and *leaves* have occurred in earlier contexts in association with violence and love-making:

> We follow the wind to the fields
> Bruising grass leafblade and corn. . . .
> > ('Lament of the Flutes', 1960)

> Shadows of sin in grove of orange,
> Of altar-penitence,
> Over me at sundown,
> Of wind on leaves, . . .
> Shadows of the stillness of the Song
> Over me at sundown
> In an empty garden
> > where
> Wounded by the wind lie dead leaves.
> > ('Lament of the Lavender Mist', 1961)

When the words 'wind' and 'leaves' occur again in 'Distances' II (1964), they suggest that the relationship between the wind and the leaves is like that between the hero and the goddess:

> For the wind, eternal suitor of dead leaves,
> unrolled his bandages to the finest swimmer . . .

The words *bandages* and *swimmer* are associated with the violent relationship between the goddess and the hero in 'Siren Limits' (first published in 1962), a poem which immediately precedes 'Distances' thematically, and ends with the hero's cry, 'Wound me, O sea-weed face, blinded like strong-room.' In the light of this appeal *bandages* become necessary because of the *wound*, and *swimming* because to approach a goddess described as sea-weed face requires some efficiency at swimming. The bandages are surely the promise of salvation in 'Distances'. After the plea for surgical healing in 'Siren Limits' IV:

> When you have finished
> & done up my stitches,
> Wake me near the altar,
>
> (*LP* p. 27)

the poet-hero wakes near Death's altar in 'Distances', though the resurrection is 'from flesh into phantom'.

It is this type of recurrence in similar contexts that gives meaning or significance to the words in the poem. Passages often chosen to illustrate the 'mere sound' of Okigbo's work are in fact meaningful if read in their contexts as part of the whole work. To offer them in isolation from their contexts is of course to divest them of much of their significance. One such passage comes from 'Distances' when the hero arrives at the threshold of discovery, as indicated by the presence of an archway – obviously the heavensgate of the first volume and the high arched gate of *Limits* III. At this point one of the two signs that are offered the hero is the following inscription by which he might recognize the path to his destiny:

> *the only way to go*
> *through the marble archway*
> *to the catatonic pingpong*
> *of the evanescent halo . . .*
>
> ('Distances' IV; *LP* p. 57)

This inscription serves the hero as a road sign. But it also gives him a picture of the heaven beyond. And because of the inadequacy of direct statement he is presented with a concrete equivalent of his conception of the world beyond through an aural and visual demonstration of its nature. What is suggested by 'catatonic ping-pong' is an image of heaven as a musical interplay of sound. The effect of the experience on the hero's mind is one of madness, a state with which he has identified himself in *Heavensgate*, and with good reason. Catatonia, a form of schizophrenia typified by stupor, is also Okigbo's metaphor for the trancelike state that precedes creation, and is appropriate as much for its sound value as for its meaning. 'The evanescent halo' is also an assurance – he can tell now that he is on the right trail by this indication, this quality of transience that he constantly associates with his 'Watermaid'. It appears in *Heavensgate* as 'matchflare in wind's breath' and in 'Distances' II as 'a cloud of incense'.

It is this accumulation of meaning which gives an essential unity to the poet's work: every additional poem expands and enlarges the meaning of the whole. Thus, hints of Okigbo's method and meaning occur even in the Canzones, although it is in *Heavensgate* that they are fully developed. In *Heavensgate* the poet-hero seeks to rediscover himself by returning to his cultural origins. He discovers that the requirement for re-entry is ritual sacrifice and repentance, and that although traditional culture is necessary for discovering himself he must accept its modification by the new culture into which he has strayed.

'Siren Limits', the first part of *Limits* (1962 and 1964) is concerned no longer with this discovery but with developing this new-found secret of the self by seeking a harmonious union of the two. So while in the earlier poem the desired union is between the poet and an ancestor, a third figure is introduced in this poem: the second self of the hero, who must be integrated with the Self if the unity of being originally sought is to be preserved. This is a variation on the earlier theme, because where the earlier hero is an incomplete man in search of rebirth, the present hero is a divided man who seeks to overcome his perpetual catatonia.

'Siren Limits' begins with a movement in which the hero, having performed the preparatory purification rites, is caught in a trance-like state, anticipating the descent of his goddess-muse, which marks the release of the lyric impulse. So the poem opens with the weaverbird image. This is followed in the second movement by the motif of growth – the poet striving for maturity and an audience. But the theme does not stop at an aesthetic commitment. The general choral tone, the oratorial structure underscored by the constant allusion to an audience and the image of the prophetic horsemen, all suggest a mantic purpose which seems to cancel the deceptive aestheticism of the method. In the third strophe 'Horsemen of the apocalypse' is a reference to 'the echoes' which earlier emerge out of the solitude to become the vehicle for voice and soul. But the line itself is an allusion to *Revelations*

6:2–8, in which the Four Horsemen of the Apocalypse represent Imperialism, War, Famine, Pestilence and Death, and they anticipate both the invasion in *Limits* VIII where, in a similar image, eagles fly over voices, and 'Path of Thunder' (1965/66), which presents in a more direct way the metamorphoses of these political nightmares. This section therefore contains hints of social themes to appear later, although it is here an integral part of a system of imagery which is less arbitrary than it seems. In the immediate context the image develops by association – the horsemen image develops from the metaphor of the selves riding the echoes. But in the wider context the symbol of the weaverbird as poet leads naturally to egg-shells for cleansing, and the forest setting provides the plant imagery developed in the next section. The plant imagery, because of its association with growth, helps to develop this theme.

The shift in *Limits* III to the construction image of reed, mortar and broken bottles is not arbitrary, because it is more appropriate for developing the new theme. In this movement the reader is introduced to a work site heaped with the fragments of experience which the poet hopes to erect into a stately pleasure-dome. The uncompleted work among the building materials is witnessed by wet mortar. The hero's quest is then resumed, dramatized here by the exploration that ends in the usual discovery by the quester that the work is as yet uncompleted. The first intimations of the reward of the quest comes as usual against the background of that transitory state between trance and consciousness:

> And this is the crisis point,
> The twilight moment between
>   sleep and waking;
> And voice that is reborn transpires,
> Not thro' pores in the flesh,
>   but the soul's back-bone.

(LP p. 25)

Identifying in this trance-like state the right state for receptiveness, the explorer abandons the care of the early section and, strongly attracted by hopes of getting quickly to his goal, he hurries on down only to have his pilgrimage terminate at the partly desired, partly disappointing goal of 'The big white elephant'. There is some self-mockery here, for the white elephant is both his goal and the penalty for his impatience.

Limits III shows how the poet symbolically transforms events into his poetry. Okigbo's note on these lines refers to 'rockpoint of CABLE' as the 'cable point at Asaba, a sacred waterfront with rocky promontory, and terminal point of a traditional quinquennial pilgrimage', and Okigbo's introduction further says that the hero's quest is inspired by the poet's own illusory pilgrimage from Nsukka to Yola. A strict fidelity to the source of the image would define the white elephant as this illusion. But reading in conformity with the nature of the poem, *white elephant* implies something more. The two principles to keep in mind here are, (1) the basic symbolist preoccupation to distil the poet's personal experiences into an aesthetic experience not necessarily related to the original experience; and in this connection we have Okigbo's assent in his interview with Serumaga,

> *Heavensgate* and *Limits* do not attempt to carry any message whatsoever . . . the poems have nothing to do with me – they live their own separate lives and when I've created a poem it is just as if I'm giving it life.[17]

(2) The second principle is implied in the first. Poems 'live their own separate lives', and should be judged strictly in terms of their attempt to *be*.

By this principle the original pilgrimage to Asaba is the cultural source providing the general idea for the poem; that is, the actual sacred pilgrimage becomes the means of mapping the hero's progress just as the poet's personal pilgrimage to Yola is the source of the hero's futile journey. But in addition to the normal religious significance which Cable Point must have for the pilgrims to Asaba, the context gives cable an additional attraction for the hero as something by which to pull the elusive white elephant. *White elephant* is not merely the frustrated end of the quest, but also ironically the original reason for setting out. It is to be explained not by the original experience, but by the immediate context of the poem as well as the wider context of the poet's other work in which it occurs. The relevant lines from this wider context are in the poem 'Lament of the Masks',[18] where they are part of the tribute to Yeats as 'Hunter of elephants/Earth tremor upon the land':

> They thought you would stop pursuing the white elephant
> But you pursued the white elephant without turning back –
> You who charmed the white elephant with your magic flute
> You who trapped the white elephant like a common rabbit
> You who sent the white elephant tumbling into your net –
> And stripped him of his horns, and made them your own –
> You who fashioned his horns into ivory trumpets.
>
> ('Lament of the Masks' III)

[17] *Cultural Events,* loc. cit.
[18] D. E. S. Maxwell and S. B. Bushrui (eds.), *W. B. Yeats: 1865–1965 Centenary essays on the art of W. B. Yeats* (Ibadan University Press, Ibadan, 1965), pp. XIII–XV.

Being specifically an elegy on a great poet, 'Lament of the Masks' sufficiently restricts the meaning of 'white elephant' to poetry, especially because of the presence of musical instruments in the poem – flute, horns and trumpets. The meaning is less restricted in other poems. But even in *Limits* III 'white elephant' implies a common view of poetry as a useless art. Yet the quest in *Limits* is not merely for poetry in the limited sense. Poetry is necessary only because it is the by-product of the quest for spiritual harmony within oneself; by itself it is useless. If there is need to corroborate this interpretation, there are two separate statements that suggest his attitude to poetry. In the introduction to *Labyrinths* Okigbo tells us that the work is 'necessarily a cry of anguish' (p. xiv) and in the interview with Serumaga, he says that 'poetry is not an alternative to living. It is only one way of supplementing life and if I can live life in its fullness without writing at all, I don't care to write' (see note 14). Together the two statements seem to make of poetry a compulsive burden, though not an essential one in itself; it is a white elephant, it seems.

Although a poet's pronouncements on poetry may help to throw light on his poetry, they cannot be pressed too much for the meaning of his poems. However, Okigbo's poems contain some hints that the hero's quest is for a unity of being. In *Heavensgate* the hero's endeavour is to reconcile the two incompatible sides of his experience. This obsession provides the constant motif which appears in various forms in the poems. In 'Distances' VI it appears as a sexual union, attained in the direct statement of 'I have entered your bridal chamber', but presented a little earlier in the image of the stream,

> I wash my feet in your pure head, O maid,
> and walk along your feverish solitary shores
>
> (*LP* p. 60)

The stream symbol is used for the same purpose earlier in *Limits* III as an image drawn from the nature of the goddess as a water-maid: she is the fountain-head of inspiration into which the hero, as her tributary, must flow:

> Hurry on down
> little stream to the lake;
>
> (*LP* p. 26)

This theme of union, with its strong cultural undercurrent, is almost exclusive to the *Heavensgate–Limits–*'Distances' group. The last occurrence of this motif in this partly cultural sense is in the second part of *Limits*, where the prophetic sunbird is killed and separated from his second self, a separation that is enacted in the divorce by violence of the twin-gods of Irkalla. Because, thematically, the undivided self has been discovered in 'Distances' and resurrected in 'Fragments out of the Deluge'[19] to suffer a traumatic experience of re-separation, when the motif occurs once more it is in a primarily psychological and private, non-cultural sense. This is in 'Elegy of the Wind', where, because the cultural source of spiritual nourishment has been discovered, the river-symbol is no longer necessary and the white goddess becomes translated into the sky:

> White light, receive me your sojourner; O milky way,
>   let me clasp you to my waist;
> And may my muted tones of twilight
> Break your iron gate, the burden of several centuries,
>   into twin tremulous cotyledons. . . .

$$(LP \text{ p. } 64)$$

Although the white goddess has undergone transformation from river goddess to sky deity here, the metamorphosis is in fact not sudden – it has been a continuous process, consistent at particular moments with the hero's needs, as in ancient mythology where gods become assimilated into other deities with similar attributes, according to the gradual revelation to the worshippers of the true nature of the deity. The various aspects of the goddess in some of these poems have been implied in earlier poems. The indifferent surgeon of 'Distances' has been anticipated by the aggressive goddess of *Limits* IV, whose cruelty in *Limits* V earns her the title 'the beast', an epithet for the Lioness of *Heavensgate*. This does not mean that the figures that occur on different occasions as Idoto and Watermaid and Death were initially conceived as identical deities. They are related conceptions merged by the necessity of circumstances into a more or less composite figure. Thus Idoto is, in the prelude to *Heavensgate*, a cultural mother – the source of which the soul seeking the origin of creative intuition must return. Watermaid is a Muse-like figure – the soul of poetic intuition. But in 'Lustra', the offering to Idoto becomes an appeal for the descent of Watermaid, the muse; and in *Limits* IV the unsolicited visitation of the goddess becomes a 'cruel' but accepted experience.

The revelation of the White Queen as Death in 'Distances' II is consistent with the nature of the quest. The consummation of the quest can come only after a passage that is in effect a rebirth ritual; hence death here is not an end but a beginning. As a passage between earthly life and immortality, it may

---

[19] An inevitable clash between theme and chronology arises in any discussion of these three sequences. Thematically the order is *Heavensgate* – 'Siren Limits' – 'Distances' – 'Fragments', although chronologically 'Distances' comes last.

best be described as the gate to heaven, or heavensgate. Just as in Ibo masquerade cult the ancestor – for the masquerader is an ancestor come back to life – returns into the ground through an ant-hole accompanied by his initiates, so the hero of 'Distances' seeks his inspirer and teacher, the goddess in the realm of the grave:

> Miner into my solitude,
> incarnate voice of the dream,
> you will go,
> with me as your chief acolyte,
> again into the anti-hill . . .

('Distances' I; LP p. 53)

This is a descent into Hades in quest of the ancestor who will teach the secrets of immortality to the acolyte. The theme of death as a process of initiation is developed by the 'anti-hill' pun. A grave physically resembles an ant-hill, and is also not really a hill because its secrets (like the ants' nest) rest in a hole. The descent into a hole (to get secrets) that both words imply makes it possible to draw an analogy with the masquerade cult, into which novices are introduced by being told that to be 'drawn down into the spirit world . . . they will be made to pass through the hole of an abwissi [akpisi] (a tiny insect) and thence be obliged to cross a very wide river on a thread'.[20] This meaning is implied in the second nativity hymn in Okigbo's poems – that of 'Distances' I in which

> . . . a voice, from very far away,
> chanted, and the chamber descanted, the birthday of earth,
> paddled me home through some dark
> labyrinth, from laughter to the dream.

(LP p. 53)

'Home' recalls the prodigal motif; that this home is arrived at only after a ferry passage through the dark labyrinth (crossing a Lethean river?) suggests the usual quest to the underworld to meet a close kinsman, although Okigbo also links the reference to labyrinth with the tortuous journey to the Aro Chukwu oracle, suggesting therefore the path to some awful knowledge.

The initiate is here making the passage through death into immortality or maturity. This seems to be the significance of the pilgrimage from Dan to Beersheba. Anozie suggests with characteristic insight, '. . . from *Death* to

---

[20] G. T. Basden, *Among the Ibos of Nigeria* (Frank Cass, London, 1921), p. 241. The different versions of 'Distances' in fact have 'ant-hole' (1964), 'ant-hill' (1965, unpublished) and 'anti-hill' (1970).

Birth?'²¹ The peculiar implication of the experience for the hero is related to his earlier experience in 'Siren Limits'. It is only through the symbol of death that true aesthetic purity can be signified; the cruelty of the rose is the fire of purification. This is suggested in the anaesthesia/aesthetics relationship. The anaesthesia of 'Siren Limits' and the aesthetic posture of the figure of Death in 'Distances' are linked as a result of the hero's awareness that he has to learn first to become insensible to feeling in order to attain a truly disinterested interest in art. The point of Okigbo's metaphysical interpretation of Joyce's aesthetic is made when Death, the object of the pilgrims' worship in 'Distances' II, is presented like a God of creation: she is 'the chief celebrant' and is therefore at the centre of the action, and yet she may be said to remain beyond or above it in her manifest indifference, since she stands 'behind them all, /... paring her fingernails ...' (*LP* p. 55).²² Death is a type of artist, and her *indifference* is like the artist's goal.

But ironically such indifference does not absolve the artist from social responsibility. The anaesthesia sought in 'Siren Limits' ('A loss of feeling of sensation'), is a means of achieving an aesthetic awareness ('perception by the senses'); it is not a rejection of moral sense but a rejection of concern for opinion, for the merely topical. So although the Self sought by the hero must be found alone, leaving no room for spectators ('I am the sole witness to my homecoming' in 'Distances' VI), such union eventually demands the artist's awareness of his responsibility to an audience, or at least his social responsibility. This is already implied in *Limits* II, where the united selves feel for audience. This responsibility to an audience is fulfilled in poems that follow 'Distances' thematically; i.e. 'Fragments out of the Deluge', 'Silences' and the poems of 'Path of Thunder'.

'Fragments out of the Deluge' starts where 'Distances' leaves off. In 'Distances' the hero achieves homecoming by being united with Death herself. 'Fragments out of the Deluge' continues from this point with the theme of the resurrection of the dead, symbolized by the image of the giant fennel branch growing out of an empty sarcophagus – according to Okigbo's note, an image from the story of a metamorphosed Pharaoh. The reference to post-diluvian survivals in the title of the poem recalls the archaeological discoveries of the Middle East sources of the flood myth. This is because the allusions are to myths of the Middle and Near East. The method however

---

²¹ S. O. Anozie, 'A Structural Approach to Okigbo's Distances', *The Conch*, (Paris) vol. 1, no. 1, 1969, p. 29.

²² An allusion to the aesthetic theory in ch. 5 of Joyce's *A Portrait of the Artist as a Young Man*. For another possible reference to Joycean theory cf. the closing lines of the introduction to *Labyrinths* (p. XIV) where the statement 'the present dream clamoured to be born a cadenced cry' recalls Joyce's 'the personality of the artist [is] at first a cry or cadence or a mood'.

derives from *The Waste Land*, which originally inspired the title of the poem. Unlike the first part of *Limits*, the original version of the second part in *Transition* nos. 6 and 7 did not have a separate title. Rather it carries as epigraph the line from *The Waste Land* (l. 430) about consoling oneself with the poetic fragments of one's efforts. The main allusion is however to the broken tablets of the Gilgamesh epic. Okigbo's use of this myth is an instance of how his borrowings are determined by the exploration of his own meaning rather by their original context. In the original version of *Limits* V the Sumerian god, Enki, is used for a purpose which, because it is not sufficiently integrated within the main concerns of Okigbo's poems, is not satisfactorily put across in the original version. Here, for example, is a possible reading of that version, starting with the appropriate knowledge of the source.

Enki, the Sumerian water god, seems to have been related to fertility, for, according to Thomas Campbell, one of his two names means 'the Lord (*en*) of the goddess Earth (*ki*)'. His symbol was an animal with the body of a fish and the foreparts of a goat.[23] Campbell suggests also that John the Baptist and the idea of rebirth through water is related to this. The relevance for Okigbo's poems is clear. The goat-fish symbol may be taken to represent the union of water and land, and it suggests the perfect spiritual union sought by Okigbo's hero who, in 'Siren Limits', presents himself as 'the he-goat-on-heat', while in *Heavensgate* the object of the union which the hero seeks is presented as Watermaid, a water goddess; this appears to fit the goat-fish symbol. The rebirth theme is apparent in the giant fennel branch, and in the circular patterns which the quest follows. The appearance of Enki in *Limits* V suggests the consummation of the union sought by the hero; and the twin-gods of Irkalla, who are male and female, and who are separated in *Limits* X, constitute another aspect of this relationship.

Gerald Moore takes 'the new branch in Enki' to be Okigbo's attempt to trace the resurgent culture of Africa to Egypt, and beyond to Sumer. Moore adds that Okigbo 'abandons the enterprise with a hint that we can never name a source for what is self-renewing'.[24] Okigbo in fact abandons 'Enki' in a more fundamental manner by substituting 'Enkidu' in the final version of the poem.

Enkidu is more consistent with the main meaning of this group of poems because it continues the central themes of the divided self and the search for immortality. Enkidu, the friend of Gilgamesh who went in quest of the ancestor from whom he hopes to get the secret of the proper ritual for immortality, becomes the second self of Okigbo's prodigal. The poet suggests

[23] T. Campbell, *The Masks of God: vol II: Oriental Mythology* (Secker and Warburg, London, 1962), p. 107.

[24] Gerald Moore, *The Chosen Tongue*, op. cit., p. 146.

that the drama is internal, and the branch here refers partly to the aspiration of the hero symbolized in the tree image of 'Siren Limits':

> Into the soul
> The selves extended their branches,
> Into the moments of each living hour
> Feeling for audience
>
> (*Limits* II *LP* p. 24)

Enkidu and Gilgamesh are usually taken as culture representatives – Enkidu as an embodiment of a hunting and food-gathering culture, and Gilgamesh as the Sumerian civilization that overcame it. Against this background, the Gilgamesh self of the hero is apparently the original protagonist, the urbanized prodigal of 'Debtor's Lane' and *Heavensgate* seeking to attain a fullness of being by complementing his western, urban orientation with his traditional, rural past.

The second part of *Limits* is thus a projection back into the past. There is a constant reference back to the time of *Heavensgate*, especially in section IX where the dog, the passageway, and the hills recall the landscape in the Jadum section of 'Initiation' in *Heavensgate*. Similarly, the oil-bean tree, an experience from the hero's past, occurs in *Limits* VIII. Having discovered his true self at last, the hero experiences anew the colonial invasion, which he was incapable of appreciating while he was still alienated from the traditional culture to which his second self was affiliated. This re-living of the communal experience of persecution is dramatized in the ravishing of the twin gods of the forest, 'the tortoise and the python', by the invaders, and this invasion takes place after the killing of the sunbird.

The python is sacred among the Ibo, as it is among some other peoples in West Africa, and it is an abomination to kill it. As for the tortoise, it should be noted that although there is evidence that it is, or may have been sacred in certain areas,[25] it does not necessarily carry a similar religious significance in this context as does the python. There is a dualism here, with the python possibly symbolizing something spiritual, and the tortoise, ubiquitous hero of African folk-tales, carrying an aesthetic or literary significance. The rapid shift from 'twin gods of the forest' to 'twin gods of Irkalla' is at first confusing because the twin gods in the two cases are identical. This is because of the intense compression of meaning. After killing the forest gods, the invaders divide the spoils of martyrdom by separating the serpent skin from the tortoise shell. Some emasculation is implied here, and possibly a reversal of the marital union achieved in 'Distances':

[25] cf. Basden, op. cit., p. 217.

> And the ornaments of him,
> And the beads about his tail;
> And the carapace of her,
> And her shell, they divided.
>
>   ('Fragments out of the Deluge' X, *LP* p. 33)

Because the action now connects with Irkalla's domain, the dead gods appear to have been subjected to the inexorable laws of the underworld – the primary state to which every creature is forced to return. The phrasing of these lines is patterned after the Sumerian hymn about the descent of Ishtar into the abode of Irkalla, queen of the underworld, and hence the action indirectly recalls the stripping of Ishtar at the seven gates.[26]

In *Limits* XII the circle of the hero's experience is completed by the return to immortality – a state only just anticipated by the graveyard fennel branch of section VI:

> But at the window, outside, a shadow:
>
> The Sunbird sings again
> From the LIMITS of the dream;
> The Sunbird sings again
> Where the caress does not reach,
>
>   of *Guernica*,
> On whose canvas of blood,
> The slits of his tongue
>   cling to glue . . .
>
> *& the cancelling out is complete.*
>
>   (*LP* 35)

This final version of the closing section is neater than the original version, although it is not without its problems of interpretation. It presents the

---

[26] See the hymn in *The Ancient Near East*, ed. James B. Pritchard (Princeton University Press, Princeton and London, 1958), p. 82.

> When the fourth gate he made her enter,
>   He stripped and took away the ornaments on her breast.
> 'Why, O gatekeeper, didst thou take the ornaments on my breast?'
> 'Enter, my lady, thus are the rules of the Mistress of the Nether World.'
> When the fifth gate he made her enter,
>   He stripped and took away the girdle of birthstones on her hips . . .
> When the sixth gate he made her enter,
>   He stripped and took away the clasps round her hands and feet.

Sunbird's resurrection as well as the immortalization of its earthly function in visual art. Picasso's *Guernica* presents an artist's criticism of violence, symbolized by the dying horse, the fallen warrior, and the agonized singing bird. There are two distinct images in Okigbo's poem. The first is the Sunbird singing from the limits of the dream. The second is the painting *Guernica* depicting war and violence on earth, with a singing bird representing humanity's only expression of hope. The bird provides the link between the two images because it symbolizes the career of the Sunbird or its function: the slits of the Sunbird's tongue cling to the glue of *Guernica's* canvas. The primary meaning here is that *Guernica* is a mirror of the outrage committed against the Sunbird – the nature of this outrage is specifically defined by the occurrence of the word 'newsprint' in the following lines from the original version:

> The newsprint-slits of his tongue
> cling to glue ...   (*Limits* X; 1962 and 1964)

This word, eliminated from the *Labyrinths* version, suggests more obviously that the killing of the Sunbird is directed at silencing him (his tongue still clings to glue in section XII of the final version: *LP* p. 35). The elimination of 'newsprint' in the final version is caused by the need for accuracy rather than by the desire for a change of meaning. Strictly speaking, the 'newsprint' area of Picasso's canvas is the body of the horse, not the tongue of the bird. Earlier in the poem there has been an emphasis on the prophetic function of the Sunbird. His publicity function, implied in 'newsprint', is evident from the analogous attributes, 'the dawn's charioteer' in *Limits* IX, the messiah and diviner of *Limits* VI, and the town crier with his iron bell in 'Hurrah for Thunder'. The image of the newsprint-tongue sticking to glue represents the most violent form of censorship. The main problem with this section is the use of *Guernica* (the painting, not the town) as a symbol of violence, so that *Guernica* is not just the visual art mirroring the horrors of an age, it is itself the image of that malevolence, and 'canvas' is both literal and figurative.

This is an instance of how the poem attempts to *be* by assimilating its borrowed images. This section shows the primacy which Okigbo gives to the poet's art above everything else: the undeniable musicality evident in the interplay of sibilants with 'i's, 'k's, and 'g's stresses the essentially aesthetic concern of the poet. In spite of this aesthetic emphasis, however, it is important, with reference to Okigbo's work, not to be too easily persuaded into accepting a view of poetry's ontology or complete independent existence. Poetry can never attain to the state of pure music because even the words it reinvests with meaning must begin their work by first infusing the poem with meaning from their original context, as in the *Heavensgate* poem, 'For Georgette', where the 'birth' either of the poet, or the poetic impulse, is heralded with

> such synthetic welcome at the cock's third siren;
> when from behind the bulrushes
>
> waking, in the teeth of the chill May morn,
> comes the newcomer.
>
> (*LP* p. 18)

By the references to Peter and Moses implied in 'cock's third siren' and 'behind bulrushes' respectively, we are introduced to the betrayal that awaits the newborn messiah or saviour. The theme of betrayal occurs in *Limits* VI – X, where it is a prelude to *Limits* X, which fulfils the martyrdom also implied in 'cock's third siren'. Later in 'Distances' the theme of salvation occurs in section IV, where the pilgrim-hero is confronted with words in the form of a crucifix as he enters the white chamber. These allusions bring their meaning along from their original context into the otherwise integrated context of the poems.

It is generally agreed that *Limits* and 'Distances' mark the end of the first phase of Okigbo's poetic career. Although 'Fragments out of the Deluge' was published before 'Distances' and as the second part of *Limits*, it is generally excluded from this phase because it does not follow the usual quest pattern, this having been completed in 'Distances'.[27] But it is still related to the group, since it is an epilogue to 'Distances'.

The first real break with this group of poems comes with 'Silences', 1963. This break is marked by the contrast between the primarily choral character of 'Silences' and the mainly personal character of what may be called the Sunbird poems. In spite of this difference, however, it is possible to trace a continuity from the Canzones through 'Silences' to 'Path of Thunder' (excluding 'Lament of the Masks', which is a different kind of poem). 'Fragments out of the Deluge' is the link in one respect. The earlier group, including 'Fragments', form a distillation of the poet's autobiography: the Canzones, as Anozie attempts to demonstrate, were influenced by the poet's movement from one employment to another.[28] The author himself provides the other sources: *Heavensgate* and *Limits* are the result of an abortive pilgrimage, 'Distances' is the result of the poet's first experience of surgery under anaesthesia. Poems in the second group are stimulated by public

---

[27] cf. Moore, op. cit., p. 171.

[28] S. O. Anozie, 'Christopher Okigbo: A Creative Itinerary 1957–1961', *Présence Africaine*, no. 64, 1967, pp. 158–67.

issues: 'Silent Sisters' by the Western Nigeria crisis and the death of Lumumba; 'Lament of the Drums' by the double tragedy of Chief Awolowo, 'Path of Thunder' by the Nigerian crisis. The link between all these is that the various combinations of the mainly personal experiences of the first group seem to lead to the various responses to the social and political tragedies of the second. 'Fragments' provides the link by the way it almost develops the personal experience of a cultural problem into a political issue – at any rate the private dilemma becomes a public one in the poem – necessarily so because the prophetic aspirations of its poet-hero enable him to fulfil the central dream of his career, that of the poet as prophet seeking an audience.

'Lament of the Masks' is different from the rest of the last poems because it does not deal with a social tragedy. Its only unity with all the other poems is that apart from making a poet the hero, it makes greater use of the technical resources of the oral tradition, like 'Lament of the Drums' and 'Path of Thunder'. In the *Oriki*, a form of Yoruba praise-poem which Okigbo adapts for this elegy,[29] gods and men and their deeds or attributes are placed in a heroic context. The praise of a great man is presented in a series of parallel or equivalent statements in which logical analogy becomes irrefutable proof, as in sympathetic magic, in which a priest's incantations are intended as persuasive argument for influencing the natural course of events. Yeats's achievement is presented in this tradition:

> How many beacon flames
> Can ever challenge the sun?. . .

> Thunder above the earth,
> Sacrifice too huge for the vulture.
> ('Lament of the Masks' II, Maxwell and Bushrui, pp. xiii, xv)

Although such direct borrowings from the oral traditions are more evident in the last poems, Okigbo was in fact continuously mindful of this tradition, although this was not always evident because of the heavier use of the more familiar traditions of European poetry. Okigbo's Orpheus-like hero began his career as a forest child in his earliest poem, 'Song of the Forest' (1957), inscribed for accompaniment with the native flute, *ubo*.

'Lament of the Drums' continues this use of the oral tradition. Following

---

[29] Although it is called a lament this poem is more of a panegyric than an elegy, as the last line of the first movement indicates. For a summary of the features of the African panegyric see chapter 5 of Ruth Finnegan's *Oral Literature in Africa* (Clarendon Press, Oxford, 1970). Finnegan however points out that both forms are closely related (pp. 147 and 149).

closely the structure of traditional funerary celebrations, the drums are moved from their place of storage into the forest clearing. Just as a European poet invokes the muse to ensure success in his great task, so the first section is an invocation imploring the relevant forces of the forest to ensure the success of a celebration to which nature herself has contributed the drums in their as yet uncreated state:

> Lion-hearted cedar forest, gonads for our thunder,
> Even if you are very far away, we invoke you:
>
> Give us our hollow heads of long-drums . . .
>
> Antelopes for the cedar forest, swifter messengers
> Than flash-of-beacon-flame, we invoke you:
>
> Hide us; deliver us from our nakedness . . .
>
> Many-fingered canebrake, exile for our laughter,
> Even if you are very far away, we invoke you:
>
> Come; limber our raw hides of antelopes . . .
>
> Thunder of tanks of giant iron steps of detonators,
> Fail safe from the clearing, we implore you:
>
> We are tuned for a feast-of-seven-souls . . .
>
> (*LP* p. 45)

The objects presented in these images have a symbolic value, being themselves the essence of what they stand for, in the true vernacular tradition. In the first tercet (the unit of this movement in spite of the 2–1–2–1 arrangement) the cedar trees which become shaped into the long-drums are lion-hearted, symbolizing nobility; and they are gonads – the germs of sound, because of their potential for the great work that drums perform, suggested in the detonator-like sound of drum thunder. In the second tercet the attributes of the materials are essential for the making of drums. The mythical context created in the poem makes it possible to accept suggestions which would be absurd in an age of science: that sound can travel faster than light, that drums telegraph messages faster than anything else because the animals which provide their skins are swifter than other animals in the forest.

The care attached to the right ritual in the collection and assemblage of the drums in the first movement suggests that the drums are not ordinary drums but the spirits of the ancestors, as is revealed in the second movement:

> Long-drums, we awake
> Like a shriek of incense,
> The unheard sullen shriek
> Of the funerary ram:
>
> (*LP* p. 46)

The mythical context is created by the fact that the poem moves at two levels, the analogical and the actual. So although an analogical relationship is established by the interpolation of the preposition 'like' which separates the awakening of the long-drums from the shrieking of incense, the two items are in fact identical in a way that they are not in reality, and the 'shriek of incense' is more than mere synaesthesia. The lines describe the invocation of the spirits of the sleeping ancestors through the ritual of drumming and animal sacrifice. The drums are linked with the ancestors by the sacrifice of the funerary ram, but they remain physically separate, until they invoke the ancestors.

Although it is the indigenous tradition that provides the means of creating meaning in the introductory sections, the basic theme is developed, as usual, with the collaboration of 'foreign' myths, as when 'a Babylonian capture' in the second section hints at the reason for the funerary rites to which the drums have been summoned. The central personage of the poem appears in the third section as Palinurus, Aeneas's helmsman, appropriate as a mythical equivalent for the sacrifice of one of the few leaders who, to use an appropriate cliché, might have steered the ship of state to safety. If the surface similarities between Okigbo's Palinurus and Eliot's Phlebas the Phoenician are mainly fortuitous, the way Okigbo develops the Palinurus theme into that of the lost leader whose incapacity renders the land waste makes this, of all Okigbo's poems, the most strongly reminiscent of *The Waste Land*. But the problem in 'Lament of the Drums' is a social or political, rather than a spiritual problem. The ritual barrenness arising from the loss of a capable leader is accounted for, in an unusually matter-of-fact manner, by making it a consequence of corruption in national leadership. As the drums of the fifth movement tell us in mythological terms,

> *The wailing is for the Great River:*
>
> Her pot-bellied watchers
> Despoil her . . .
>
> (*LP* p. 50)

This spoliation is the cause of the priestly horror with which the poet witnesses the desecration of the sanctuary earlier on in the third movement:

> *Nothing remains, only smoke after storm –*
> *Some strange Celaeno and her harpy crew,*
> *Laden with night and their belly's excrement,*
> *Profane all things with hooked feet and foul teeth –*

(LP p. 47)

It is this return to primary issues that lifts the poem beyond immediate social or political affairs, so that the ultimate emphasis in the poem is achieved through the motif of the waste land:

> *The wailing is for the fields of crop:*
>
> The drums' lament is:
> They grow not . . .
>
> *The wailing is for the fields of men:*
>
> For the barren wedded ones;
> For perishing children . . .[30]

(LP p. 50)

The theme of sick leadership with its accompanying pathetic fallacy, which together make up the waste-land myth, becomes Okigbo's means of creating art out of political events in a poem like 'Come Thunder', the most important of a group of unrevised last poems.

'Come Thunder' is much less obscure than the earlier poems, partly because of the poet's long acquaintance with the myth-making technique, but mainly because the subject itself is less complex – a public issue. There is a consistent use of the image of the war-stricken city and the stricken countryside, but the waste-land theme is present only as a motif; the central image develops as apocalyptic signs of the approaching climax of a social tragedy:

[30] This piece is a direct translation from the Sumerian song 'Lament of the Flutes for Tammuz'. Although appropriate for Okigbo's purpose, it is less an original piece of composition than other passages. The version in Donald Mackenzie's *Myths of Babylonia and Assyria* (Gresham, London, 1915), p. 88, is closer to Okigbo's adopted version than the more accessible translation in Frazer's *The Golden Bough*. Here is part of Mackenzie's version:

The wailing is for the herbs: the first lament is, they are not produced . . .
The wailing is for the perishing wedded ones; for the perishing children . .

> The drowsy heads of the pods in barren farmlands
> > witness it,
> The homesteads abandoned in this century's brush fire
> > witness it:
> The myriad eyes of deserted corn cobs in burning
> > barns witness it:
> Magic birds with the miracle of lightning flash on
> > their feathers . . .
>
> The arrows of God tremble at the gates of light,
> The drums of curfew pander to a dance of death.
>
> > > (*LP* p. 66)

The nature of the problem requires prophetic utterance, and the poet's earlier dream of the social function of poetry finds fulfilment. There is a directness and a simplicity of verbal arrangement here which contrasts with the allusiveness of the earlier poems; and the poem retains the absorbing incantatory music that is typical of Okigbo's poetry. But it also has one other effect that is peculiar to his works, the strange feeling of familiarity which one has when confronted with a literary medley. For just as 'Hurry on down' appears to come from the title of John Wain's novel, so titles and phrases from works of art become the basis of the poetic phrase in 'Come Thunder', one of the poems in 'Path of Thunder' (which is itself the title of one of Peter Abrahams's novels): Chinua Achebe's *Arrow of God*, Tchicaya U Tam'si's *Brush-fire*, C. P. Snow's *Corridors of Power*; to say nothing of Strindberg's or Holbein's *Dance of Death* or the strains from *Paradise Lost* in 'gates of light'. In short, at the end of his career Okigbo was like the dog's mouth, never at rest; a restless reader and tireless assimilator of disparate experiences, whom we already glimpse at the beginning, with the difference that in the development of his craft he has tempered the poet's aristocratic disdain for an audience without lowering his standard of performance. The poet's plastic energy has fused the phrases into his poetic system, so that they don't stand out as 'borrowings' or what one critic calls 'blatant liftings'.[31] Instead borrowing becomes usage, and blatant lifting becomes the exploitation of material from an accumulating store of individual contributions to language, for language is after all communal property.

There is a view that Eliot never had any beneficial effect on a budding poet. This depends on whether the poet makes the literary fragments sufficiently malleable for construction work or whether he remains a collector of literary fragments:

[31] O. R. Dathorne, 'Ritual and Ceremony in Okigbo's Poetry', *Journal of Commonwealth Literature*, no. 5, July 1968, p. 81.

Banks of reed.
Mountains of broken bottles.

& the mortar is not yet dry . . .

(*Limits* III; *LP* p. 25)

Eliot himself argued that the young poet who hopes to mature should begin
his career by modelling his work on that of a poet most suited to his situation
and temperament. Okigbo found this model in Eliot, who originally made
the synthesis between the two main traditions possible for him. But while
retaining the method Okigbo moved beyond the direct influence of his model.
At the end of his career the oral tradition was already speaking with a stronger
voice. One other achievement was the greater clarity and conciseness of the
revised versions. For example, in 'Siren Limits' IV the periphrasis of 'No
shield is lead plate against you' in the original version gives way to the simpler
more direct 'No shield is proof against her' of the final version (*LP* p. 27).

One limitation of Okigbo's work has been the very personal nature of his
approach to poetry. Okigbo himself was aware of this limitation, for his chief
ambition was to attain the type of impersonal or dramatic poetry described
by Eliot in 'The Three Voices of Poetry' (1953) as 'the voice of the poet . .
when he is saying, not what he would say in his own person but only what
he can say *within the limits* of one imaginary character addressing another
imaginary character'[32] (italics mine). 'Silences' and 'Distances' are dramatic
in this sense. The value of this kind of poetry is to help create an internal
logic for the poem. The derivativeness of 'Lament of the Drums' does not
matter because it has enough of this internal coherence. Okigbo's method is
often elliptical. Ellipsis can be an invitation to conjecture and deduction, and
a poet's notes – which should not be part of the poem – may invite a probing
for biographical meanings; dramatic poetry can help check such an approach.
But Okigbo often negates his effort at impersonality by too often coming
into the drama in his own person as poet. In *Limits* X a blind dog howls at
his godmother, Eunice, who is singing a lullaby somewhere back in the poet's
childhood (*LP* p. 32). The possessive pronoun refers to the poet here, not
the dog. The poet's notes point to the childhood background of the poem,
thus suggesting that a range of personal experience not open to the reader
remains within the closed circle of the poet's world. But although the poems
suffer from a too-romantic concern with the poet as hero, it is in the mastery
of sound and the sense of structure that Okigbo's art triumphs.

[32] T. S. Eliot, *On Poetry and Poets* (Faber, London, 1957), p. 89.

7 J.-J. Rabéarivelo:
A Poet before Négritude

▼▼▼▼▼▼▼▼▼▼▼▼▼▼▼▼▼▼▼▼▼▼▼▼▼▼▼▼▼▼▼▼

CLIVE WAKE

RABÉARIVELO's poetry provides a corrective to the view that francophone African poetry developed exclusively from the *négritude* poets. At the same time it provides an interesting comparison with some of the English-speaking poets who developed their poetry without becoming 'exiles'. Although African and Malagasy literature in French came into being essentially after the Second World War, the seeds of the literary renaissance in the French-speaking African colonies were sown by Senghor and others in the 'thirties in Paris, even if publication had to wait on the whole until after the war. Poets like Senghor and Tchicaya U Tam'si have made substantial and important contributions and David Diop has had a great influence on the new tradition of protest poetry. While seeking to give their work an African basis, the poets have drawn freely and with profit on the mainline French poetic movements. Yet, well before this movement got under way, the Malagasy poet Rabéarivelo, in the comparative isolation of the Madagascar of his day, had published a number of volumes of poetry of great interest and considerable quality. Although born only five years before Senghor, his short life was over in 1937 before Senghor's star had begun to rise. His poetry, like that of his successors, is a product of the colonial situation, and it is interesting to see how he has treated the same themes, but without the admixture of ideology, to be taken up later. While not essential to an understanding and appreciation of the poetry, knowledge of Rabéarivelo's personal circumstances within the colonial context provides a clearer perspective on his achievement. His earliest rhyming poetry owed much to nineteenth-century poets such as Baudelaire and the early Mallarmé. He read the minor French poets of his own generation, but was later attracted to the work of Jules Supervielle, a 'loner' (but an important one) whose poetry had an affinity with the mainline Surrealists. With his discovery of Supervielle, Rabéarivelo abandoned the use of rhyme for the twentieth-century practice of free verse. This in turn enabled him to incorporate in his mature poetry the techniques and themes of the traditional Malagasy *hain-teny* poetry. He carried this 'symbiosis' (to use Senghor's term) to a high level of mastery, while at the same time exploiting, in a particularly moving way, one of the most prevalent themes of the twentieth century – the individual's sense of imprisonment and deprivation in an alien world.

Clive Wake is a specialist in French literature. He taught in Rhodesia, and with John Reed produced one of the first and most successful introductions to modern African poetry. He is well known for his studies of French African literature. He is now a senior lecturer at the University of Lent, Canterbury, England.

By the mid-1930s, Léopold Sédar Senghor, Aimé Césaire and other young Caribbean and African intellectuals had launched the concept of *négritude* and had begun their involvement in the anti-colonialist movement which was to lead to the flowering of a new, black literature in French in the post-war period. Meanwhile, in Madagascar, a young poet, Jean-Joseph Rabéari-velo, was writing some of the most outstanding poetry in French of the decade, but, driven by the despair brought on by his feeling of isolation in an oppressive and unsympathetic colonial atmosphere, unable to break out of his intellectual prison, he committed suicide in 1937, at the age of thirty-six. Only four years older than Senghor, had he lived he would have undoubtedly grown in stature as a poet after the war and, who knows, overshadowed the men who are now the acknowledged *doyens* of modern African poetry in French. Instead, we are obliged to consider Rabéarivelo as a poet of the pre-war, pre-independence period, the victim of colonialism, while Senghor and Césaire represent the victory of the post-war struggle against the stifling effect of colonialism and the white man's culture. They could see the light at the end of the tunnel, whereas Rabéarivelo could not, and it is this factor which, in each case, underlies and differentiates the mood of their poetry. This, too, probably explains why Rabéarivelo has suffered from relative neglect, a poet a little *en marge* of the literature of the day. But he is important, being the only poet in French Africa who has expressed through the medium of the creative sensibility what it was like to endure the full brunt of colonialism.

Some of his work has been translated, a few of his poems are usually included in anthologies of African poetry;[1] but he is only rarely mentioned in critical studies of contemporary African literature, and, apart from one or

[1] Here is a complete bibliography of Rabéarivelo's poetry. *La coupe de cendres* (Pitot, 1924); *Sylves* (Imprimerie de l'Imerina, 1927); *Volumes* (Imprimene de l'Imerina, 1928); *Presque-Songes* (Vidalie, 1934); *Traduit de la Nuit* (Mirages, Tunis 1935); *Chants pour Abéone* (H. Vidalie 1937); *Vieilles Chansons des Pays*

two studies in French – one thinks mainly of Robert Boudry's helpful, but short study, *J.-J. Rabéarivelo et la Mort*, published in 1958[2] – he has received no close attention from the critics, especially as a poet. Robert Boudry's book, valuable as it is, is concerned primarily with Rabéarivelo the man and victim of colonialism, and not to any significant extent with his poetry. Even in Madagascar, one wonders whether sufficient efforts have been made to preserve his memory and, what is more important, to ensure the survival of his work. His name has been given to a *lycée* in Antananarivo, it is true, and a new edition of his later and most important poetry was published in 1960,[3] but the national library does not possess copies of all his work, and the whereabouts and fate of his unpublished manuscripts are uncertain.[4] His tomb, in the family village of Ambatofotsy, a few miles outside Antananarivo, was so overgrown with tropical bushes when I visited it in 1963 that it was almost impossible to get near it.

Robert Boudry shows quite convincingly how deeply Rabéarivelo's sensibility was marked by his own experience of the colonial situation, producing in the poet's personality the distortion that was to condition the themes of his poetry. The colonizer's experience of colonialism is totally unlike that of the colonized individual, and it is therefore difficult for him to appreciate the effect it has on the latter. The nearest the modern Western European has come to this experience was the Nazi occupation of the last war, but even this is not an exact parallel because the occupation did not last long enough to affect too deeply the mentality of the people in the occupied countries. In any case, they knew, or believed, that they would sooner or later drive the occupier out. This belief in the eventual expulsion of the occupier was firmly held by the young African and Caribbean intellectuals living in Paris in the 'thirties, but they were inspired and encouraged by the cosmopolitan atmosphere in which they lived and by the sympathy they received from influential French intellectuals and politicians working at the heart of the French power

---

[2] R. Boudry: *J.-J. Rabéarivelo et la Mort* (Présence Africaine, 1958).

[3] J.-J. Rabéarivelo: *Poèmes-Presque-Songes, Traduit de la Nuit* (Les Amis de Rabéarivelo, Antananarivo 1960), abbreviated in this essay to PS/TN.

[4] These include, chiefly, his diaries, which he called his *Calepins bleus*.

d'Imerina (Imprimerie Officielle, 1939); *Des Stances oubliées* (Liva, 1959). Unless otherwise stated, the place of publication is Antananarivo. There is only one volume of translations devoted to Rabéarivelo's poetry alone: *24 Poems*, translated by Gerald Moore and Ulli Beier (Mbari, Ibadan 1962). Several poems in translation are included in *Modern Poetry from Africa*, edited by Gerald Moore and Ulli Beier (Penguin, 1963) and in *A Book of African Verse*, edited by John Reed and Clive Wake (Heinemann, 1964). There is a generous selection of Rabéarivelo's poems in the original French in *An Anthology of African and Malagasy Poetry in French*, edited by Clive Wake (Oxford University Press, 1965).

structure. Rabéarivelo certainly enjoyed the encouragement of a few enlightened but not very influential Frenchmen living in Madagascar, but the isolation of the island and its distance from Europe meant, on the one hand, a more autocratic and short-sighted colonial administration, and, on the other, a more tenuous thread of sympathy between French intellectuals in Paris and the lonely Malagasy poet. This sense of isolation is everywhere present in Rabéarivelo's work, as, for example, in the image of the solitary bull trapped in the middle of the vast, empty space around him. Rabéarivelo longed to visit France, but was never able to realize his ambition. Something of his distress can be seen in the voluminous correspondence he maintained, ever hopefully, with fellow writers in France and in other parts of the world. But few of them could really sense the anguish of his appeals to them, or if they did, they must have felt unable to do anything about it. In one of his later poems, entitled 'Imprimés' (from *Presque-Songes*), he meditates on his longing to break free from his island prison and to realize his 'désir d'errer/jusqu'au bout du monde'.

Joseph-Casimir Rabéarivelo (he later changed his first names to Jean-Joseph) was born on 4 March 1901 in Antananarivo. He was the only child of a devoted mother. He was educated at Catholic mission schools, but when he left school, his knowledge of French was still far from perfect. One of the most remarkable features of his career was the way in which he set out to master French so completely as to finally emerge as a poet with an extraordinary sense of French language, style and versification. He was a voracious reader, so that, without advanced formal instruction, he turned himself into a highly cultured Malagasy Frenchman, and in this respect resembles Senghor. Earning his living in a colonial society which provided very few openings for the indigenous people, however well-read, was a problem throughout Rabéarivelo's life, and for long periods he was without work. Eventually, in 1923 or 1924, he obtained a post as proof-reader at the Imprimerie de l'Imerina, where he remained until his death. He married in 1926, and fathered five children. Like Victor Hugo, he was particularly devoted to one of his four daughters and, again like Victor Hugo in similar circumstances, he was shattered when she died suddenly in 1933. There can be no doubt that her loss had a profound effect on his poetry, which, round about this time, took on a completely different orientation. In 1937 he had high hopes of being chosen to represent Madagascar at the *Exposition Universelle* in Paris. Unfortunately, the short-sighted colonial authorities decided that a group of basket-weavers would be more representative of the island's culture, and on 22 June 1937, Rabéarivelo, overcome by his disappointment, took poison.

The decision not to send the poet to Paris was certainly the immediate cause of his suicide, but it could only be the climax of a lifetime of despair and frustration. In addition, Rabéarivelo's extremely introspective and highly touchy personality made him one of those men for whom life is a constant burden. Robert Boudry, who was a friend of the poet, lays great stress on this factor.

> Très émotif, susceptible et même ombrageux, il attachait une importance extrême à de petits détails, surtout quand ils intéressaient son amour-propre . . . Il aimait qu'on le loue à sa valeur et souffrait profondément de sa situation inférieure. L'humiliation lui faisait mal. Jalousement indépendant, avide de jouissances, sensuel à l'excès, intellectualisé en diable, ce bout d'homme possédait une vitalité extraordinaire mais ne ménageais guère sa santé.[5]

His introspection and his pride, naturally enough, intensified his isolation. He sought escape in a couple of romanticized love affairs and, worse still, in drink, drugs and gambling. Poor enough as he was, his excesses worsened his own misery and that of his family. One can only admire his wife Mary for standing loyally by him through it all, but, being a simple and uncomplicated woman, there was little she could do to help him on the intellectual or emotional levels.

A striking feature of Antananarivo in the 'twenties and 'thirties was the flourishing literary atmosphere, parochial necessarily, but alive and, for Rabéarivelo, able to provide a minimum of intellectual stimulus.[6] Two leading French poets of the period spent a certain amount of time in Madagascar in the French colonial service. They were Jean Paulhan, whose book *Les Fleurs de Tarbes* was an important contribution to French poetic theory in its day, and Pierre Camo, whose friendship and encouragement were of immense significance to Rabéarivelo's poetic development. Jean Paulhan's book on the Malagasy popular poetry of the *hain-teny* is still invaluable both as a study and because of the translations it contains.[7] The leading Malagasy and expatriate poets of the day contributed to two important literary magazines. The first of these was Pierre Camo's *18° Latitude Sud*, which ran from 1923 to 1927. Its two series comprised a total of twenty-two numbers. Much of Rabéarivelo's early poetry was first published in *18° Latitude Sud* and his first volumes of poems were sympathetically reviewed by Pierre Camo. The second of these magazines was named *Capricorne*; it was jointly edited by Rabéarivelo and another Malagasy poet of mixed descent, R.-J. Allain. There were six numbers, between October 1930 and March 1931 –

[5] Boudry, op. cit., p. 36.
[6] For a bibliographical account of the Malagasy literary scene before the war, see: C. Wake and J. Reed: 'Modern Malagasy Literature in French' (*Books Abroad*, Winter, 1964).
[7] J. Paulhan: *Les Hain-Tenys* (Gallimard, Paris, 1939). First published in 1913.

not a very long life, but long enough to include the publication of many new poems by Rabéarivelo. Perhaps the most interesting feature of this magazine, however, was the *Notes* – reviews and commentary on new books of poetry written by Rabéarivelo, under the romantic pseudonym of A. Valmond. They even include a review by the poet of one of his own volumes, of which he was pleased to make the following comment: 'et ce Rabéarivelo qui commence enfin à sortir de son indifférence et à s'occuper de sa gloire. Mais nous y reviendrons. En attendant, béni soit qui l'y a décidé'.[8] These articles provide some helpful information about the poet's own tastes in modern poetry at the time.

All this serves to illustrate the fact that Rabéarivelo lived in an intense atmosphere of poetry and literature, which explains the obsession everywhere in his work with the notion of the poet and of poetry. As Boudry writes, 'la littérature est devenue pour lui "la nourriture", la vraie, l'essentielle'.[9] Poetry, more than drugs and drink, represented for him the way out of his prison, but it could never be more than a dream, never the reality.

Rabéarivelo's early poetry is strikingly different from his later work (the turning point occurring in the early 'thirties). His first three volumes of poems are strongly, and very obviously, influenced by the French poets he currently admired. In his review of *Sylves* (1927), Pierre Camo observed:

> Enfin nous avons les *Sylves* du poète malgache J.-J. Rabéarivelo, dont les premières pièces que gâtent des imitations maladroites, sont rachetées par les dernières, dites *Poèmes d'Iarive*, d'inspiration et de facture plus vraies et plus réussies parce qu'issues de source plus personnelle et plus terrienne.[10]

Yet, seen against his later poems, even those Pierre Camo here admires seem imitative and immature. References in the poems of this period, dedications, and, above all, specific comments in his *Notes* for *Capricorne* all give us a clear enough indication of his literary interests at the time. The main influence is obviously that of Baudelaire and Mallarmé; this is evident both from the vocabulary and the imagery (he has, for example, a predilection for the *azur* of the early Mallarmé) and from the tone of his verse. The contemporary poets he admired were not, as one might have expected, the *avant-garde* Surrealists, but now largely forgotten minor poets such as Derème, Vérane, Ormoy, Chabaneix and Fagus, whom he calls 'les poètes les plus délicieux et les plus parfaits de leur génération . . . la succession de Moréas et de Toulet';[11] in other words, the inheritors of the by-then outmoded

---

[8] *Capricorne*, no. 3, décembre 1930, p. 141.

[9] Boudry, op. cit., p. 47.

[10] *18° Latitude Sud*, nouvelle série, no. 10, 23 novembre 1927, p. 20.

[11] *Capricorne*, no. 4, janvier 1931.

Symbolists. Had Rabéarivelo remained devoted to their wistful melancholy (which so suited his own temperament), to their conventional versification and to their general lack of inspiration or relevance to their own age, he would never have developed into the truly original poet he eventually became. All the same, they served a useful purpose in providing him with his apprenticeship in French prosody, without which he might not have been able to move over to his final style with so much assurance.

Curiously enough it is in this early poetry that Rabéarivelo seems closest to the poets of *négritude*, not so much in style as in his explicit statement of the tension between his acquired French culture and his native Malagasy culture. Like Senghor – but nearly ten years earlier than he – Rabéarivelo expresses what virtually amounts to a preference for the borrowed culture, while lamenting the decline and the increasing inaccessibility of his Malagasy culture. He experiences what he refers to, in one of these poems, as the 'exil au sol natal'.[12] Less effectively than Senghor at this stage, he laments his inability to reconcile the two cultures.

> Qui donc me donnera de pouvoir fiancer
> l'esprit de mes aïeux à ma langue adoptive,
> et mon coeur naturel, calme et fier au penser
> pervers et sombre de l'Europe maladive.
>
> (*Volumes*, p. xxxiv)

He is torn between 'la piété qu'on doit aux morts que l'on oublie/et mon ferme désir de vivre en le génie/de l'Emyrne qui meurt' (*Volumes*, p. lxviii) and 'l'Europe froide où va le meilleur de toi-même' (*Volumes*, p. xlii), but one cannot help suspecting that this is more of a dramatic attitude than a deeply rooted tension (again reminiscent of Senghor), for he would quite clearly prefer, at this stage of his life, to achieve some kind of identification with Europe.

> Si le monde a changé, si ma voix elle-même
> renonce à ta musique, ô parler ancestral,
> et que, sous le sillon du clair Navire Austral,
> elle chante selon une langue que j'aime,
>
> le sang héréditaire et l'âme de mes morts,
> sève toujours vivante en l'arbre qui décline,
> m'aiment à jamais comme, sur la colline,
> le vent du sud qui souffle au coeur des ficus tors;

---

[12] *Sylves, Sonnets et Poèmes d'Iarive*, 2, p. lxviii.

> et je te suis semblable, ô beau rosier de France
> qui, fleurissant au flanc d'un tombeau de chez nous,
> fiances aux églantiers au feuillage roux
> la pureté perdu, hélas, de ton essence!
>
> > (*Volumes*, 'Coeur et Ciel d'Iarive',
> > no. 4, p. xciii)

In another poem he notes what is for the Malagasy a third facet of this tension, the fact that the people of Madagascar's high plateau are descended from Polynesian ancestors.

> O mon coeur amoureux de trois zones du monde:
> l'Europe froide où va le meilleur de toi-même,
> l'Inde au ciel aussi rose et bleu que ton poème,
> et l'Afrique, ta source limpide et profonde,
>
> nul arbre n'a plongé ses vivaces racines
> dans le sol différent de trois vergers contraires!
> Fixe ton choix sur l'une ou l'autre de ces terres,
> bien que toutes, dis-tu, gardent tes origines!
>
> > (*Volumes*, 'Coeur et Ciel d'Iarive',
> > no. 3, p. xcii)

There is a rhetorical quality about this early poetry which is the product of the poet's self-conscious adoption of a stance, and the language of other men which he uses to express it. Occasionally there are signs of his later, mature manner, as, for example, his habit of addressing himself ('tu'), as if his poetry were a dialogue between two sides of himself. It indicates its essential introspection. All his poetry reflects a deep fascination with nature, but the difference in the use he makes of it in the early and later poetry could not be more fundamental. Trees already obsess him in his early poetry, but, whereas in the later poetry it is the tree unspecified that is for him a place (much like Yves Bonnefoy's 'vrai lieu' or 'patrie', in fact), in this early poetry trees are named and act merely as symbols. Several of the poems in *Volumes* are about trees, both indigenous and imported, and on them he bases his meditation on the 'exil au sol natal' theme. A typical example is the poem entitled 'Filao'.

> Filao, filao, frère de ma tristesse,
> qui nous viens d'un pays lointain et maritime,
> le roi imérinien a-t-il pour ta sveltesse
> l'élément favorable à sa nature intime?

Tu sembles regretter les danses sur la plage
des filles de la mer, de la brise et du sable,
et tu revis en songe un matin sans orage
glorieux et fier de ta sève intarissable.

Maintenant que l'exil fait craquer ton écorce,
l'élan de tes rejets défaillants et sans force
ne dédie aux oiseaux qu'un reposoir sans ombre,

tel mon chant qui serait une oeuvre folle et vaine
si, né selon un rhythme étranger et son nombre,
il vivait du sang qui coule dans mes veines!

(*Volumes, Arbres 9*, p. lxxiii)

Some of the poems are about specifically Malagasy or African trees – 'Aviavy', 'Zahana', 'Hasina', 'Manguier', 'Bougainvillea', 'Amontana' – while others are foreign – 'Laurier', 'Lilas', 'Oranger'.

I have deliberately quoted fairly liberally from these early poems because they are not generally accessible. It is virtually impossible to find copies of the early volumes outside Madagascar. It would, indeed, be a great service to Malagasy literature, and to the whole of contemporary African literature, if a Malagasy scholar could be found to edit an edition of Rabéarivelo's complete works, and if the Malagasy government were to subsidize such a venture. Otherwise the time may not be far off when it will be impossible to trace certain of the poet's works. Apart from work already published, there is a certain amount of unpublished material, including his diary, the *Calepins bleus* as he called it, parts of which are quoted by Robert Boudry in his book.

Rabéarivelo's early poetry is fairly obvious; there is little depth of feeling in it, and what feeling there is is mainly rhetorical. Neither the texture of the poetry nor its themes are particularly subtle or complex. The poet uses a borrowed literary language and style to express an experience of which he is not yet himself deeply conscious. However, between the publication of *Volumes* in 1928 and *Presque-Songes* in 1934, Rabéarivelo's poetic sensibility underwent a profound transformation, and with it the quality and style of his poetry. During this period he abandoned the conventional metres, fixed-form poems, and borrowed language of his early poetry, substituting for them a masterly use of free verse and a totally new approach to imagery. Most significant of all, he was, suddenly (or so it seems), in possession of a subtly complex, rich and vital personal poetic world, completely coherent and sure of itself. The explicitly stated tensions of his cultural exile gave way to the more complex insights of the poet's intuitive perception of himself and of his place in the world.

How can one explain this transformation? It was probably due to the merging of several factors at a time when, having reached the maturity of his thirtieth birthday, he acquired a deeper, more conscious insight into himself and the world around him. This was probably the crucial reason for the change, the catalysing factor, but there were other, external factors which no doubt played their part. It seems likely, for instance, that Pierre Camo encouraged Rabéarivelo to bring his poetry more into line with the more predominant and important trends in contemporary French poetry; namely, the poetry of the Surrealists and related poets, whose poetry was characterized by the use of free verse and a new attitude to the image, the 'stupéfiant image', as Aragon called it. It is almost certain that, around 1930, Rabéarivelo discovered the poetry of Jules Supervielle, not himself a Surrealist but nevertheless representative of the new trends in French poetry. To some extent the attraction for the Malagasy poet may have been Supervielle's own colonial origins, but at a more significant level, it represented a marriage of similar minds which sparked off Rabéarivelo's realization of what he really wanted to do in his poetry. There is a clear similarity between Supervielle's use of free verse and the style adopted by Rabéarivelo in *Presque-Songes*. Several poems in *Gravitations*, which Supervielle published in 1925, are distinctly reminiscent of Rabéarivelo's *Presque-Songes* and *Traduit de la Nuit*. Such, for example, is Supervielle's poem entitled 'Echanges':

> Dans la flaque du petit jour
> Ont bu les longs oiseaux nocturnes
> Jusqu'à tomber morts alentour
> Au dernier soupir de la lune.
>
> Voici les flamants de l'aurore
> Qui font leur nid dans la lumière
> Avec la soie de l'horizon
> Et le vent doré de leurs ailes.[13]

At the head of the first poem of *Traduit de la Nuit* (1935), there are four lines from Supervielle's poem 'Vivre', which give us our chief clue to this influence and to the origins not only of much of Rabéarivelo's new imagery, but also of his new vocabulary. The four lines quoted by Rabéarivelo are the opening of the poem:

> Pour avoir mis le pied
> Sur le coeur de la nuit

---

[13] J. Supervielle: *Gravitations* (Gallimard, Collection *Poésie*, Paris 1966), p. 159. Cf. also 'Tiges', p. 124 of the same edition.

> Je suis un homme pris
> Dans les rets étoilés.

Because of the light they shed on Rabéarivelo's new style, it may be worth quoting the rest of Supervielle's poem:

> J'ignore le repos
> Que connaissent les hommes
> Et même mon sommeil
> Est dévoré de ciel.
>
> Nudité de mes jours,
> On t'a crucifiée;
> Oiseau de la forêt
> Dans l'air tiède, glacés.
>
> Ah! vous tombez des arbres
> (Gravitations, p. 153)

Two of Rabéarivelo's favourite verbs, *tituber* and *chavirer*, are to be found in Supervielle's poems, but so too are the images of birds, trees, sky and stars common to both of them. The most striking similarity between the two poets, however, is their delightful sense of fantasy, the sort of fantasy which enables Supervielle to write:

> Attention! voilà l'homme qui bouge et qui regarde à droite et à gauche;
> Le voilà qui se lève et sa face crépite comme torche résineuse,
> Le voilà qui s'avance foulant les hautes herbes du ciel.
> Son ombre ne le suit plus, comme sur la Terre fatiguée,
> Et le voilà qui se mire dans la lune où il ajuste son regard,
> Et qui donne au loin les ordres dont toute sa voix est comblée.
> ('Au Creux du Monde', Gravitations, p. 190)

As with Supervielle, Rabéarivelo's fantasy is very largely associated with the night sky, and Supervielle's image of 'les rets étoilés' is used almost word for word by the Malagasy poet. Yet the final impact of their poetry is very different. There is, ultimately, a certain intellectual quality and a remoteness about Supervielle's poetry, which is quite unlike the warmer, more intuitive, more total fantasy of Rabéarivelo. Supervielle's vision, moreover, is a vaster one, embracing man's relations with the universe; it is, ultimately, a metaphysical poetry. Rabéarivelo's vision, on the other hand, remains primarily concerned with himself, and his fantasy world is an imaginative projection of his own struggles and torments. Supervielle's 'je' is a good deal less personal than Rabéarivelo's 'tu', which, by its very nature, is the expression of a deeper introspection.

The foreign influence was not, however, the only one. Perhaps at about the same time as he fell under the spell of Supervielle, Rabéarivelo came to realize the value for his own poetic creation of the translations he had been making for some years from the indigenous *hain-teny*. Versions of his translations had been published in the late 'twenties in Camo's *18° Latitude Sud*, and later in *Capricorne*. Before he died, Rabéarivelo collected his translations together, and Robert Boudry supervised their posthumous publication in 1939 under the title *Vieilles Chansons des Pays d'Imerina*. Paulhan had, of course, published his own translations a number of years earlier, but, although they are set out in verse form (whereas Rabéarivelo's are in prose), Rabéarivelo's versions are far more successful as French poems. This is essentially because Rabéarivelo has succeeded in blending the style of the Malagasy original with the French into which he translates them.

There has been a great deal of controversy about the correct definition of the *hain-teny*. Both Rabéarivelo and Flavien Ranaivo (a living Malagasy poet who writes French poems based on *hain-teny*)[14] have contested Paulhan's claim that they are love poems distilled from proverbs. They claim that the *hain-teny* are not proverbs and that they contain a wider range of themes than that of love alone. There is no place to consider this controversy in detail here, but there is no doubt that the love theme does occur in a very large number of *hain-teny*. Like African traditional poetry generally, the *hain-teny* belong to the oral tradition, and they are handed down from generation to generation, with new ones being composed all the time. They usually take the form of a dialogue between lovers, or of a speech addressed by one lover to another. When not in dialogue, the antithetical form is still present in the contrasting of two objects, aimed at illustrating a truth. This is why they often resemble proverbs. They are not always easily comprehensible to the uninitiated because they consist mostly of metaphors which resemble riddles (reminiscent of a similar love of riddles on the African continent). The foreign reader is inevitably struck by the vividness of the imagery. It may be helpful to the reader if I give one or two examples. Here is one taken from Rabéarivelo's *Vieilles Chansons*, followed by another example from Paulhan's book, on a similar theme, so as to illustrate the different methods each poet has used to render them into French. ·

[14] Ranaivo has published three volumes of verse. For examples of his work in English translation, see Reed and Wake, op. cit., and for a selection in the original French, see Wake, op. cit.

– Près de la jarre, mes paroles s'égarent; au pied du manguier, je ne laisse de m'étonner.

– Si vous êtes étonné, moi, je suis surprise! Passant devant la maison de votre femme, j'ai reçu tout à l'heure des cailloux mais ne me suis pas retournée; j'ai recu des injures, mais n'ai pas répondu. Aimez votre femme, mais moi ne m'abandonnez pas.

(*Vieilles Chansons*, no. XVII)

> Que je meuse Rainatoa
> J'ai passé devant la maison de votre mari
> Je l'ai salué, il n'a pas répondu.
> Je lui ai demandé pardon, il n'a rien dit.
> Que veut dire tout cela?
> N'ayez pas d'inquiétude.
> Je séparerai le jour d'avec la nuit
> La nuit sera à lui
> Le plein jour à vous.

(*Les Hain-Tenys*, p. 96)

Malagasy names usually say something, mostly in metaphorical form, and, unlike Paulhan, who leaves them as they are, Rabéarivelo frequently translates them, thus heightening the poetic effect of his version.

> – Un seul coup de tonnerre dans l'Ankaratra, et
> les orchidées d'Anjafy fleurissent, et pleure et pleure
> la Fille-de-l'oiseau-bleu, et ricane et ricane
> Celui-qui-ne-craint-pas-le-châtiment-du-mal!

(*Vieilles Chansons*, no. XXVIII)

The influence of the *hain-teny* is sometimes quite obvious in the poems of *Presque-Songes* and *Traduit de la Nuit*. Examples are the three 'Naissance du Jour' poems and 'Flûtistes', where the direct address and the use of parallel action and antithesis are typical of the *hain-teny*. These four poems are considered to be among Rabéarivelo's finest, and are the most frequently represented in anthologies of African poetry. 'Fruits' is an excellent example of the way Rabéarivelo has almost exactly transposed the structure of the *hain-teny* into a modern poem in French.

> Tu peux choisir
>   entre les fruits de la saison parfumée;
>   mais voici ce que je te propose:

deux mangues dodues
où tu pourras têter le soleil qui s'y est fondu.
Que prendras-tu?
Est-ce celle-ci qui est aussi double et ferme
que des seins de jeunes filles,
et qui est acide?
Ou celle-ci qui est pulpeuse et douce comme un gâteau de miel?
L'une ne sera que violentes délices,
mais n'aura pas de postérité,
et sera étouffée par les herbes.
L'autre,
source jaillissant de rocher
rafraîchira ta gorge
puis deviendra voûte bruissante dans ta cour,
et ceux qui viendront y cueilleront des éclats de soleil.

                                                    (P S/TN p. 38)

Sometimes the influence of the *hain-teny* is only partially present, as, for example, in Rabéarivelo's frequent use of rhetorical interrogation. It is also possible to recognize in the dialogue of the *hain-teny*, as illustrated in the poem just quoted, the origin of Rabéarivelo's practice of dialoguing with himself, with the exception that Rabéarivelo's dialogue is introverted, whereas that of the *hain-teny* is not. The influence of the *hain-teny* does, however, go deeper than technical practice, and is closely associated with the poet's attainment of maturity as an artist. A distinctive feature of the traditional *hain-teny* is an air of remoteness, almost of detachment, which has the effect of apparently depriving the poems of all emotive force. This characteristic seems to have been carried over by Rabéarivelo into his own mature poetry, where the deeply subjective and emotive themes acquire an extraordinary air of detachment, as if to purify them. The early poetry was rhetorically emotional, and therefore ineffective. The later poetry really expresses the poet's feelings directly, but does so with a control that saves them from falling into romantic self-pity and sentimentality. The detachment so typical of the *hain-teny* is probably to a large extent due to the fact that they are popular poems, known to and repeated by everyone in the community. It must in some measure at least derive from the great use of metaphor and symbol, which helps to objectify the poet's emotion, and it is this practice which Rabéarivelo has carried over into his own poetry. His poetry is not intended for popular enjoyment, even though it draws on a popular verse-form for some of its inspiration. The terrain of the *hain-teny* is the village and the market-place; Rabéarivelo's world is contained within the secret of his own heart. As he himself writes:

Il y aura un jour, un jeune poète
qui réalisera ton voeu impossible
pour avoir connu tes livres
rares comme les fleurs souterraines,
tes livres écrits pour cent amis,
et non pour un, et non pour mille.

(PS/TN p. 108)

In his mature poetry, Rabéarivelo uses his imagery in a way reminiscent of the contemporary Surrealists, especially Eluard, another poet fascinated by the 'paysage intérieur'. Like Rabéarivelo, Eluard had a great predilection for nature imagery or, more specifically, for the image of the landscape. The image is always, or nearly always, the centre of the poem. The object which provides the first element in the metaphor, the reality, is not mentioned. Only the image survives. The result is that the poem, through its imagery, is at one extra remove from the poet himself, since the element directly linking it with the poet is omitted. This creates a strangely remote, altogether independent world. Rabéarivelo draws nearly all his imagery from nature but, although his outlook is largely that of the romantic – self-centred, introspective – they are not affective images but nearer to objective symbols. The important thing about his nature imagery is that it is drawn entirely from his native Malagasy landscapes, and it is therefore thoroughly real to his imagination. Indeed, on the visual level alone, his imagery gives the reader a remarkably vivid impression of the Malagasy countryside. He has a marvellous eye for the detail that captures the essence of what he is describing, as in this image of a spider:

Lente
comme une vache boiteuse
ou comme un taureau puissant
aux quatre jarrets coupés,
une grosse araignée noire sort de la terre
et grimpe sur les murs
puis s'arc-boute péniblement au-dessus des arbres,

Jette des fils qu'emporte le vent,
tisse une toile qui touche au ciel,
et tend des rets à travers l'azur.

(PS/TN p. 112)

What poet has better captured the impression made on the eye of the near object up against the much greater but distant background? And one marvels at the vivid evocation of the spider's clumsy movements.

Rabéarivelo's nature imagery is drawn from three areas: firstly, the night and the day, with the moon, the sun, the stars, the dawn and so on, seen both temporally and spatially; secondly, the landscape itself, with its prairies and deserts, inhabited by cattle, swept by the wind and enclosed by the horizon; thirdly, forests, trees, birds and flowing water (such as springs and rivers). These three areas of imagery are frequently kept distinct from one another, but they are also intermingled, producing the fantasy effect which is such a striking feature of Rabéarivelo's poetry. This applies particularly to the intermingling of the first and second groups, so that cattle are seen as grazing on the prairies of the night sky – 'se dispersent les troupeaux stell-aires,/puis rentrent dans leur parcage inconnu' (PS/TN p. 47), or the sky is seen as part of the landscape – 'les clairs de lune bondissant dans les forêts' (PS/TN p. 49).

> Les pâtres sont là-bas, ils escaladent le ciel.
> Il y a des herbes nouvelles sous leurs pas,
> il y a des fruits irréels autour d'eux,
> et des sources cachées qu'ils cherchent.
>
> (PS/TN p. 107)

This fantasy, which is more often than not achieved by the simple device of personification, is largely responsible for the surrealist effect of much of Rabéarivelo's imagery: 'je pourrai cueillir les matins en fleurs au bout de la tige brisée des soirs' (PS/TN p. 55). One of the most beautiful poems Rabéarivelo wrote illustrates this effect – 'Naissance du Jour':

> Avez-vous déjà vu l'aube aller en maraude
>   au verger de la nuit?
>   La voici qui en revient
>   par les sentes de l'Est
>   envahies des glaïeuls en fleurs:
>   elle est tout entière maculée de lait
>   comme ces enfants élevés jadis par des génisses;
>   ses mains qui portent une torche
>   sont noires et bleues comme des lèvres de fille
>   mâchant des mûres.
>
> S'échappent un à un et la précèdent
>   les oiseaux qu'elle a pris au piège.
>
> (PS/TN p. 42)

This poem recalls Rimbaud's poem to the dawn, 'Aube' (*Les Illuminations*). Like Rimbaud's, too, Rabéarivelo's poetry and imagery are very strongly characterized by a delicate, perceptive and loving sense of wonder. Indeed, Rabéarivelo was a kind of Malagasy Rimbaud. Both poets subjected themselves to a 'dérèglement de tous les sens' – although Rabéarivelo's was not 'raisonné' as Rimbaud's was – in search of an absolute. Yet, when it is brought down to its essentials, one discovers a child in quest of love and security. The sense of fantasy and wonder, the delight and delicacy of touch, the freshness and joy of Rabéarivelo's mature poetry reflect the childlike imagination discovering the world as it were for the first time, and marvelling at its beauty. The child, symbol of the poet, is the only human being who is to be found in Rabéarivelo's poetic world, apart from the poet himself and occasional references to his family or to poets he admired. It is a child aware of suffering and of the need to protect his secret from the world.

> Je sais un enfant,
>   prince encore au royaume de Dieu,
>   qui voudrait ajouter :
>   'Et le Sort, ayant eu pitié de ces lépreuses,
>   leur a dit de planter des fleurs
>   et de garder des sources
>   loin des hommes cruels.'
>
> ('Cactus', PS/TN p. 50)

Rabéarivelo's poetic universe is the world of the child for another reason, just as it was in Rimbaud's poetry. The world he evokes in his poetry is an attempt to recreate the innocence and purity of childhood, and, as with the romantics, he sees the poetic function as the means, not merely the symbol, of realizing this desire. Rabéarivelo's poetry is dominated by two basic images: the image of the descent into the lost world, and the image of the return to reality.

> Sentir, croire que des racines te poussent aux pieds
> et courent et se tordent comme des serpents assoiffés
> vers quelque source souterraine,
> ou se rivent dans le sable
> et déjà t'unissent à lui, toi, ô vivant,
> arbre inconnu, arbre non identifié,
> Qui élabores des fruits que tu cueilleras toi-même.
>
> (PS/TN p. 99)

It is essentially a descent into the subconscious world of the self in search of a lost secret. It is an unknown, unexplored world, 'immatériel', for him alone. He penetrates, in his poetry, as in a dream, deep into the night sky or into the forest, bush or tree, 'en quête d'un rêve au bout du monde' (PS/TN p. 117), hoping to trap the bird which is the symbol of the object of his quest and return with it to reality. Rabéarivelo's 'Bateau Ivre' is a long poem entitled 'Haute Futaie', from which I quote the first three stanzas.

> Je ne viens pas pour saccager les fruits
>   que tu tends, sur tes cimes inaccessibles,
>   au peuple des étoiles et à la tribu des vents,
>   non plus pour arracher tes fleurs que je n'ai jamais vues,
>   dans le but de m'en vêtir ou d'en cacher quelque honte que j'ignore,
>   moi, l'enfant des collines arides.
>
> Mais je me suis soudain souvenu dans mon dernier sommeil
>   qu'était toujours amarrée avec les lianes de la nuit
>   la vieille pirogue des fables
>   qui tous les jours faisait passer mon enfance
>   des rives du soir aux rives du matin,
>   du cap de la lune au cap du soleil.
>
> Je l'ai ramée, et me voici en ton coeur, ô montagne végétale!
>   Me voici venu pour interroger ton silence absolu,
>   pour chercher le lieu où les vents éclosent
>   avant d'ouvrir des ailes trouées chez nous –
>   trouées par le filet immense des déserts
>   et par les pièges des villes habitées.
>
> > (PS/TN p. 53)

This poem contains all the constituents of Rabéarivelo's journey. The imagery may vary within the limits of the three areas already mentioned, but the essentials are always the same. There is always great emphasis on the need to keep it secret:

> Scelle fortement tes lèvres afin que n'en sorte
>   aucune des choses que tu voies,
>   mais que ne voient pas les autres!
>
> > ('Fièvre des Iles', PS/TN p. 37)

Always, too, it takes place as if in a dream, the realm *par excellence* of the subconscious self, where he is carried by 'une minuscule pirogue à balancier/ achetée dans une île lointaine que le rêve seul habite' (PS/TN, p. 55). Hence the titles *Presque-Songes* and *Traduit de la Nuit*.

The poet seeks the still, quiet centre where he will be safe. It is the world of those childhood legends and fables that once stimulated his imagination and carried him beyond mean reality. If one may be allowed to refer to it in terms of the now hackneyed Freudian notion, it is a return to the safety of the night of the maternal womb, in search of his origins, of the 'grotte' from which he has come. Life is a kind of exile from the night. There is a constant tension, however, between the night, the heart of which he rarely, if ever attains, and the need to return to the light of day, of reality. Dawn always comes to destroy the illusion: 'les coqs de tous les villages/ . . . auront vaincu et dispersé/ceux qui chantent dans les rêves/et qui se nourrissent d'astres' (PS/TN p. 94). Day is the great enemy of night, come to pillage and lay it waste. Like the poet Eluard, Rabéarivelo contrasts night and day, but whereas for Eluard day is good and night is bad, the symbolism is the reverse for Rabéarivelo. He contrasts, too, the prairie and the desert, the hidden abundance of the underground spring with the dry surface of the desert. These are not new symbols, but they are so much part of the poet's own everyday existence that they acquire a new vitality. The core of this imagery is the idea of birth and revelation, and so, too, images of fecundity abound – the winds scatter the seeds and the plants germinate and grow, the sky is full of stars. The earth is cultivated: 'les monts et les plaines cultivés par mon étoile' (PS/TN p. 34); life is finally born: 'L'enfant de cette ombre parturiante/qui se repaît de lactogène lunaire' (PS/TN p. 99).

But it is the poem that is born, not the poet. This descent into the self, back into the womb of the night, is essentially a quest for the real, or ideal self, which is the poem, the created object, totally unrelated to the child that was originally born into the daylight world of harsh reality. The bird is the main image here. It hides in the heart of the forest, in the heart of the tree or of the night, and the poet penetrates this world – 'le vrai lieu', to use Yves Bonnefoy's term again – in search of the bird. He lays traps for it and hopes to bring it back with him. It is, always, the 'oiseau immatériel' – 'innombrables les fables qui entourent l'éclosion de cet oiseau immatériel qui tombe puis reprend son vol' (PS/TN p. 66). They are

> ces oiseaux pacifiques
> Qui grandissent au coeur du paysage fantomatique
> Ils paissent l'ombre,
> ils picorent la nuit.
>
> ('Images Lunaires', PS/TN p. 39)

In one poem, entitled 'Les Trois Oiseaux', he enumerates three kinds of birds – the aeroplane, the man-made bird that belongs to the harshness of human reality; 'l'oiseau de chair' which, like the poet, has to battle with the material world to secure its place among the leaves of the tree; and, thirdly,

Celui qui est immatériel, lui,
charme le gardien du crâne
avec son chant balbutiant,
puis ouvre des ailes résonnantes
et va pacifier l'espace
pour n'en revenir qu'une fois éternel.

(PS/TN p. 33)

Like its song – 'balbutiant' – the bird is fragile, 'titubant au coeur des branches', until, with the growing sureness of its song, like the finished poem, it conquers space and eternity. In other words, Rabéarivelo is concerned with the poetic experience, and the man out to trap the bird is equivalent to the poet in quest of the poem. The first poem of *Presque-Songes*, placed at the very beginning of his mature poetry, links, in its title and imagery, the world of the poet's creativeness and the imagery he draws from nature.

Lire

Ne faites pas de bruit, ne parlez pas:
    vont explorer une forêt les yeux, le coeur,
    l'esprit, les songes . . .

Forêt secrète bien que palpable:
    forêt.

Forêt bruissant de silence,
    Forêt où s'est évadé l'oiseau à prendre au piège,
    l'oiseau à prendre au piège qu'on fera chanter
    ou qu'on fera pleurer.

A qui l'on fera chanter, à qui l'on fera pleurer
    le lieu de son éclosion.

Forêt. Oiseau.
    Forêt secrète, oiseau caché
    dans vos mains.

(PS/TN p. 28)

There is, in the image of the trapped bird, a hint of the sadness of the creative act. The bird seeks to elude its hunter, like the poem eludes the poet, so it must be taken by violence and brought back to the world of reality, which is unworthy of it. More often than not, it is impossible to bring it back; the poem cannot survive in the light of day. The poem written on the page, held up to the vulgar gaze, is nothing as compared to the experience which produced it, for it is a secret, intimate experience, which cannot stand up to scrutiny. This is, in fact, another aspect of Rabéarivelo's contradictory emotions – the tension between the secret self, which he wishes to preserve, and the longing to be famous and recognized as a poet. This is a recurrent theme in his poetry. The poem is 'une stèle lumineuse/que l'artiste aura érigée sur sa tombe invisible' (PS/TN p. 44).

Yet, although he sees the poem as like 'un arc-en-ciel reliant deux continents' which are incompatible, the emphasis in nearly all his poems of this period is on the beauty and the wonder of the place where the poem lies hidden, and there is no great expression of anguish or tragedy. The poet is sure of the poem, and his poetry is a defiance flung in the face of reality, which he can now afford to ignore. There is, however, one striking poem in which one senses the poet's dissatisfaction with himself, particularly with his 'dérèglement de tous les sens', which he sees as undermining his poetry. It is a difficult poem, although one of his best known, and may be worth closer examination.

> Quel rat invisible
> Venu des murs de la nuit,
> Grignote le gâteau lacté de la lune?
> Demain matin,
> Quand il se sera enfui,
> Il aura là des traces de dents sanglantes.
>
> Demain matin,
> Ceux qui se seront enivrés toute la nuit
> Et ceux qui sortiront du jeu
> En regardant la lune,
> Balbutieront ainsi:
>
> 'A qui est cette pièce de quat'sous
> Qui roule sur la table verte?'
> 'Ah! ajoutera l'un d'eux,
> L'ami avait tout perdu
> Et s'est tué!'
>
> Et tous ricaneront
> Et, titubant, tomberont.
> La lune, elle, ne sera plus là:
> Le rat l'aura emportée dans son trou.

(PS/TN p. 90)

The poem was probably written in 1933, inspired by a particularly disastrous night spent drinking and gambling, which he recorded in his diary. An image in this diary entry links the incident directly with the poem:

> Ai joué comme un forcené jusqu'au matin. Ai bu comme le sable la mer. A minuit tout ce que j'avais sur moi était brûlé après une apparence éphémère de chance ... Rentré aussitôt pour prendre tout ce que nous avions, ma femme et moi, d'argent liquide ... J'ai tout perdu encore et ce sont des Chinois et des Indiens qui m'ont eu ... Rentré seulement à 4h 15, rond et saoul comme la lune ... Et voici que nous sommes une fois encore obligés de recommencer notre vie.[15]

The poem can be interpreted as an expression of his realization that by drinking and gambling his life away, the poet drives himself towards despair and death (already the mention of suicide) and at the same time forfeits the power of creation. The rat, as a symbol, is the opposite of the bird, and represents the destructive force from underneath, emerging from the night (the dream world), where it, too, lives, to mutilate and carry off the moon (equivalent, in the night sky, to the bird at the heart of the tree and to the poem). The death of the poet and the death of poetry are simultaneous. Rabéarivelo talks about his death in many other poems, but he always asserts his belief in the power of his poetry to survive him and, one day, to bring him recognition. This is because, usually, he sees himself as excluded against his will by the world in which he lives, but on this occasion he seems to be acknowledging that his own escapism is itself a destructive force within him.

There is one last symbol that ought to be mentioned. The bird is the symbol of the poem. The bull – *taureau, boeuf, zébu*, even *vache* – is the symbol of the poet in a number of poems. It is shown as grazing on the prairies of the night sky or on the real prairies of the Malagasy countryside, frustrated by the desert to which it is sometimes confined, unable to reach the horizon of the night which lies, always, ahead of it – 'le taureau voit un désert qui s'étend jusqu'aux frontières de la nuit' (PS/TN p. 59). Its power (compare, for example, the poem entitled *Zébu*) represents the creative instincts of the poet, its vulnerability the poet's subjection to his environment, and especially to men.

> Il vient d'un parc s'étendant au bord du soir
> et s'engage entre deux voies lactées.
>
> Le fleuve de la lumière ne l'a pas désaltéré,
> et le voici qui boit avidement au golfe des nébuleuses.
>
> ('Le Boeuf Blanc', PS/TN p. 41)

[15] Boudry, op. cit., p. 49.

Poetry, the poem and the poet are the obsessive themes of Rabéarivelo's mature poetry. The love theme is hardly present at all, and it is interesting to observe that, although he was considerably influenced by the *hain-teny*, essentially love poems, he did not adopt their main theme. Most of his poetry deals with the poet's quest for the poem in its secret place, but the theme of the artist as artificer is not neglected, and there are some striking references to it, perhaps the most effective of all in the poem entitled 'Une Autre':

> Fondues ensemble toutes les étoiles
>> dans le creuset du temps,
>> puis refroidies dans la mer
>> et sont devenues un bloc de pierre à facettes.
>> Lapidaire moribonde, la nuit,
>> y mettant tout son coeur
>> et tout le regret qu'elle a de ses meules
>> qui se désagrègent, se désagrègent
>> comme cendres au contact du vent,
>> taille amoureusement le prisme.
>
> Mais c'est une stèle lumineuse
>> que l'artiste aura érigée sur sa tombe invisible.

> (PS/TN p. 44)

In other poems, the object carved is a musical instrument, the flutes in the poem entitled 'Flûtistes', or the valiha in the poem of the same name. The night, the source of the poem, is at times equated with the poet himself, as in the poem quoted above, and in another poem he refers to the night as 'le vitrier nègre' (PS/TN p. 106).

> Et tu assistes à son supplice quotidien
>> et à son labeur sans fin;
>> tu assistes à son agonie de foudroyé
>> dès que retentissent aux murailles de l'Est
>> les conques marines –
>> mais tu n'éprouves plus de pitié pour lui
>> et ne te souviens même plus qu'il recommence à souffrir
>> chaque fois que chavire le soleil.

> (PS/TN p. 106)

It is a theme that reflects Rabéarivelo's enormous thirst for achievement. The striking beauty of the imagery, the remarkable sense of wonder and appreciation of the world around him often obscure the conflict at the heart of the poem. But the essential quality of his poetry is one of hope and faith in his talent, belief that one day it will find its justification. *Presque-Songes* and *Traduit de la Nuit* both end with poems that affirm this belief –

> Mais quel triomphe certain
> m'annoncent déjà tous ces signaux
> que terre et ciel s'envoient
> à l'orée du sommeil:
>
> dans nos cités de vivants
> jusqu'aux plus humbles huttes
> répondent aux appels de feu
> jaillis des étoiles naissantes. (PS/TN p. 119)

Rabéarivelo was an individualist in the way the poets of Senghor's generation were not. Rabéarivelo's experience of colonialism produced a reaction of turning inward, since the poet could not break out of his prison in any other way. Senghor's generation were aware of themselves as the spokesmen of all black men, and their poetry was therefore outward-turning. The evolution of Senghor's poetry is totally different from Rabéarivelo's. The early Senghor was inclined towards introspection, driven to it by his initial sense of exile and loneliness in Paris, but very soon it turned outwards as his sense of responsibility towards other men increased. His poetry is self-centred, but he wants it this way, because he has chosen to be the ambassador of his people, who must keep their gaze turned on him. Rabéarivelo's early poetry shows signs of an objective concern with the cultural tensions created by colonialism, but he found it impossible within the narrow confines of his prison world to see beyond his own predicament and, in his mature poetry, had to create a freedom within himself. This could only exacerbate the tensions, with the final tragic result of suicide.

But Rabéarivelo's positive contribution to modern African poetry in French is nevertheless considerable. Before the doctrine of *négritude* sought, by conscious practice, to create a specifically African poetry, Rabéarivelo had, unconsciously, welded together trends in modern French poetry and the traditional Malagasy *hain-teny*, and built his edifice on the solid ground of the Malagasy countryside, to produce a poetry of striking originality.

> Tu t'étonnes en suivant des yeux cet oiseau
> qui ne s'égare pas dans le désert du ciel
> et retrouve dans le vent
> les sentiers qui mènent à la forêt natale. (PS/TN p. 83)

Index